Messages
to Canada

Shoghi Effendi,
aged 22 years

Dear & Valued co-workers:

The brilliant success achieved by the Canadian Bahá'í Community, marking the triumphant conclusion of the Plan formulated on the morrow of the emergence of the Community as an independent member of the international Bahá'í Family, is to be regarded as a milestone

. . . .

That they may acquit themselves of their task, as befits their high station in this great spiritual adventure, that they may enrich their heritage, + noise abroad the fame of the Cause of Bahá'u'lláh through a whole-hearted + valiant participation in this world-girdling spiritual Crusade, is the object of my constant prayer + one of my cherished hopes.

Shoghi

Handwriting of Shoghi Effendi

Messages
to Canada

Shoghi Effendi

Bahá'í Canada Publications

BAHÁ'Í CANADA PUBLICATIONS
7200 Leslie Street, Thornhill, Ontario, L3T 6L8
(905) 889-8168
(905) 889-8184 (fax)
E-mail: secretariat@cdnbnc.org

First published in 1965
Second edition 1999

Photographs from the Bahá'í National Centre Archives, Canada

Canadian Cataloguing in Publication Data

Shoghi, Effendi
  Messages to Canada

2nd ed.
Includes index.
ISBN: 0-88867-112-1

1. Baha'i Faith - Canada. I. Title.

BP364.M47 1999   297.9'3   C98-932110-X

Printed in the United States of America
in cooperation with Palabra Publications

Contents

Foreword

Bahá'ís everywhere will feel a deep sense of gratitude to Canada's National Spiritual Assembly for its decision to republish *Messages to Canada*, letters written by or on behalf of Shoghi Effendi, which has been out of print for all too many years. The new edition will be welcomed even more enthusiastically because of the fact that the compilation as now made available has grown from the thirty communications constituting the original publication to a total of over two hundred letters and cables addressed to the National Spiritual Assembly itself, to Local Spiritual Assemblies and groups, to committees, and to a great many individual Canadian believers.

Clearly, the task of identifying and assembling this large body of new material and of integrating it into the original volume has been a long and painstaking labour of love on the part of the editors. No more appropriate occasion could be imagined for the launching of the resulting work than the fiftieth anniversary of the establishment of Canada's National Spiritual Assembly as an independent Institution of the Bahá'í Faith and "ninth pillar" of the Universal House of Justice. To remember that historic occasion is to ponder deeply the significance of the body thus created. This meaning is powerfully expressed in words which Amatu'l-Bahá Rúḥíyyih Khánum addressed to the first national convention assembled in the drawing room of her girlhood home in Montreal:

> Whenever one thinks of Canada one thinks of cultivation. Out of her virgin forests, her wildernesses, her barren North lands and lakes, has already been wrung a great and promising nation. The darkness of nature, as the Master said, has given way to cultivation and out of imperfection has arisen the splendour of government, industry, trade, settlement, and the arts and sciences of human life. But spiritually the land is still dark, promising, but dark. Primarily the measure of spirituality radiated

by your national body will be the measure of Bahá'u'lláh's
light directly available for Canada. For He created the concept of your institution. You exist because of the functions
He desired you to perform, and your fundamental func-
tion is to be the spiritual heart of Canada.

On April 30, 1949, barely twelve months after the new National Spiritual Assembly had come into existence, it was formally
incorporated by special Act of Parliament, an event twice hailed
by Shoghi Effendi in the documents published here as "a magnificent victory unique in the annals of East and West". In retrospect,
the achievement provided a dramatic illustration of the immense
potentialities with which, as the Guardian repeatedly reminded
Canadian believers, Providence has endowed their community and
their country. Today, as Canadian Bahá'ís contemplate the results
of fifty years of struggle and sacrifice they begin to catch a glim-
mer of the dazzling panorama that lay open to the eyes of Shoghi
Effendi as he penned the words of appeal, advice, and encouragement that constitute the heart of this book: Local Spiritual Assemblies established in the most remote corners of a vast land—the
second largest on the face of the planet; an enviable record of
work carried out quietly but with great effect by succeeding generations of Canadian pioneers and travel teachers in every part of
the world; an outpouring of funds that has nourished the activities
of the Cause at its World Centre and throughout the globe and that
truly merits the term sacrificial; the impetus given to the international community's proclamation of Bahá'u'lláh's message by Canadian Bahá'í creativity in the arts and the media; and the growing
involvement in the work of the Faith on the part of believers from
Canada's many ethnic and cultural backgrounds, a hope which is
the unflagging theme of so many of Shoghi Effendi's letters.

Canadian readers who note the Guardian's poignant references
to the suffering of their fellow Bahá'ís in the land of their Faith's
birth will derive a feeling of profound satisfaction from the leadership which both their community and their nation have since demonstrated in mobilizing international condemnation of such per-

secution, in providing homes for several thousand of the victims, and in winning the agreement of many other nations to similarly open their own doors.

Above all, given the letters' urgent emphasis on the qualities of "loyalty", "vigilance", and "unswerving fidelity", Canadian Bahá'ís will reserve their deepest expressions of gratitude to Bahá'u'lláh for the Divine protection which, since the moment of the Faith's arrival in their country a hundred years ago, has so remarkably shielded their community from all efforts to undermine its record of unyielding commitment to the Covenant.

All of these developments were possible because of the hours of patient care which Shoghi Effendi devoted to the community's development at the very dawn of its collective history as a distinct national community. It was the blazing ardour of these messages that inspired Canadian Bahá'í pioneers to endure years of isolation in Arctic posts, remote island settlements, and regions of the earth which seemed initially to display as little in the way of spiritual receptivity as they offered with respect to the comforts of life. It was letters in this book—cherished treasures in homes across the country, treasures grown fragile through constant re-reading—which awoke in individual believers the courage to look within themselves for capacities quite outside their daily experience. Through the guidance the messages contained, Local Spiritual Assemblies learned gradually to be patient not only with the failings of the communities entrusted to their care, but also with the slow processes of their own institutional growth.

At all times, Shoghi Effendi held up before the eyes of Canadian believers—conditioned by everything in their culture to the virtues of modesty and prudence, and confirmed in this mindset by sobering historical experience—the breathtaking mandate which has been conferred on them by the Centre of the Covenant. They must strive to appreciate, he insisted, that they are a "co-heir" of the Tablets of the Divine Plan, "chosen prosecutors" of that Plan, "sole partner" and "chief ally" of their sister community in the United States in its worldwide implementation, and endowed with that "primacy with which the twin Bahá'í national com-

munities labouring in the North American continent have been
invested by the unerring Pen of the Centre of Bahá'u'lláh's Covenant".

Whenever response was unduly slow or energies flagged,
Shoghi Effendi was in no way reluctant to press those matters which
deeply concerned him. Perhaps the most vexed single issue was
the difficulty which the National Spiritual Assembly appeared to
have in acquiring a suitable site for its first Mashriqu'l-Adhkár
and even an appropriate property for its national Ḥaẓíratu'l-Quds.
As delay followed delay and one after another of the Assembly's
optimistic expectations proved illusory, letters from the Guardian's
secretaries expressed growing concern. Eventually, Shoghi Effendi
himself addressed the subject in the course of a major message in
1955:

> [The] purchase of the site of the Mother Temple of
> the Dominion of Canada and the establishment of the na-
> tional Ḥaẓíratu'l-Quds constitute a double task that can
> brook no further delay, as the entire Bahá'í World, having
> hailed the erection of such an indispensable institution in
> no less than eighteen countries scattered throughout the
> continents and oceans of the Globe, is now intently fixing
> its eye on this community, so richly blessed by 'Abdu'l-
> Bahá. . . .

Principally, however, one is struck by the gentleness and re-
straint that the messages display over failures which, however serious in themselves, were clearly seen by Shoghi Effendi as the
result not of obduracy or folly, but of ineptitude on the part of a
very young community desperately concerned to learn and to fulfil the expectations of the incomparable figure on whom all its
love and hope were fixed.

A startling feature of Shoghi Effendi's letters to Canada—and
indeed of the Tablets of 'Abdu'l-Bahá that inspired them—is their
linking of the spiritual destiny of the country with its brilliant material future. Repeatedly, the Guardian returns to the theme of the
Master's emphasis on this dual process. In an especially provoca-

tive passage, he points to the vital role which, in the fullness of
time, the Bahá'í community itself is destined to play not only in the
nation's spiritual development, but in its social and economic advance:

> May this community, the leaven placed by the hands
> of Providence in the midst of a people belonging to a na-
> tion, likewise young, dynamic, richly endowed with mate-
> rial resources, and assured of a great material prosperity
> by 'Abdu'l-Bahá, play its part not only in lending a notable
> impetus to the world-wide propagation of the Faith it has
> espoused, but contribute, as its resources multiply and as
> it gains in stature, to the spiritualization and material
> progress of the nation of which it forms so vital a part.

Here, we touch with that mystery that 'Abdu'l-Bahá termed
"the secret of Divine civilization". Increasingly, Bahá'ís will feel
impelled to consider the impact on Canadian consciousness of
Shoghi Effendi's messages and the long term effects on the nation's
life. Prior to World War II it might well have been impossible to
identify a society more provincial, more resolutely self-absorbed
than that of Canada. Today, in its place, stands a nation for whom
a global perspective is the norm, that has established a perhaps
unparalleled record of service to the cause of international peace-
keeping, and that is justly renowned for its willingness to provide
economic assistance without attaching to it political or other conditions.

Readers will note that the major messages in the book were
all written during the nine year period—1948 to 1957—which
coincided with this great turning point in the orientation of Canada's
people. The letters' immediate effects can be traced in the lives of
only the several hundred persons to whom they were directly addressed. Their broader influence, an influence deriving its force
from the direct intervention in Canadian history of the Centre of
Bahá'u'lláh's Covenant, was prefigured in words with which
'Abdu'l-Bahá described the significance of the brief but incalcula-
bly precious days He spent in the country:

The time of sojourn was limited to a number of days, but the results in the future are inexhaustible. . . . Again I repeat, that the future of Canada, whether from a material or spiritual standpoint, is very great. Day by day civilization and freedom shall increase. The clouds of the Kingdom will water the seeds of guidance which have been sown there.

Douglas Martin[1]
Haifa, 28 February 1998

Preface

It is with immense joy that we release this new edition of *Messages to Canada*. The publication of this commemorative edition of communications from Shoghi Effendi is particularly momentous in this auspicious year when the Canadian Bahá'í Community celebrates the hundredth anniversary of the introduction of the Faith of Bahá'u'lláh to Canada and the fiftieth anniversary of the election of Canada's independent National Spiritual Assembly.

The edition published in 1965 contained thirty letters and cablegrams, which, other than the Guardian's first letter to Canada, were concentrated in the period after Canada's National Spiritual Assembly came into being. Since then, a substantial number of additional letters from the Guardian to individuals, Groups and Local Spiritual Assemblies, as well as to the National Spiritual Assembly, have been collected and catalogued. As a result we are pleased to include 278 letters and cablegrams in this edition.[2]

The letters contained in this volume are written by the Guardian or on his behalf by his various secretaries. Those written by the Guardian himself have a unique character and a greater authority than messages written on his behalf, but the latter constitute authoritative Bahá'í text, as noted in a letter dated 25 February 1951, written on behalf of the Guardian to a National Spiritual Assembly: "Although the secretaries of the Guardian convey his thoughts and instructions and these messages are authoritative, their words are in no sense the same as his, their style certainly not the same, and their authority less, for they use their own terms and not his exact words in conveying his messages."

The messages are presented in chronological order. In accordance with guidance of the Universal House of Justice, addressees and other individuals have not been identified, except in circumstances where "it would seem strange or inappropriate to omit a particular believer's name." All cablegrams received from Shoghi Effendi have been presented in the original form and without interpolation.

The variety of spelling, capitalization and punctuation used by the Guardian's secretaries has been standardized to the form most often used by the Guardian himself. The texts remain as written, and have been checked against the originals or authenticated copies of originals. The names used in the text to designate various groups have been retained, notwithstanding that these designations are no longer in common use.

We would like to thank Judith Oppenheimer in the Archives office of the Bahá'í World Centre, and Roger Dahl in the National Bahá'í Archives of the United States, for providing additional texts beyond those in our own archives. We would like to extend our deep appreciation to the diligent and enthusiastic project manager, Ailsa Hedley, who operated under the supervision of an advisory committee of the National Spiritual Assembly. We are also grateful for the proofreading and research assistance of Pixie MacCallum, Jayne Long, Michael Rochester, Jean McKeever, Anne Banani and Sarah Banani.

National Spiritual Assembly of the Bahá'ís of Canada
April 1998

Foreword to the 1965 edition

Few tasks have given such pleasure to the National Spiritual Assembly as the publication of this book. The thirty messages which it contains are collated from letters and cablegrams sent to the Canadian Bahá'í community by Shoghi Effendi, Guardian of the Cause. They span virtually the entire thirty-six years of his ministry, but the reader will not fail to note that apart from the first letter (written in January 1923, shortly after Shoghi Effendi assumed his responsibilities at the World Centre) the messages are concentrated in the nine years from 1948 to 1957. The explanation lies, of course, in the fact that prior to April 1948, Canadian and American Bahá'ís were members of a single community embracing the two countries. The great body of messages addressed to that community have found permanence in several other volumes,[†] and are now a part of the heritage of the entire Bahá'í world. The Canadian National Spiritual Assembly has long desired to contribute to that inheritance this final share of the trust left to it by the Guardian. No more fitting occasion could be found than the inauguration of the first of the global plans designed by the Universal House of Justice and inspired by just such undertakings as form the subject of much of this book.

For those believers who were members of the Faith before November 1957, this book will have a special dimension. For them, the messages will always be *letters*, inseparable in memory from climactic moments at conventions, conferences, and assembly meetings; for some among them, they will be even more closely interwoven with memories of the personal decisions which helped to translate the plans of the messages into the reality of a worldwide community; for a fortunate few, these letters will speak with

---

†*Bahá'í Administration, The World Order of Bahá'u'lláh, The Advent of Divine Justice, The Promised Day is Come, Messages to America*

an unforgettable voice and face and hands remembered from all too brief evenings at the dinner table in Haifa. The messages have significance, however, far beyond the circumstances in which they were issued. Perhaps the most obvious, to a Canadian, is the unique contribution which they make to the history of the Cause in this country. As a nation, Canada has not had a strong sense of mission or identity, and its history has frequently appeared to be a sequence of reactions to events occurring in other countries. For Canadian Bahá'ís, however, the messages of Shoghi Effendi and the statements of 'Abdu'l-Bahá on which they are based provide glimpses of the foundations of their community and of its mission in the world which are the very essence of history. Shoghi Effendi speaks in moving language of the promises of 'Abdu'l-Bahá; of the role of the Canadian community as "co-heir" with the American believers to the Tablets of the Divine Plan; of the "imperishable record of international service" associated with such names as May Maxwell and Sutherland Maxwell, Marion Jack, Fred Schopflocher, Louis Bourgeois, and Rúḥíyyih Khánum, "my helpmate, my shield . . . my tireless collaborator"; of the "initiation of [Canada's] glorious mission, far beyond the borders of the Dominion"; of the significance of the 1949 Act of Parliament incorporating the National Spiritual Assembly, a "magnificent victory unique annals East West"; and of the special role which the community must play in the establishment of the Faith among aboriginal peoples and particularly among the Eskimos.

Ultimately, however, the messages are the property of the Bahá'í world community. On the one hand, they provide authoritative guidance for both individuals and assemblies on issues which in several instances may have been dealt with nowhere else. On the other, they speak in a spirit of understanding which will infinitely reward any effort to appreciate and express it. Local assemblies, like national assemblies, will benefit from a study of the Guardian's repeated urging that we "avoid . . . rules and regulations" as stifling to "the spirit of the Cause", and deal instead with each case on its individual merits in the light of the principles of the Faith. The individual believer will be interested in the reflection in several of the letters of 'Abdu'l-Bahá's appeal that we refrain from moral judgements on other people. Assemblies and individuals alike will not fail to remark the extreme caution which the Guardian counsels us to use in the disciplinary functions of an administrative body. Finally, the letters provide a remarkable glimpse into the world of the spirit in such passages as those in which the Guardian stresses the long term significance of the goals established in the remote and inhospitable regions of Canada's northland.

In one of the most challenging passages of this book, Shoghi Effendi writes: "Above all, the utmost endeavour should be exerted by your Assembly to familiarize the newly enrolled believers with the fundamental and spiritual verities of the Faith, and with the origins, the aims and purposes, as well as the processes of a divinely appointed Administrative Order. . . . For as the body of the avowed supporters of the Faith is enlarged . . . a parallel progress must be achieved, if the fruits already garnered are to endure, in the spiritual quickening of its members and the deepening of their inner life."

There can be no doubt in the mind of anyone who has read them that these messages themselves provide a priceless opportunity for the spiritual quickening to which their author refers. They constitute a part of that imperishable legacy which, without a written Will, the Guardian of the Cause has left to the entire world, a legacy which will continue to enrich future generations of Bahá'ís throughout the centuries of this Dispensation.

National Spiritual Assembly of the Bahá'ís of Canada
Riḍván, 1964

Introduction to the 1965 edition
By Hand of the Cause, John A. Robarts

The communications in this book were written by Shoghi Effendi to the Bahá'ís of Canada, mostly through the National Spiritual Assembly. The first message dated January 2nd, 1923, the Guardian wrote when he was twenty-five years old, and in the beginning of his ministry. The others, dating from April 1948, when Canada became an independent Bahá'í Community, continued until almost that tragic day of his death, November 4th, 1957.

'Abdu'l-Bahá, in His Will and Testament, wrote of Shoghi Effendi, His eldest and dearly loved grandson: "Salutation and praise, blessing and glory rest upon that primal branch of the Divine and Sacred Lote-Tree, . . . the most wondrous, unique and priceless pearl that doth gleam from out the Twin surging seas; . . . Well is it with him that seeketh the shelter of his shade that shadoweth all mankind . . . as he is the sign of God, the chosen branch, the Guardian of the Cause of God. . . ."

Until 1948, the Bahá'ís of the United States and Canada had been one Community. In April of that year, acting upon the instructions of the Guardian, we passed the stage of infancy, attained the status, and assumed the functions, of an independent existence within the Bahá'í World Community. We held our own National Convention in the Maxwell Home, in Montreal, elected our National Spiritual Assembly, the ninth in the Bahá'í world, and were given a Five Year Plan by the Guardian. We proudly became the ninth pillar of the Institution of the Universal House of Justice.

The Five Year Plan called for the incorporation of our National Spiritual Assembly; the establishment of National Bahá'í endowments; doubling the number of our fifteen Local Spiritual Assemblies and raising to one hundred the total number of localities where Bahá'ís reside; the constitution of a group in Newfoundland and the formation of a nucleus of the Faith in Greenland, and the participation of Eskimos and Red Indians in membership to share administrative privileges in local Institutions of the Faith in

Canada.

For the mere handful of Bahá'ís scattered across Canada, this Plan seemed a colossal task. But, as a reading of these messages will reveal, the Guardian knew the goals were attainable. He gave us a glimpse of his great vision of the Cause. He reminded us of the promises of 'Abdu'l-Bahá: "The future of the Dominion of Canada . . . is very great and the events connected with it infinitely glorious. . . ." He showed us that dedication and service to the Cause of God must come first in our lives. His stirring appeals, his unwavering faith in us, his love and his prayers for us, his keen interest in the execution of all phases of the Plan, his constant encouragement, his sympathy and understanding in our difficulties, his deep appreciation, gratitude and pride in every victory, his reminding us of the promises of Divine assistance, brought us to April 1953, with our Five Year Plan completed.

To our sixth National Convention he cabled: "Overjoyed grateful triumphant conclusion Five Year Plan most momentous enterprise launched Canadian Bahá'í history initiated morrow emergence independent existence Canadian Bahá'í Community. . . ."

In that same cable he announced details of our part of the Ten Year World Crusade, "constituting prelude mightier undertaking designed consolidate magnificent victories achieved homefront inaugurate Community's historic mission beyond confines Dominion. Ten Year Plan its valiant members now embarking upon enabling them push outposts Faith northernmost territories Western Hemisphere associating them members seven other sister Communities raising aloft banner Faith Pacific Islands. . . ."

These messages contain both instruction and inspiration. The Guardian gave us a deeper understanding of the Faith. We are very proud that he paid such loving tributes to a number of Canadian Bahá'ís: Sutherland and May Maxwell, their daughter now Amatu'l-Bahá Rúḥíyyih Khánum, Siegfried (Freddie) Schopflocher, Marion Jack, and others.

While we suffered the devastating loss of our cherished Guardian at almost the halfway point of the Crusade we are happy that the goals have been achieved. We know that he will be overjoyed and grateful for the triumphant conclusion of his Ten Year World Crusade, "the greatest spiritual drama the world has ever witnessed". We will now go forward with our fifty-five sister Communities of the Bahá'í world to establish the Kingdom of God upon the earth.

A fuller perspective of the work of Shoghi Effendi is obtained by reading these messages in conjunction with those he wrote before 1948, to the Bahá'ís of the United States and Canada, and from 1950, to the Bahá'ís of the world. For thirty-six years he was the Divine Tree that shadowed all mankind. He was the most wondrous, unique and priceless being. He was indeed the Guardian of the Cause of God.

O my loving friends! After the passing away of this wronged one, it is incumbent upon the Aghsán (Branches), the Afnán (Twigs) of the Sacred Lote-Tree, the Hands (pillars) of the Cause of God and the loved ones of the Abhá Beauty to turn unto Shoghi Effendi—the youthful branch branched from the two hallowed and sacred Lote-Trees and the fruit grown from the union of the two offshoots of the Tree of Holiness,—as he is the sign of God, the chosen branch, the Guardian of the Cause of God, he unto whom all the Aghsán, the Afnán, the Hands of the Cause of God and His loved ones must turn.

—Will and Testament of 'Abdu'l-Bahá, 11

The Guardian's First Letter to Canada

January 2, 1923

The Guardian's First Letter to Canada

2 January 1923

THE BELOVED OF THE LORD AND THE HANDMAIDS OF THE MERCIFUL THROUGHOUT CANADA

C/O THE MEMBERS OF THE SPIRITUAL ASSEMBLY IN MONTREAL

Dear friends!

It is a great pleasure and privilege to me to enter into direct and I trust permanent correspondence with those faithful friends of 'Abdu'l-Bahá, who, though few in number and scattered over that vast and flourishing country, will I trust act as a powerful leaven to the mass of that spiritually-minded people.

Though its people be firmly entrenched in their religious sectarianism and strongly attached to their religious doctrines and traditions, yet who can doubt that with courage and persistence, kindliness and wisdom, the all-conquering words of Bahá'u'lláh can fail to break down all these barriers of prejudice and religious exclusiveness and conquer this long-standing stronghold of sectarian belief!

Surely the efficacy of the universal Teachings of Bahá'u'lláh, as applied to the cherished and time-honoured religious traditions of the East, has been sufficiently demonstrated to justify at present our confident hopes for the future and speedy reawakening of that land.

May the small company of the steadfast followers of 'Abdu'l-Bahá in Canada be filled with the outpourings of the Divine

Grace that are being showered so mightily in these days upon the friends of God the world over, and may they arise with undiminished fervour to carry out to their fullest measure the last wishes and instructions of our departed Master for that great and flourishing Dominion!

With all good wishes,

Your brother and co-worker,
Shoghi

The Early Years

1923-1937

The Early Years

20 April 1923

THE BELOVED OF THE LORD AND THE HANDMAIDS OF THE MERCIFUL THROUGHOUT THE
DOMINION OF CANADA

C/O THE SECRETARY TO THE MONTREAL SPIRITUAL ASSEMBLY

My dearly beloved friends!

I was deeply interested and immensely gratified to read the newly received messages and letters from that distant land, all testifying to the growth of a new spirit of enthusiasm and fellowship recently kindled in the hearts of those few, yet earnest, workers for the Cause of Bahá'u'lláh. The report sent to me recently by the Secretary of the Montreal Spiritual Assembly, as well as the letters which our beloved spiritual sister, Mrs. Schopflocher,[3] has received from America, all gave me the assurance that a new era of spiritual activity is dawning upon the people of that land. May the repeated promises of 'Abdu'l-Bahá regarding the ultimate religious revival of that spiritually conservative country, and the universal and whole-hearted response of its people to the Call of Yá-Bahá'u'l-Abhá be speedily fulfilled!

It behoves us, now that the signs of that glorious and promised Day are fast appearing, to arise, with utter selflessness, unity and determination, to promote and consolidate the Work which He has Himself established in the heart of that vast Dominion, and prove ourselves, by our wisdom, moderation, and constancy, worthy of the many bestowals He has showered upon us in the past. If we but follow in His Way, regard at all times the dignity of the Cause, guard sedulously its unity and vital principles, and exercise the utmost endeavour to keep its Spirit pure, effective, and unobscured, then, and only then, can we hope to achieve the immediate spread and triumph of the Cause.

Our beloved Bahá'í sister, Mrs. May Maxwell,[4] the pioneer of the Cause in Canada, will soon be with us in the Holy Land, and I trust that after her visit to the Three Holy Shrines, she may be enabled to return, invigorated and refreshed, ready to continue, in collaboration with you all, the great mission which the Master has destined her to fulfill in this world. May I assure you again of my constant prayers for your success, and of my desire to hear from you all, individually and collectively, regarding the progress of your labours, and the plans you contemplate for the further advancement of the Movement in those regions.

I am your brother and co-worker,
Shoghi

&

[13] December 1923

To THE MONTREAL ASSEMBLY

ASSURE YOU MY PRAYERS AND AFFECTIONS.

SHOGHI

&

1 February 1924

To AN INDIVIDUAL BELIEVER

My dear Bahá'í Sister,
Your spiritually beautiful letter of December 16th sent through our beloved brother, Mr. F. Schopflocher[5] to our dear Guardian, Shoghi Effendi, has been received. He was deeply impressed with the spirit of your devotion and attachment to the Holy Cause of God and lofty aspirations to serve humanity which is the fundamental aim of the Bahá'í Movement.

He has instructed me to answer your letter and convey to you his loving greeting. He assures you that he remembers you in his ardent prayers at the Holy Shrine of our Master, 'Abdu'l-Bahá, so that you may day by day grow stronger and stronger in your understanding the realities of the heavenly teachings.

Shoghi Effendi approves of your consideration for your husband. He hopes that through your wise conduct and loving-kindness to him, he will also gradually understand the significance of the Holy Cause. People are not naturally against the Truth. There are obstacles between them and the Truth. These obstacles must be wisely removed and then they surely will be attracted to the Cause. The magnet for this attraction is real love and tolerance towards the ideas and customs of the people. We must follow our Lord, 'Abdu'l-Bahá, who taught us to be well-wishers of mankind disregarding religious and racial differences. Our love must be so spacious as to engulf the whole of the people of the world. With love and only with unlimited love we have been and will be able to conquer the hearts of the people and direct the current of their sentiments along the channel of the happiness of mankind and thus usher in the era of the regeneration of man. It is unlimited love which is the Elixir that turns the common metals of the human being into pure gold.

Dear sister, the Jewish nation are a religious people. They are strong in their faith. When they become Bahá'ís, they are apt to become strong in the Cause too. We have thousands of Jewish Bahá'ís in Persia, who have broken the barriers of exclusiveness from other people and are most active in the service of the Cause. Shoghi Effendi's desire is that you ought still to be more considerate and kind to your husband and relatives. This is Bahá'í spirit.

For several days we have had the pleasure of having our dear brother, Mr. Schopflocher,[5] with us. We are impressed deeply with his love, devotion and sincerity or in other words, with his Bahá'í spirit. We are sure that when he returns to Canada, through the inspiration he has received from his personal touch with our beloved Guardian and from the Holy Shrine of our Master, he will be able to reach the hearts of the people with a greater power than ever before.

Be assured dear sister, that I will not also forget you in my humble prayers and I am cherishing the hope that you will succeed in bringing up your dear children to become good Bahá'ís and servants of the world of humanity.

With Bahá'í love and greeting, I remain,
                    Your humble brother in His love and service,
                                        'Azizu'lláh S. Bahadur

My dear Bahá'í sister:
It is true that you are labouring for our beloved Cause under
difficult and trying conditions, yet you realize, I am sure, that
by so doing you are treading the Path our Beloved has pursued
throughout His heroic life, that your fortitude, your persever-
ance, your services, your loyalty to Him will be abundantly
rewarded in the world to come in His Divine Presence. Be then,
cheerful, radiant and resolute and persevere to the very end
and be assured of my constant and ardent prayers for your
happiness, prosperity and spiritual advancement. My beloved
Fred, that living torch, lit by the spirit of our departed Master,
joins me in praying for you at His Shrine.
                                                        Shoghi

ം‿ഛ

                                        4 February 1924

THE BELOVED OF THE LORD AND THE HANDMAIDS OF THE MERCIFUL THROUGHOUT CANADA

Esteemed fellow-labourers in the Vineyard of God!
My close companionship during the last few days with that
zealous and promising disciple of 'Abdu'l-Bahá, our dearly
beloved Mr. Schopflocher[5] has served to remind me of my Ca-
nadian friends, who are destined and chosen by Bahá'u'lláh to
prepare the way for the ultimate triumph of His Cause in that
great and vast Dominion.
I have received from him the assurance of your warm and
abiding affection, of your unflinching faith and noble resolve
to carry on the work so heroically begun by the Báb, and so se-
curely established by Bahá'u'lláh, and so widely and power-
fully promoted by His beloved Son 'Abdu'l-Bahá. In my hours
of association with your beloved representative I could not
but feel deeply impressed by the sweetness of his nature, his

ardour, his humility and selflessness, his clear understanding of, and entire devotion to, the interests of our beloved Cause. True, his has not been the privilege to gaze at our Beloved's face, yet who that has seen him can but for a moment doubt that his soul is aglow with the flame of our Master's love, that in him the Spirit of our departed Master abides in all its power and beauty?

I am confident that his radiant heart is but the reflecting mirror of that undying Fire, lit by our Beloved's hand in the heart of your country, and destined one day to blaze forth and illumine all the Dominion of Canada—nay the whole of the Western continent. My prayers at the three Holy Shrines are that the Almighty may guide you and enable you to adhere steadfastly to the admonitions and counsels of our All-Wise Master, that you may combine and harmonize the essential qualities of prudence and courage, discretion and candour, dignity and lowliness, fidelity and goodwill, that thus you may guard His Cause and promote its interests at all times and under all conditions.

I am glad to convey to you the glad news of the improving health of that loved one of God, our dear Mrs. Maxwell.[4] That pioneer worker of the Cause, so precious an asset to the Movement in Canada, will soon be in your midst, refreshed and restored. I am waiting with intense expectation to see your individual activities and talents all merged into one motive force, sustained by your combined efforts, directed by a unified purpose, and inspired by one common aim. Then will the showers of His grace rain upon you, and the unfailing promises of 'Abdu'l-Bahá be speedily and effectively fulfilled.

That His Word will eventually be spread and firmly established none of us can ever doubt; my only yearning and hope is that we may through sustained effort and prayer be graciously aided to hasten by our words and deeds the advent of this glorious and long-awaited Day.

Your true brother in His service,
Shoghi

16 October 1924

TO AN INDIVIDUAL BELIEVER

Dear Bahá'í Sister,

Your highly spiritual letter of August 24th written to our beloved Guardian, expressing your deep attachment to the Beloved of our hearts and His Will, arrived and impressed him very much. He was also very glad to learn that the dear friends are doing their best to make Green Acre the focal centre from which the heavenly Teachings may radiate to all parts of America.

Yesterday he instructed me to write a few words in answer to your letter conveying his profound affection to you and make you and your beloved husband assured that he remembers you both in his ardent prayers at the Holy Shrines. He wishes you both to be always two burning sparks in the Cause of God so that you may kindle the love of God in anybody with whom you may come in contact. He expects you also to often write to him and tell him how you are.

The Greatest Holy Leaf, the Holy Mother and the other Holy Leaves are well and send you their tender love. They pray for your happiness and success too.

Your humble brother in His love,
'Azizu'lláh S. Bahadur

৩৯৯৫

January 1926

TO AN INDIVIDUAL BELIEVER

My dear Mr. . . . :

After reading your short yet delightful letter, Shoghi Effendi passed it over to me to acknowledge its receipt. He was most pleased to hear that the Cause has lately aroused some interest among the people in Canada. This has been the case everywhere. This last world war together with the treaty of peace and its consequences have taught humanity that unless national, religious and political prejudices be abolished, unless universal brotherhood be established, unless spiritual civilization be given an equal footing with material civilization and thereby change the standard of individual, national and international morality, the world is doomed to failure and society to utter destruction. Confirming this idea, Mr. Lloyd George, in one of his late addresses, stated that one morning he had invited some church dignitaries for breakfast to Downing Street. Their talk was about the real need of England. The church dignitaries were almost unanimous in their view that the real need of England was a political revival. Mr. Lloyd George, who was the only layman present, and was at that time the British Prime Minister, stated that the real and only need of England was a religious revival, because religion changes the character of the individual, and once the individual changes the nation changes, and once the nation changes the government has to change and follow a new code of laws in its dealings towards other nations. Thus we see that even those who hold the reins of world politics believe that religion is essential for human welfare. If so what religion is more broad in its views, more liberal in its ideas, and more modern and scientific in its principles than the Bahá'í Religion?

The reason why the Cause has not spread more than it has is that the world up to the present has not really felt its critical position and the friends not done their best. It is the duty of the Bahá'ís, the world over, to study the Teachings, become versed in the principles and history of the Cause, catch the spirit of the Movement and then arise to service. This was the Master's last word of command, this is Shoghi Effendi's first desire.

Whenever Shoghi Effendi visits the Blessed Shrines, and kneels at those Sacred Thresholds, he earnestly prays and asks God to help the friends in this great work and pave the way for their service. Had it not been for his tremendous work, Shoghi Effendi would have written to the friends individually and nerved them to action. Yet his correspondence with the Assemblies does not permit him as yet to attend to the letters of the individual friends, so he tells us who are around him to take up that part of his work and put on paper what he communicates to us orally.

At present we are having Mrs. Maxwell[4] and Mrs. Schopflocher[3] with us. They tell us about your Assemblies in Canada and the wonderful success you have had in teaching and interesting the people. I really hope your group will increase from day to day and achieve great things in the path of God.

With best wishes to you as well as to your family, I beg to remain,

Yours most sincerely,
Ruhi Afnan

ᖇᘓᖇ

9 August 1926

To an individual believer

My dear Mr. . . . :

Shoghi Effendi wishes me to acknowledge the receipt of your letter dated June 19th 1926. The sentiment it expressed, the feeling it revealed, the words used all seemed to go down into one's heart. Here stands the Bahá'í Cause with absolute need of true and ardent servants who are ready to raise its call and invite the heedless people to the acceptance of its teachings. Few are those who have already taken their allegiance to the Master. But even smaller in number is that group of those who have also the freedom to go out and teach it to others.

There is, however, one hope. God is not heedless to the sighings of the soul. When we desire such an altruistic thing, when we pray for it ardently and truly seek some outlet for the realization of our hopes, sooner or later the occasion will present itself. We are told that the way to Paradise is thorny, but we are also assured that if we persist we shall attain it and obtain our victory.

So, Shoghi Effendi prays that, though at present circumstances may prevent you from rendering those services you desire, you will keep up the hope and await that moment. It will undoubtedly come and bear you the fruit of anxious waiting. The Master surely knows your heart's desire and grants it to you; especially as it is for better service to His Cause.

With deepest love I remain,

Yours in His Name,
Ruhi Afnan

My dear brother:
Your touching letter has been read by me with deep sympathy and interest and my prayer will henceforth be offered for you that strength may be given you to withstand and overcome the trials that are sent you by the All-Wise for your ultimate deliverance, regeneration and victory. Do not despair, remember the sufferings of our Beloved and rest assured in my sympathy, affection and prayers for you. Persevere in your labours for our beloved Cause.

Shoghi

෯෯

2 December 1926

To the Montreal Assembly

ASSURE CANADIAN FRIENDS LOVINGLY REMEMBERED AS-CENSION NIGHT.

SHOGHI

෯෯

10 December 1926

To an individual believer

Dear co-worker:
Your welcome letter, breathing the spirit of loving devotion to the interests of humanity, has touched my heart.
I am greatly pleased to learn of your awakened interest in the Divine Message Bahá'u'lláh has given to the world, and of your keen desire to investigate and study it. You have truly grasped its essence when you characterized it as a Faith so new and fresh in its vitality and yet so old in the truth upon which it is based.
I am convinced that as you travel, whether in America, Europe, Asia, or Australasia, and get in contact with its fervent and devoted followers in the divers regions of the world you will increasingly realize the unique potency, the trans-

forming power, the all-unifying force which distinguish the Bahá'í Faith from the religious and humanitarian movements of this age.

I shall be delighted to meet you in 'Abdu'l-Bahá's home here in the Holy Land, and I cannot tell whether future developments will enable me to seek a much needed rest during the hot summer months. If I can at all manage to get the rest I need, I will certainly be back by the middle of October at which time I trust you will be able to visit Palestine.

I wish to assure you of my best wishes for your success, happiness and spiritual advancement and of my joy and hope to accord you a warm welcome in our home.

Your true brother in the service of God and humanity,
Shoghi

৩০৫

10 March 1927

TO AN INDIVIDUAL BELIEVER

Dear Bahá'í Friend,

The beloved Guardian has asked me to write to you on his behalf, and to tell you how very pleased he is that you have been able to form a Spiritual Assembly in Vancouver, after the inspiring visit of Mrs. Maxwell.[4]

He will earnestly pray for confirmation and blessing for your Assembly, that its members may become ever more detached and illuminated, so that all may become living witnesses to the truth, and may be enabled to spread widely the knowledge of these Divine Teachings which are now so vitally necessary for the healing of the spiritual sickness of the world.

Please accept my warm good wishes for your Assembly. Many years ago, about thirty years ago I should think, I visited your beautiful city! It was then fully planned out, but few houses were built.

Your sincere fellow-worker in this great service,
Ethel J. Rosenberg

My dear co-worker:
I cannot let this letter go without adding a few words in
person and assure you of the great joy and encouragement
which your letter has brought me. I will most lovingly and fer-
vently pray for your group that it may grow from strength to
strength and develop into a radiant and powerful centre of
Divine Guidance and fellowship. Persevere in your efforts and
let not inevitable obstacles dishearten you in your pioneer
labours.

Your true brother and well-wisher,
Shoghi

ৡঌ

12 April 1927

To an individual believer

Dear Bahá'í Brother,
Shoghi Effendi thanks you very much for your letter to him
dated March 20th 1927.

He rejoices to hear that through the influence of your devout
and Christian parents and family your life has been guided by the
Hand of God, until you have now received and accepted the message of God in this Day and the inspired teachings of the Bahá'í
revelation.

You are indeed most blessed through receiving at this time in
your life, when you are entering upon the full responsibilities and
duties of manhood—these sacred teachings and principles—
which should be an inspiration to you to put forth your utmost
efforts to draw other souls into this radiant light.

As you realize, these principles can only be rendered attractive when they are exemplified by a life lived wholly in accordance
with these heavenly counsels. Then they will have their full effect.
Many years ago, when as a young believer I asked of the beloved
'Abdu'l-Bahá instructions as to the method of teaching and attracting souls to the Light—He replied in a beautiful Tablet de-

scribing the life of detachment, purity, and dedication to the service of God, which should be lived by the one who was desirous of teaching. And now, in this time of grave difficulties and trials which surround all the peoples of the world, our first duty is to teach, and gain adherents for our Bahá'í Faith and the life-giving precepts and principles given to us by Bahá'u'lláh, and the beloved Master 'Abdu'l-Bahá.

'Abdu'l-Bahá once said to me that we should use the *Hidden Words* as a mirror—comparing our actions and thoughts with what is there revealed—and if they did not match, so to speak, and fully reflect these Divine Counsels—then we must change our actions and conduct until they were in perfect harmony and agreement with these heavenly exhortations.

With all Bahá'í greetings, and wishing you every success in your endeavours,

Your sincere fellow-worker in this great Service,
Ethel J. Rosenberg

My dear spiritual brother:
Your letter has brought joy to my heart. I will pray for you from the bottom of my heart that the Beloved may pour upon you His richest blessings, guide your steps, sustain your faith, deepen your understanding, and remove every obstacle from your way. I urge you to study the Teachings and particularly 'Abdu'l-Bahá's Some Answered Questions *and Dr. Esslemont's* Bahá'u'lláh and the New Era, *two of the outstanding books in our Bahá'í Literature. I hope to meet you some day in Haifa in the Beloved's home.*

Your well-wisher,
Shoghi

༺◈༻

13 April 1927

Dear Spiritual brothers and sisters:

Shoghi Effendi wishes me to acknowledge the receipt of your letter dated March 18, 1927. He hopes and prays that through your endeavours and the Master's ever-showering blessings you will succeed to make of this first Convention held in Canada a true and brilliant success; that the result of the conferences will be to begin a new era in the spiritual life of that land, and hoist the flag of peace and brotherhood as never before.

There are some important questions that await immediate settlement and we hope that the deliberations made there will give them a true and final solution. In short the eye of the Bahá'í world is now anxiously following the steps you are taking and the decisions you are to attain.

The members of the Master's family are all well and join in wishing you the greatest success. Their only hope rests in seeing the friends set aside their petty differences and in one accord and with a firm determination carry the burdens bequeathed to them by their dear Master.

Yours in His Service,
Ruhi Afnan

My dear and valued co-workers:

I fear this letter will reach you after the closing of the Convention, but I hope it will serve to assure you of the necessity of adopting for future Conventions the essential method of a full, frank and unhampered consultation between the National Assembly and the assembled delegates. It is the vital duty of the delegates to unburden their hearts, state their grievances, disclose their views, and explain their motives. It is the duty of the National Assembly to give earnest, prompt and prayerful consideration to the views of the delegates, weigh carefully their arguments and ponder their considered judgements, before they resort to voting and undertake to arrive at a decision

according to the dictates of their conscience. They should ex-
plain their motives and not dictate, seek information and in-
vite discussion.

Wishing you the fullest success,
Shoghi

ত্ত্ব

4 May 1927

To AN INDIVIDUAL BELIEVER

Dear Bahá'í Friend,
Shoghi Effendi desires me to thank you very much for your
letter mailed April 14, 1927.

He is so glad to hear all that you tell him of your visit and of
the inspiration it has been to you, and he earnestly hopes that, as
you say, "Inshá'lláh" the way will be opened for you to make another visit when he may have the pleasure of meeting you face to
face.

He is truly grieved to hear of the serious accident which befell
your little daughter, and he prays that no ill-consequences may
arise from it. He has been thinking very much of the Convention
held for the first time in Montreal, and is hoping that it will bring
about great results which will be of much benefit for the progress
of our beloved Cause.

He will pray at the Holy Shrines for you and your family, and
the dear friends around you, that you may receive abundantly the
Divine blessing and guidance in all the efforts you are making to
attract souls to this heavenly Light. The Greatest Holy Leaf and the
Holy Family send you their warm love and greetings.

Your fellow-worker in this great service,
Ethel J. Rosenberg

My dear and precious sister in 'Abdu'l-Bahá,
Your sweet letter has brought joy to my heart. To feel that
such an ardent, enlightened and devoted soul is tirelessly en-
gaged in diffusing the Spirit of the Faith in that land is a great
relief and encouragement to me. I too deplore my inability to
meet you face to face at the Beloved's home. My thoughts how-

*ever were directed to your needs and wishes during your stay
in Haifa, and I will continue to pray for you from the depths of
my grateful heart, that the Beloved may guide you, comfort
you, sustain you and pour upon you His rich and manifold
blessings. Hoping to meet you some day in the not distant future,*

Your true brother,
Shoghi

ৎৡৡ

25 August 1927

To an individual believer

Dear Friend,

Our dear Guardian has instructed me to acknowledge the receipt of your letter dated July 22nd and to express to you his grati-
fication at your determination to arouse the student generation to
an intelligent understanding of the tenets of the Faith.

He admires your resolution to abandon all thought of a material career and to consecrate all your energies to the services of
our beloved Cause.

You are most welcome to visit the Holy Land in case you find
it feasible, but whether you are able to come or not, an intensive
period of study in the light of the Bahá'í Teachings seems, to our
beloved Guardian, a necessary preliminary to your work. He hopes
and prays that you will in time prove yourself to be an exemplary
advocate of the universal teachings of the Bahá'í Cause.

Wishing you every success in your endeavours,

Yours very sincerely,
R. Rabbani

My dear and valued co-worker:
*Your welcome letter was a cheer and inspiration to my
heart and I will follow with eager interest the progress of your
labours for the promotion of God's sacred Cause. Do not feel
depressed if obstacles arise in your path. I will pray that the*

Holy Spirit may guide you and sustain you in your noble endeavours.

> *Your true brother,*
> *Shoghi*

ৎৡৣ

27 October 1927

My dear Bahá'í Friend,

I thank you so much on behalf of our dear Guardian for your very kind letter of May 19th together with the interesting enclosures you had sent.

Unfortunately pressure of work and later his absence for the summer from Haifa prevented him to have your letter answered earlier.

Your account of the Bahá'í Convention at Montreal, the measure of its success and the hopes and aspirations that it had raised in the hearts of the friends and delegates assembled there, was indeed most gladly welcomed, and our Guardian awaits with expectant eyes to see those hopes realized in this coming year.

Naturally it depends mostly upon the individual effort of the friends, their zeal and enthusiasm which must sustain their endeavours in serving this great Cause. Shoghi Effendi will be always glad to hear from you and trusts hopefully in the success of your work.

With heartfelt greetings from the members of the family and loving assurances of our Guardian's prayers for you,

> Sincerely in His service,
> Soheil Afnan

My dear co-worker:
Although much pressed by a multitude of cares and responsibilities, I find time to assure you personally of my genuine interest in your work, and of my fervent prayers for your success. May the Beloved guide your steps, remove every ob-

*stacle from your path, and enable you to fulfil your heart's
desire.*

Your true brother,
Shoghi

ৡৡ

7 March 1928

To an individual believer

My dear Friend,
I am instructed by Shoghi Effendi to thank you for your welcome letter of February 17th.

He read with interest and pleasure your short account of the
stages you had passed ever since your youth, the thoughts and
feelings that occupied you in your earnest pursuit of what could
bring you contentment and peace. He is now gratified to learn that
the path you chose when you were still so young in years has finally led you to the Fountain-head from which you can drink deep
and which can satisfy the genuine hunger of your soul. He would
be very glad to help you in the study and understanding of the
Bahá'í teachings and would welcome you as a fellow-worker in
the happy task of carrying to others the "Light" that we have seen
and in trying to reflect in our humble lives the glory that it claims.

He would be always interested and glad to hear from you and
of your doings and trusts that the Bahá'ís in Montreal will find in
you a devoted, sincere and able friend and collaborator.

He wishes me to assure you of his heartfelt good wishes and
prayers, that you may succeed in the realization of all that your
earnest soul asks for.

With many greetings and loving regards,
Sincerely in His service,
Soheil Afnan

My dear co-worker:
*I wish you from all my heart the fullest success in your
efforts to teach and spread our beloved Cause, and trust that
you may some day undertake the pilgrimage to the Holy Land
and visit the Bahá'í sacred Shrines and thus obtain a clearer*

vision of the mission and significance of the Faith.
                                                Your true brother,
                                                      Shoghi

                          ༄༅ྃ

                                          26 April 1928

TO AN INDIVIDUAL BELIEVER

My dear . . . ,

I am instructed by Shoghi Effendi to thank you for your letter of the 9th instant.

He was very much touched by your letter so full of hope, of faith and encouragement and he does not doubt for a moment that the Bahá'í youth of today, they are the men upon whom shall fall one of the happiest and yet one of the most difficult duties that the Cause requires of us, and it is in them that he lays his greatest hope for the future.

That is why the assurance of your hope to do your part is so deeply appreciated and he would be always glad to co-operate with you.

He is very glad to learn of the possibility of your visit to Haifa in the near future, and he wishes me to extend to you a most hearty welcome. It will be a pleasure to him to hear from you and of your doings and he trusts, that in the near future, you will render valuable and permanent services to a Cause that is so near and dear to your heart.

Assuring you always of his good wishes and prayers and with happy greetings for the Riḍván festivals,

                                                Sincerely yours,
                                                Soheil Afnan

My dear co-worker:
I just wish to add a few words in person in order to assure you of my deep interest in the efforts you exert for the advancement of our beloved Cause. I will supplicate for you Divine Guidance and assistance, that you may be graciously as-

sisted to fulfil your heart's desire.

Your true brother,
Shoghi

꒰ঌ

6 May 1928

TO AN INDIVIDUAL BELIEVER

My dear Bahá'í Sister,

I am instructed by our Guardian to thank you for your welcome letter of April 13th with enclosure.

He was much interested in what you had written him as regards oil mines in your and neighbouring properties and I must say at the beginning that he has been deeply touched by the spirit in which you had written your letter and by your desire that in accordance with Bahá'í teachings, if the mines prove valuable, the proper proportion may go for public Bahá'í utilities.

Whether the lots prove valuable commercially or not, the fact still remains that your gesture in writing to our Guardian is truly worthy of a Bahá'í and is sufficient to prove your eagerness to apply the teachings of the Bahá'í Faith and not profess it by name.

As regards the exploitation of the lots, and their value from a practical point of view, of course our Guardian would not wish to say much and would advise you to seek expert advice on the subject. Perhaps in the few words he will append to this letter, he will suggest the name of one of the friends who could help and advise you in the matter.

Please accept the love and good wishes of the Master's family for yourself, your husband and children and permit me to assure you of Shoghi Effendi's heartfelt greetings.

Sincerely yours in His service,
Soheil Afnan

My dear co-worker:
I advise you to consult our dear, trusted and capable brother in the Faith, Mr. Roy Wilhelm,[6] who I feel will be only too glad to assist you with his advice regarding a matter that may prove

beneficial to the interests of our beloved Cause. I will pray for your success from the bottom of my heart.

Your true brother,
Shoghi

໑∽໑

10 October 1928

Dear Mr. . . . :

Shoghi Effendi wishes me to acknowledge the receipt of your letter to him dated August 7th. He very much appreciates the constant efforts you are making in arousing the interest of the friends on the subject of the Temple. Those who are fortunate enough as to attend the Convention should on their return home carry with them the spirit they have experienced there and inform the friends of the decisions that the delegates came to, so that a concerted effort be made and a unity in thought and action be obtained at least along the main issues of the year.

Shoghi Effendi hopes that the Montreal Assembly will succeed to play an important part in establishing and manifesting that wonderful spirit.

He also wishes you to extend to the friends there, especially the members of your family, his best wishes and greetings. Please convey my deepest regards to . . . .

Yours very sincerely,
Ruhi Afnan

With the assurance of my best wishes for you and steadfast prayers for your success,

Your true brother,
Shoghi

໑∽໑

25 October 1928

My dear Mrs. . . . ,

I am directed by Shoghi Effendi to thank you for your letter of September 17th which he was very glad to receive.

He was much interested and touched with your spiritual yearnings and the way in which the Master's spirit had filled your heart and satisfied it. It shows well your sincerity and eagerness to become a worthy channel for His grace and a worker in His Cause.

Shoghi Effendi appreciates deeply your wish to co-operate with him in serving the progress of the Bahá'í Faith and he welcomes you as a valued sister and fellow-worker.

He is always glad to hear from you and awaits your good news of progress in Edmonton. He trusts that some day you will be able to come to Haifa where you would be gladly welcomed.

With much love and greetings and assuring you always of Shoghi Effendi's prayers and good wishes,

Sincerely yours in His service,
Soheil Afnan

My dear co-worker:

I will supplicate for you the blessings of the Almighty and trust that in the days to come you will render inestimable services to the sacred Threshold. The Beloved will surely guide you in your efforts and will strengthen you in the fulfilment of your task.

Your well-wisher,
Shoghi

৽৽৽

20 March 1929

My Dear Mr. . . . ,

Shoghi Effendi wishes me to hasten and thank you for your good letter of February 23rd which he has been so glad to receive.

The news of the co-operation of the Bahá'í young men and women in Montreal, their establishment of a group for study and discussion, the sane and sober expression of their methods as expressed in the programme you had enclosed, and their thoughtful and enthusiastic outlook upon the future, all these have helped to create the liveliest hopes and the deepest satisfaction in the heart of our Guardian. It is indeed with no little pleasure that he welcomes the active co-operation of his young friends in Montreal, and he sincerely trusts that with an adequate study of the proper teachings and its spiritual significance coupled with a sufficient knowledge of the problems and perplexities that the world is beset with, you will be able to render great services to the Cause and therefore to humanity.

He considers it a splendid idea to keep in touch and if possible communicate with other youth organizations in Canada and the United States. It may open immense fields for service at a time when beneath a casual indifference there often lies searching and serious thought.

Shoghi Effendi wishes me to express his appreciation of your own personal efforts and to ask you to convey his sincere good wishes to every member of your group. It will be always a pleasure to him to learn of your work and for your communications he will always have time.

Assuring you of his affection and prayers,

Sincerely yours,
Soheil Afnan

My dear and precious co-worker:

I was delighted by the tone of your letter, and the news it conveyed and the assurances it gave greatly heartened me in my task. The youthful and eager workers for the Cause in Montreal occupy a warm place in my heart. I will remember their hopes, their plans, their activities in my hours of prayer at the Holy Shrines. I urge them to study profoundly the revealed utterances of Bahá'u'lláh and the discourses of 'Abdu'l-Bahá and not to rely unduly on the representation and inter-

*pretation of the Teachings given by the Bahá'í speakers and
teachers. May the Almighty sustain you and guide you in your
work.*

Shoghi

ৎৄৄ৻৶

4 June 1929

To Siegfried Schopflocher[5]

Dear Fred:

Shoghi Effendi wishes me to thank you for your letter dated
May 19th as well as for the trouble you have undertaken to obtain
for him the papers. The colour seems to be the most fitting and he
hopes to receive them in due time. In case he leaves for his summer vacation he will not be here when they arrive but proper care
will be taken of them, you may rest assured.

Shoghi Effendi as well as the others were very glad to hear of
your election as member of the National Spiritual Assembly. The
spirit of co-operation you have been showing and the wonderful
sacrifices you have been making are fully appreciated by the friends
and your election is only a token of that.

We all hope and pray that you may succeed in your work,
both materially and spiritually, for as you have shown the object of
both is the advancement of the interests of the Cause.

In close may I assure you of Shoghi Effendi's prayers and extend to you his loving greetings.

Yours ever sincerely,
Ruhi Afnan

My dear and precious co-worker:
*I deeply appreciate the effort you have exerted in connec-
tion with my request and I wish to assure you that I am much
pleased and satisfied with the quality and colour of the paper
you enclosed. I am also delighted to learn of your election as
member of the National Assembly and I am sure that your participation will greatly contribute to the success of its delibera-*

*tions. Assuring you of my affection, appreciation and prayers
and with my best wishes and loving greetings to Kitty[3] whose
services I shall never forget,*

Your true brother,
Shoghi

ৎৡৎ

20 September 1929

My dear Mrs. . . . ,

I am directed by our Guardian to thank you for your letter of
July 9th.

He has read your letter with great interest and pleasure and
he admires its spirit—so frank, so thoughtful and as regards the
Cause, with such abounding hopefulness.

In connection with your dear husband, Shoghi Effendi would
consider it in full and happy accord with the expressed desire of
the Master that every man should have some permanent work.
Much as he desires to see you both devote your entire energies to
a well thought out, progressive and attractive presentation of the
Cause—a thing he feels we lack lamentably—he would be very
pleased to see your husband follow what the Master often repeated
even to His own immediate family, namely the necessity of a pro-
fession. Of course you know that He always said His had been
mat-making.

As to your entrance to Reed College as an undergraduate, he
also feels that it would be a very nice idea if it is possible and if it
meets with the wishes of your husband. No one could think more
than the Master did of the great need for capacity, knowledge and
a broad scientific outlook in the service of the Cause, but as against
the hard and dry intellectuals, he wished such knowledge to be
coupled with an intense love for the welfare of humanity. Perhaps
the enlightened world already suffers because it has too much of
the former and very little of the latter, but could it be that we suffer
a bit because we have too much of the latter and too little of the
former?

I am also asked to express Shoghi Effendi's deep appreciation of your kind sentiments and of your husband's and your own burning desire to devote your hearts and thoughts to the progress of the Cause.

With warm regards and greetings to you both.

Sincerely yours,
Soheil Afnan

With the assurance of my best wishes and prayers for you at the Shrine of Bahá'u'lláh,

Your true brother,
Shoghi

ৡৢ

5 January 1930

To AN INDIVIDUAL BELIEVER

Dear . . . :

You cannot imagine the great pleasure it gives me to acknowledge the receipt of your letter to Shoghi Effendi dated October 18th, 1929. It reminds me of those meetings I attended in Montreal and of the wonderful friendships I cultivated among its Bahá'í group.

Shoghi Effendi wants me to assure you of his prayers for he has great hopes in those young persons who do not let their worldly desires and needs stand in their way in serving the movement and spreading its teachings. He hopes that in due time your numbers will increase and you will count among your group youthful souls who are determined to work for the inauguration of the era of peace and goodwill.

Shoghi Effendi hopes that you will not merely interest the young people that come to your meetings, but that you will also exert your efforts in awakening them to the full import and station of Bahá'u'lláh, for it is only by coming in touch with the source of light and inspiration that a soul can appreciate the full significance of the Cause. The task is surely harder but the fruits will be so much greater.

Please convey Shoghi Effendi's love and greetings to all the friends especially those of the young people who are working with you.

With best wishes I remain,

Yours ever sincerely,
Ruhi Afnan

With the assurance of my loving prayers at the Shrine of Bahá'u'lláh for the success of your much-appreciated endeavours,

Your true brother,
Shoghi

֎

3 January 1932

TO FRED SCHOPFLOCHER[5]

KINDLY CABLE APPROXIMATE SIZE COST AND TIME REQUIRED RESTORATION TEMPLE MODEL LOVE.

SHOGHI

֎

18 January 1932

TO AN INDIVIDUAL BELIEVER

Dear Mr. . . . :

Shoghi Effendi gave me your letter of December 20th, 1931, sent through the kindness of Mr. Dewing, to read. First let me say that Shoghi Effendi would like me to extend to you his loving greetings and assure you of his prayers. He sincerely hopes that you will ever be guided and assisted in your work as well as in your services to the Cause.

Concerning the Tablet of the Master explaining one of the doctrines of Sufism, which He revealed during His youth at the demand of Ali Shawka Pasha: this is published in the second volume of His Tablets published in Egypt. Unfortunately it has not been

translated into English. It is an epistle of about fifty pages, otherwise I would have attempted to translate it for you. It is not however very important from a Bahá'í point of view for He says at the
end that His object was merely to state the Sufi view and not to
criticize it in the light of the Bahá'í teachings. Moreover, the task
would be very difficult for I am unfamiliar with the terminology
used. It needs a scholar on Sufism to render the Tablet into English.

Mr. Dewing is now with us in Haifa. He has given us very encouraging news about the progress of the movement in Montreal,
especially in the work that the young people are doing. I sincerely
hope your daughter . . . is taking an active part, for I am sure she
could do much. Please give her my love and express to her this
hope of mine. Please remember me also to Mrs. . . . .

 With best wishes,

Yours ever sincerely,
Ruhi Afnan

*With the assurance of my loving and fervent prayers at the
Holy Shrines for your welfare and spiritual advancement,*

Your true brother,
Shoghi

10 February 1932

To Fred Schopflocher[5]

ACCEDE REQUEST PROFOUND LOVING APPRECIATION.

SHOGHI

1 April 1932

To an individual believer

 Dear Mr. . . . :
 Shoghi Effendi wishes me to acknowledge the receipt of your
letter dated March 11th, 1932 as well as the enclosed copy of the

report of the activity of the Bahá'í young people in Montreal. He is sure that Mr. Horace Holley[7] will find in it many interesting facts to incorporate in his review of the progress of the Faith during the last two years.

Shoghi Effendi was very glad to read it and obtain first hand information as to the way the young people in Montreal have succeeded to attract many souls and inspire them with the spirit of service to our beloved Faith. Once the youth learns that this Cause is their Cause, and that through it they can ensure their future social tranquillity and spiritual progress, then they will arise and consecrate their life to the promotion of this Faith. And as you clearly state in your report, no one can awaken the youth of the world to a consciousness of this road to salvation except from their own numbers—youths already inspired with the Bahá'í spirit.

Shoghi Effendi will remember you and the other members of your group in his prayers, and ask for you all divine guidance and help in this all-important task.

Yours ever sincerely,
Ruhi Afnan

May the Beloved of our hearts bless richly your efforts, deepen your understanding of the truth and principles of His Faith, remove all obstacles from your path, and enable each one of you to render inestimable services to His Cause. I will pray that each one of you may be graciously assisted to become a living embodiment of the ennobling principles inculcated by the Message of Bahá'u'lláh.

Shoghi

ॐ

26 April 1932

To the Bahá'ís of Montreal

Dear Bahá'í brothers and sisters:

Shoghi Effendi wishes me to acknowledge the receipt of your joint letter dated March 21st, 1932. He trusts that, with the aid and blessings of the Master, you will succeed to realize your hopes and create a great impetus among the friends that will ultimately lead towards the completion of that noble and beautiful edifice. It is only through such a general sacrifice that we can bring that task to a successful completion.

Consider what a wonderful prestige we will create for the Cause in the eyes of the public! At a time when stupendous undertakings are being given up for lack of funds, when all the human institutions are crumbling down and failing to inspire hope in their followers, the world will see our Temple completed, not through the donations of wealthy people, but through the sacrifices of humble souls who have the love of God burning in their hearts.

In Persia the Cause was established through the blood of the martyrs shed in its path; in the West it seems it shall prosper as the result of constant sacrifice on the part of its handful of followers. It is only by dedicating our life to the Cause of teaching and our means to establish its Institutions that the Faith of Bahá'u'lláh will conquer the West.

In his moments of prayer at the blessed Shrines Shoghi Effendi will think of you and ask God to guide and assist you. The spirit of the Master, he trusts, will enable you to advance the cause of peace and good-will in that city and at the same time make you set an example of service for all the friends in that continent.

With best wishes and loving greetings,

Yours ever sincerely,
Ruhi Afnan

Dearly-beloved co-workers:

I was greatly touched by your message and wish to assure you in person of my deepest appreciation of your collective and untiring efforts for the spread of our beloved Cause. The Bahá'ís of Montreal are often in my thoughts and occupy a warm and abiding place in my heart. They are the object of my continued prayers at the Holy Shrines, and constitute the vanguard of that spiritual host which will, in the fullness of time, achieve signal victories for the Faith of Bahá'u'lláh in that

promising country. May they, by their high, their self-sacrific-
ing endeavours, be enabled to contribute a notable share to
the heroic efforts which the American believers are now exert-
ing for the completion of the Mashriqu'l-Adhkár,

> *Your true brother,*
> *Shoghi*

༄༅

20 August 1932

Beloved Friends in the Faith of Bahá'u'lláh,

Shoghi Effendi was deeply touched by your letter of July 18th, 1932 and he has charged me to thank you on his behalf and express his lively appreciation of your heartfelt sympathy at the great loss which the Faith has come to suffer through the sudden passing of the Greatest Holy Leaf.

Your beautiful words, which eloquently testified to your genuine love for our departed Khánum, have immensely relieved the burden of sorrow that weighs so heavily upon our Guardian's heart and have given him the assurance that the friends are amply sharing his grief at this cruel hour. For in this great calamity his share is, perhaps, the greatest as he had found in the Greatest Holy Leaf the only one who could sustain his energies and inspire him with hope and vigour. Her departure, at this critical hour, will, undoubtedly, continue to be deeply felt for many long years.

The removal of her physical presence from our midst, however, though a source of immeasurable sorrow, will ultimately serve to rekindle the flame of faith in our hearts and inspire us with a fresh resolve to promote and safeguard the very best interests of the Cause. Through intense sufferings and hardships this Faith of God has been able to win its immortal victories and it has always welcomed such moments of profound and well-nigh demoralizing sorrow as providential means whereby its vitality can be best safeguarded.

Might not this calamity serve to intensify our devotion to the Cause and by deepening our spiritual insight make us worthy instruments for the promotion and the consolidation of the Faith?

The Guardian is anxiously waiting to see the friends once more united and whole-heartedly striving to spread those teachings and principles through which an ailing humanity can alone find the real path to salvation.

Yours in His Service,
H. Rabbani

Dear and precious co-workers:
I am greatly touched and relieved by your message. I value the sentiments you have expressed and I will pray that the Almighty may guide and sustain you in your efforts to follow in her footsteps and to perpetuate the memory of her glorious life.

Your true brother,
Shoghi

 So

10 September 1932

Beloved co-workers in the Faith,

It was with a great satisfaction and joy that Shoghi Effendi received your message of condolence dated August 5th, 1932 written through Mr. E. Harrison, your secretary. He was greatly pleased to see how faithfully the friends are sharing his grief. His sole comfort now is to see you all as ever devotedly working for the realization of our departed Khánum's dearest wishes. Surely, from the Realm Beyond she is watching over us all and is continuously sending us her blessings. May we prove worthy of such manifold bounties.

Shoghi Effendi hopes that this overwhelming grief caused by the unexpected ascension of the Greatest Holy Leaf will serve to release forces of such vigour as would tend to speed up and consolidate the work so gloriously undertaken by our American friends.

Assuring you all of his best wishes and of his fervent prayers for your spiritual advancement.

Yours in His Service,
H. Rabbani

Dear co-workers:

The messages of sympathy, sent by an Assembly which has distinguished itself by its eminent services to the Cause, has brought solace and strength to my heart and eased the burden of my sorrow. I value the sentiments you expressed, and the assurances you gave me. I will continue to pray for you from the depths of my heart. Persevere, and never allow the sense of your grievous loss to damp your zeal or to influence your determination to prosecute the task to which you are committed. I will pray that you may be enabled to perpetuate the glorious memory of our beloved Greatest Holy Leaf, and to diffuse, far and wide, the knowledge of her inspiring life.

Shoghi

ॐ

21 October 1932

TO AN INDIVIDUAL BELIEVER

Dear Mr. . . . :

Shoghi Effendi wishes me to acknowledge the receipt of your letter dated September 12th, 1932. He was very glad to know that the teaching work was progressing fairly rapidly and that there is all reason to hope that good results will be obtained. In his moments of prayer at the Shrines he will think of you as well as of the other members of the committee and ask for you all divine guidance and confirmation in the very important work you are directing.

As regards the meaning of the Bahá'í Covenant: The Guardian considers the existence of two forms of Covenant both of which are explicitly mentioned in the literature of the Cause. First is the covenant that every prophet makes with humanity or more definitely with His people that they will accept and follow the coming Manifestation Who will be the reappearance of His reality. The second form of covenant is such as the one Bahá'u'lláh made with His people that they should accept the Master. This is merely to establish and strengthen the succession of the series of Lights that appear after every Manifestation. Under the same category falls the covenant the Master has made with the Bahá'ís that they should accept His administration after Him.

The Guardian has on various occasions made it clear that the friends should abstain from voting for any political posts unless this abstinence would be considered as civil disobedience and punishable by law which I believe does not exist anywhere.[8]

To divide the inheritance as it is prescribed by Bahá'u'lláh we have to divide it into 2520 shares. But we can also divide it into forty-two shares (not forty as you mention in your letter). Then every one of the beneficiaries will take so many of these shares. These numbers form like a highest denominator for the different fractions which represent the shares of the different individuals that will benefit in case of intestacy. In case of the non-existence of one class of inheritors the *Aqdas* mentions how it should be divided. As a general rule a part goes to the House of Justice, a part to the children.

As to your fourth question, Shoghi Effendi believes that it is preferable not to confuse the methods explained by the Master with present systems. They may have many resemblances but also many points of difference. Moreover these general statements we have in the teachings have to be explained and applied by the House of Justice before we can really appreciate their significance.

Assuring you of Shoghi Effendi's prayers and best wishes I remain,

Yours ever sincerely,
Ruhi Afnan

May the Beloved bless richly your efforts, deepen your un-
derstanding of the essentials and distinguishing features of
the Faith and enable you to promote its interests far and wide,
                                              Your true brother,
                                                        Shoghi

᭪

                                              1 June 1933

To AN INDIVIDUAL BELIEVER

Dear . . . :
If Shoghi Effendi knew the address of the place where you
order his stationery for him he would surely not give you that
trouble. But unfortunately he does not, and knows what a pleasure it gives you to render him this added service.

He will, therefore, be very thankful if you order for him two
thousand papers and two thousand envelopes of each of the two
specimens I enclose for you—that is two thousand of the white
sheets with the red engraving of the Greatest Name, and two thousand of the creamy colour paper with the blue engraving. Please
remember that the envelope of the white sheets only have the Greatest Name on the back, while the other kind of envelope is ordi-
nary and without the Greatest Name.

The Guardian sincerely hopes that the Convention now sitting
will inaugurate a new era in the history of the Cause in America
and that momentous decisions will be taken. His thoughts are all
with you and he wishes you success from the bottom of his heart.

Assuring you of his prayers and deep appreciation for the services you are constantly rendering to the Faith, I remain,
                                              Yours ever sincerely,
                                                    Ruhi Afnan

᭪

8 March 1934

TO SIEGFRIED SCHOPFLOCHER[5]

*BAHÁ'Í WORLD GREATLY INDEBTED YOUR OVERWHELM-
ING SHARE PROMOTING ITS NATIONAL INTERNATIONAL IN-
TERESTS ABIDING LOVE GRATITUDE.*

SHOGHI

❧

30 April 1934

TO AN INDIVIDUAL BELIEVER

Dear Bahá'í Friend,

The Guardian wishes me to acknowledge on his behalf the
receipt of your letter dated April 5th with enclosure, and to convey to you his appreciation of your efforts for the spread of the
Message. He is gratified to learn of your contact with the . . . family, and particularly with that gentleman whom you found to be
somewhat receptive to the Teachings. Your close association with
him, and with the other members of his family, who seem to have
been so severely afflicted by some sad events, will, it is hoped, win
them to the Cause and open before them a new field of constructive activity. His prayers on your behalf and on behalf of them all
will be specially offered to Bahá'u'lláh that through His grace and
mercy you may be strengthened and illumined, and be given the
necessary inspiration to serve His Cause.

With sincere greetings and best wishes,

Yours in His service,
H. Rabbani

*With the assurance of my prayers for your welfare, your
success and spiritual advancement,*

Your true brother,
Shoghi

❧

3 December 1934

To an individual believer

Dear Bahá'í Friend,

The Guardian has directed me to acknowledge on his behalf the receipt of your welcome letter dated November 16th, and to renew his appreciation of your efforts for the spread of the Message in your locality. His prayers for the success and expansion of your labours in this field are being continually offered to the Almighty, that through His blessings and guidance you may be assisted in effectively attaining your goal.

In regard to Mr. . . . , Shoghi Effendi is deeply grieved to learn that his difficulties have not yet been solved. He hopes and prays that through your kind help and encouragement, as well as through the assistance of God, he will soon be enabled to overcome the obstacles which beset his path.

He wishes me also to assure you of his supplications on behalf of Mr. . . .'s cousin, that your hopes and wishes for him may each and all be fulfilled. He would advise you to persevere in your efforts for attracting him to the Cause, and for enabling him to eventually enlist himself under its banner.

With loving greetings and good wishes,

Yours in His service,
H. Rabbani

May the Almighty bless your efforts, guide your steps and enable you to promote the interests of His Faith,

Your true brother,
Shoghi

 ৩৽৶

18 June 1935

To an individual believer

Dear Bahá'í Friend,

I am directed by our beloved Guardian to acknowledge on his behalf the receipt of your deeply-appreciated letter dated May 22nd, together with the enclosed report written by you on this year's Annual Convention which he has specially enjoyed reading, and for which he wishes me to convey to you his deepest thanks. Your report is, indeed, quite comprehensive and highly illuminating, and must have been surely read with profoundest interest and appreciation by those who have not had the privilege of attending the sessions of the Convention. You have, therefore, rendered a real and most valuable service to them in this connection.

With regard to your suggestion relative to the translation of Bahá'í literature from Arabic into English by orientalists, Shoghi Effendi does not think it advisable the friends should take such a step at present. He feels that the matter of translations, particularly when it involves the rendering of the writings of Bahá'u'lláh and the Master, is such a difficult and highly responsible task that only believers who are deeply versed in Arabic and English, and who are also thoroughly familiar with the Writings, can possibly undertake it.

With the assurance of his best wishes, and of his prayers for your guidance and welfare, and with cordial greetings to you and to all the friends in Montreal,

Yours in His Service,
H. Rabbani

Dear and valued co-worker:
Your highly illuminating report is a service for which the friends should feel truly grateful. I value your services and above all the spirit that prompts you to render them. I will continue to pray for your success from all my heart.

Your true brother,
Shoghi

ৡৡ

To CHARLES MURRAY[9]

Beloved Bahá'í Brother,
The Guardian has directed me to acknowledge on his behalf the receipt of your letter, and to express his thanks and apprecia-

tion for the efforts you are exerting for the spread of the Cause throughout Prince Edward Island. He can well realize the nature and number of the obstacles that face you in your arduous labours for the attainment of this task. But he feels confident that your perseverance, and your utter devotion to the cause of teaching will enable you to gradually fulfil this most cherished desire of your heart. Although alone and unaided, you can be certain that the invisible hosts of Bahá'u'lláh are continually helping and guiding you in your labours.

Shoghi Effendi hopes that Mrs. Emeric Sala's[10] visit to your centre will serve to impart to your heart a fresh encouragement, as well as a more powerful incentive to carry on your work for the Cause.

In his prayers and meditations at the Holy Shrines he will specially supplicate the Almighty on behalf of you both, that your efforts for the spread of the Teachings may be continually enriched and may bear full fruitage.

With every good wish and loving greetings,

Yours in His service,
H. Rabbani

May the Almighty bless, protect and sustain you in your labours for the spread of His Cause, deepen your understanding of its distinguishing features, and assist you to render memorable services to the sacred Threshold,

Your true brother,
Shoghi

ง๛

17 March 1936

TO FRED SCHOPFLOCHER[5]

BAHÁ'ÍS WORLD OVER INDEBTED TO YOU FOR YOUR PREPONDERATING SHARE IN SUPPORTING INSTITUTIONS OF FAITH IN ITS FORMATIVE PERIOD PUBLICATION BAHÁ'Í WORLD IS YET ANOTHER EVIDENCE OF SUCH GENEROUS

SUPPORT ASSURE YOU ABIDING GRATITUDE LOVING RE-
MEMBRANCE LOROL[3] AND YOUR DEAR SELF.

SHOGHI

༄༅

11 December 1936

TO F. ST. GEORGE SPENDLOVE[11]

Dear Mr. Spendlove,

The Guardian is in receipt of your welcome message of the 19th November with enclosures, and is indeed pleased to learn that you have joined the staff of the Royal Ontario Museum of Archaeology in Toronto. For although he had suggested to you at the beginning to return to England, provided it would be financially possible, he now feels that your stay in such a town as Toronto where there is as yet no well-established group of believers can be equally fruitful and of high value to the promotion of the teaching work. Do not feel worried, therefore, if circumstances did not prove to be favourable to your return to England. In Canada there are still so many places to which the Message has not yet been carried. It is perhaps as virgin a soil as many parts of Great Britain. The essential for you now is to make every effort in order to increase the number of confirmed souls in Toronto and thus pave the way for the formation of an Assembly in that centre.

The Guardian is pleased that your labours in this connection will not be unaided, but will be reinforced through the close and continued collaboration of Messrs. William Suter[12] and Gerrard Sluter,[13] the only active believers besides you in Toronto. It is his fervent hope that your united endeavours will greatly stimulate the promotion of the teaching work in that centre. May Bahá'u'lláh send down upon you His confirmations, and assist you in the attainment of this supreme objective.

Assuring you and them of the Guardian's ardent supplications on your behalf at the Holy Shrines,

Yours in His Service,
H. Rabbani

Dear and valued co-worker:

I wish to assure you in person of my deep appreciation of the work you are so devotedly accomplishing in Toronto. My hope, indeed my prayer, is that you may be graciously assisted to establish a group of fervent believers who will form a nucleus and foundation for a flourishing spiritual Assembly. Persevere in your pioneer efforts and rest assured.

Your true and grateful brother,
Shoghi

ϟ

12 April 1937

To THE MONTREAL BAHÁ'Í COMMUNITY

DEEPLY TOUCHED MESSAGE ASSEMBLED FRIENDS PRAYING REALIZATION HIGHEST HOPES.

SHOGHI

Canada's Involvement in the First Teaching Plans

1937-1948

Canada's Involvement in the First Teaching Plans[14]

27 June 1937

To the Bahá'ís of Vancouver

Dear Bahá'í Friends,

Our beloved Guardian has been inexpressibly touched by your letter of April 28th, which you have so kindly addressed to him on the occasion of his marriage,[15] and he wishes me to hasten to assure your community of his heartfelt appreciation of the sentiments of devoted love and loyalty you have expressed, all of which he dearly prizes indeed.

It is his fervent hope that in recognition of this priceless honour that the Almighty has chosen to bestow upon the community of Canadian believers your group will unitedly arise and will endeavour with firm determination to lend every support possible to the extension of the teaching work throughout all the provinces of Canada, so that the glorious promises given by 'Abdu'l-Bahá regarding the future of the Cause in that land may be speedily and completely realized.

The Guardian is truly delighted to know of the contribution your group has made to the teaching fund of the National Spiritual Assembly, and trusts you will continue extending every assistance you can to the nation-wide teaching efforts of the American believers. He is praying from the depth of his heart that whatever steps you may take for the furtherance of this sacred Cause may be crowned with complete success.

Again with his best and deepest thanks for your message,

Yours in the Cause,

H. Rabbani

*May the Almighty fill your hearts with joy and gladness,
fulfil your highest hopes, and enable you to consolidate your
present-day achievements,*

Your true and grateful brother,
Shoghi

৩৹৻৻

11 August 1937

Dear Bahá'í Brother,

The Guardian wishes me to thank you for your welcome letter
dated June 9th informing him of your plan to visit Europe in the
next fall and requesting his permission to also visit Haifa. He would
be indeed delighted to meet you in the Holy Land, and cherishes
the hope that your pilgrimage to the Holy Shrines will fill you with
renewed energy and a stronger determination than ever to serve
and promote the interests of the Faith in your country.

As regards Mrs. . . . ; the Guardian thinks it preferable that she
should stay in Canada and concentrate heart and soul on the promotion of the teaching work there.

Assuring you both of his keenest appreciation of your services
in Montreal, and reciprocating your very warm greetings,

Yours in the Cause,
H. Rabbani

*May the spirit of this great and invincible Faith enable you
and your dear wife to surmount every obstacle and to expand
continuously the area of your activities and to deepen the be-
neficent influence which you exert upon the souls of those
whom you wish to attract to this glorious Revelation.*

Your true and grateful brother,
Shoghi

৩৹৻৻

11 February 1938

To an individual believer

Dear Miss . . . ,

The Guardian has been most pleased to receive your message of the 23rd January last informing him of your absolute acceptance of the Bahá'í Cause, and pledging yourself to devote all your time and energies to its service.

He rejoices to know that through the devoted and valuable efforts of dear Mrs. Ives[16] a group of thirteen believers has been formed in Moncton, and he cherishes the hope that this truly splendid start that has been made will be followed up by careful and well-planned teaching activity. He would urge you and each one of your fellow-believers to gird the loins of endeavour in this path, and to exert yourselves day and night until this supreme task is accomplished.

He will specially pray on your behalf at the Holy Shrines, that you may meet with increasing success in your activities for the spread of the Faith in Moncton and in the adjoining centres, and that your highest hopes of serving the Cause may be thus fulfilled.

Assuring you also of his prayers on behalf of dear Mrs. Ives, and all the friends in Moncton, and with loving greetings,

Yours ever in His service,
H. Rabbani

May the Almighty Spirit of Bahá'u'lláh watch over, sustain, and inspire you and your dear co-workers in that promising centre, and enable you to proclaim His Faith and establish the basis, and extend the range of its God-given institutions,
Shoghi

꙳

27 February 1938

To an individual

Dear Miss . . . ,

Shoghi Effendi was indeed pleased to receive your letter of the ninth instant, and has read its contents with attention and deep interest.

He was particularly rejoiced to know of the experiences you have passed through, and to realize that they all have served to draw you nearer to the Bahá'í Cause. He cherishes the hope that the spiritual forces latent in your heart will continue gaining in intensity and will lead you eventually to fully recognize and whole-heartedly embrace the Message of the New Day.

Now that you have opened your heart to the light of Divine Truth, and have not resisted the flow of Divine grace into it, you should consider it your duty to also endeavour consciously and persistently to investigate the Teachings, so that your mind also may comprehend them. Personal effort is indeed a vital prerequi-site to the recognition and acceptance of the Cause of God. No matter how strong the measure of Divine grace, unless supple-mented by personal, sustained and intelligent effort it cannot be-come fully effective and be of any real and abiding advantage.

Shoghi Effendi hopes therefore that you will continue in your efforts to study the Bahá'í Teachings, and trusts that through such deep and concentrated study you will become increasingly pen-etrated with their spirit, and will be led to eventually embrace the Faith.

With loving thanks and greetings,

Yours sincerely,
H. Rabbani

May the Almighty assist you to deepen your understanding of the fundamental verities of His Faith and enable you to pro-mote its teachings far and wide,

Shoghi

ᎧᏬᎧ

17 March 1938

To AN INDIVIDUAL BELIEVER

Dear Mr. . . . ,
The Guardian was indeed pleased to receive your letter of the

25th February, and to know of your safe return to Montreal, and to realize that the impressions you had carried back from your visit to the Holy Land are still very vivid in your mind. He hopes as years go by your realization of the great privilege you have had of visiting these Holy Spots will deepen, and that you will be increasingly stimulated as a result to work with added devotion and with a clear vision of the task that lies ahead of you.

It is now that you are back home that you can look at your visit in its true perspective, and appreciate its full significance. Gradually you will also be able to find the answer to certain questions which may still puzzle you. These inner struggles of the soul are indeed a necessary part of the spiritual development of a believer, and if faced and overcome with resolute will and deep faith they can be of an immense asset to his growth in the Cause. You need not feel perturbed therefore, but be confident that the outcome of the experiences you have been passing through will be to further strengthen and enlighten your soul, and to make it worthy of the love which you cherish for Bahá'u'lláh and His Faith.

The Guardian will specially remember you in his prayers at the Holy Shrines, asking the Beloved to continue showering upon you His richest blessings and His most inestimable favours.

With warmest greetings and good wishes for a happy Naw-Rúz to you and your dear wife,

Yours in His service,
H. Rabbani

May the Almighty, Whose Cause you are promoting with such earnestness, devotion and diligence, guide every step you take, remove whatever obstacles may hinder the progress of your work, and enable you to render memorable services to His Faith in the days to come,

Your true brother,
Shoghi

22 April 1938

To an individual believer

Dear Bahá'í Sister,

It is with profoundest sorrow that the Guardian has learned from your letter of March 29th that your mother is suffering from an acute case of cancer, and he wishes me to hasten to assure you of his brotherly sympathy in this truly grievous situation with which you are faced.

He feels that although the physicians have found the disease too advanced, and pronounced her condition as hopeless, you should still endeavour, by means of sustained and concentrated prayer, to bring about her cure. Now that no material effort can be of any effectiveness you still have one more way open before you, namely that of prayer, and you should therefore continue to supplicate from all your heart that, if it be God's Will, your mother may be restored to full health, and regain all her forces.

Bahá'u'lláh has revealed special prayers for both spiritual and material healing, and it is therefore your bounden duty to use such prayers on behalf of your mother, and thus put all your trust in the all-sustaining and all-healing power of God. It matters not whether you are endowed with high spirituality or not. The essential is that you pray with sincerity and with full purity of heart, and with the one desire of knowing and accepting His Will.

The Guardian too will pray for your mother at the Holy Shrines, that she may be given strength, patience and faith to meet her destiny with absolute courage and complete fortitude.

Yours in His Service,
H. Rabbani

May the Almighty Giver bestow upon you and your dear mother His richest blessings, sustain you in your activities and cares, strengthen your determination, and fulfil your highest hopes in the service of His Faith.

Your true brother,
Shoghi

☙

3 May 1938

TO SIEGFRIED SCHOPFLOCHER[5]

Dear Mr. Schopflocher,

Your communications of February 11th and April 14th with enclosure have been received and read with the closest attention by the Guardian.

He has noted with deep satisfaction in your last letter that the sum which you had pledged to contribute to the National Fund has been fully paid, and he has every hope now that, as a result of your most generous donation, the National Spiritual Assembly will be in a position to meet its financial obligations with regard to the Temple, and that the ornamentation work on that beautiful Edifice will henceforth progress without the least interruption.

The Guardian is also pleased to hear of the remarkable results Lorol[3] is obtaining during her teaching travels to various parts of the States, and particularly in California. Her great zeal, and the talents she is displaying in the teaching field are indeed assets to the teaching force in America, which the friends cannot but value and fully utilize.

With loving remembrances and all good wishes to her and to your dear self,

Yours sincerely in His Service,
H. Rabbani

Dearest Fred:

I cannot refrain from adding a few words in order to assure you of my special, most loving, and fervent prayers for you, that in the course of this year and those following your services will acquire still greater prominence, effectiveness, and wider range, and thus ennoble the unique record that will ever remain associated with your name in the annals of the Faith of Bahá'u'lláh.

Your true and gratified brother,
Shoghi

17 July 1938

Beloved Bahá'í Sister,

I am instructed by our beloved Guardian to acknowledge with thanks the receipt of your letter dated June 17th, which you had been requested to address to him by the St. Lambert Assembly conveying your condolences and sympathy on the occasion of the ascension of the Holy Mother. He indeed values the feelings of profound sorrow which you have expressed at her passing, and will pray that the grief which has so sadly overtaken your hearts may be transmuted into a peaceful and abiding joy, and stimulate you to greater heights of service to our beloved Cause.

The Guardian wishes me to take this opportunity of extending through you to the newly-elected Assembly in St. Lambert the expression of his cordial good wishes and heartfelt congratulations upon your first local elections during last April—which occasion, he believes, marked an important event in the history of the Faith in Canada. He now hopes that through your efforts other centres in the vicinity will be gradually opened to the Cause, and that henceforth through the instrumentality of our Canadian believers, who though few in numbers are so aflame with the desire to serve and who have already rendered such eminent services in the field of teaching, that through them the promises of our beloved Master regarding the glorious future awaiting their country will be completely fulfilled.

The Guardian will specially pray on behalf of you all that your Assembly may steadily develop, and be enabled to accomplish its allotted task under the Seven Year Plan, which is now being vigorously pursued and actively supported by all the friends throughout America.

Yours sincerely in His service,
H. Rabbani

May the Power that directs, permeates and animates this Faith, ever sustain you in your magnificent efforts and meri-

torious activities for its spread, and aid you to fulfil the dearest wish of your hearts,

> *Your true and grateful brother,*
> *Shoghi*

༄༅

26 January 1939

To AN INDIVIDUAL BELIEVER

Dear Bahá'í Brother,

Your welcome communication of the 18th December has duly reached the Guardian, and he is indeed rejoiced at your determination to work in the field of pioneer teaching. Your offer is the more welcome and appreciated in view of the increasing demand for pioneer activity necessitated by the heavy responsibilities assumed by the American believers under the teaching program of the Seven Year Plan. During the two years that have elapsed since the inauguration of this teaching campaign considerable progress has been achieved and exemplary self-sacrifice, determination and courage evinced by the believers. But the ground that still remains to be covered is so vast that much greater resourcefulness and consecration than have so far been displayed are needed on the part of every responsible Bahá'í individual and group if this teaching programme is to be fully carried out and completed at its appointed time.

Your offer to assist in ensuring the realization of this teaching task is therefore most opportune, and will be received with profoundest gratitude by all the friends, and in particular by the National Spiritual Assembly, who have been repeatedly urging the believers to offer their services in the field of pioneer teaching.

While the Guardian would advise you to definitely settle in one of the provinces of Canada where there are no resident believers, he prefers to leave it to your discretion as to what particular town or locality in these provinces you should choose to fix your permanent residence.

In case you find such plan impracticable however he would suggest that you should teach instead in either one of the Republics of Central America where the teaching work has very little advanced so far.

This is, of course, in case you find it financially and materially feasible to undertake the journey which is both long and arduous. The Guardian leaves the final decision to you, that you may act as you deem best under your present circumstances. But he will pray, in the meantime, that you may be guided in choosing the best and wisest plan, and be assisted in carrying it through with the fullest vigour and determination.

Assuring you once more of his best thanks for your most cordial and inspiring message,

Yours in His Service,
H. Rabbani

Dear co-worker:
I will assuredly and most fervently pray for you in your new field of service, whatever it may be, and feel certain that if you persevere the blessings of Bahá'u'lláh will be showered upon you. I deeply appreciate the spirit that so powerfully animates you, and am proud of your aims and of your determination. Rest assured and be happy.

Shoghi

ॐ

22 April 1939

To HOWARD COLBY IVES[17]

Dear Mr. Ives,

Your valued letter of the 15th March has duly reached our beloved Guardian, and he was pleased to note that you had safely received his message, as well as the six ringstones, which he hopes you have found satisfactory.

He was also considerably rejoiced to know that Mr. and Mrs. Robarts,[18] for whom you had asked his special prayers in your last letter, have joined the Toronto Bahá'í Community, and are progressing so well spiritually. He will continue to remember them in his prayers that they may keep on deepening in their devotion and love for the Cause, and that also they may receive ever-widening opportunities of promoting its truth, and of extending its foundations in their centre.

The Guardian wishes me to take this opportunity of assuring you also of his best wishes for the success of your efforts in connection with your projected book on the Cause—which production, he hopes, will soon be completed and ready for publication, and will, through its circulation, help in further reinforcing the teaching work throughout the States.

May Bahá'u'lláh bless your painstaking and devoted exertions in His path, and fulfil your heart's highest aspirations in service to His Faith.

With the season's warmest greetings,

Yours most sincerely,
H. Rabbani

Wishing you ever-increasing success in your incessant and highly meritorious labours for the spread of the Faith and the consolidation of its institutions,

Your true brother,
Shoghi

ڡۍ

28 April 1939

To AN INDIVIDUAL BELIEVER

Dear Bahá'í Sister,

Your welcome letter of the 17th March addressed to our beloved Guardian has been duly received, and it pleased him very deeply indeed to know of your appointment as chairman of the Temple Guide Committee, in which capacity, he hopes and will fervently pray, you will be able to render outstanding services to the Faith.

The work which the Bahá'í guides at the Temple are called upon to undertake is truly difficult and delicate, and requires such combination of qualities as sound knowledge of the Teachings, ability, tact and wisdom for their adequate and effective presentation as few believers can claim to possess. Only those who are considered well equipped, both intellectually and spiritually, should be selected for this type of work, and it is the duty of the Temple Guide Committee to exercise the utmost care in making such selection.

Those serving as Temple guides should, in all their contacts with the visitors, maintain the full dignity of the Cause, and provide the inquirers with accurate information regarding the Faith, and stress the universal aspects of the Teachings such as world unity, and its various implications. Political questions and all controversial subjects touching current political affairs should be strictly avoided. The conflicting political systems and philosophies of the day should neither be praised, nor censured, but the fact should be stressed that whatever the political regime under which it is enforced no purely national programme can be considered as adequate and self-sufficient. It is on the higher plane of international co-operation that the problems and difficulties now facing the world should be discussed and solved, and nothing short of the fire of a universal ordeal can succeed in infusing the right spirit in the hearts of the masses and leaders alike.

The station of Bahá'u'lláh, and the significance of the age in which He has appeared, together with the supreme and infallible remedy which His Teachings offer to ailing humanity should be equally stressed, in a clear and unequivocal language.

Those inquirers who are found to be receptive should be given more detailed information, and presented, on demand, with comprehensive and authoritative literature on the Faith.

With regard to your activities in connection with the training and education of Bahá'í children: needless to tell you what a vital importance the Guardian attaches to such activities, on which so much of the strength, welfare and growth of the Community must necessarily depend. What a more sacred privilege, and also what a weightier responsibility than the task of rearing up the new generation of believers, and of inculcating into their youthful and receptive minds the principles and teachings of the Cause, and of thus preparing them to fully assume, and properly discharge the weighty responsibilities and obligations of their future life in the Bahá'í Community.

The Guardian wishes you and your dear co-workers in this field continued success in your highly-meritorious services, and will specially pray for the guidance and confirmation of your efforts. He further wishes me to assure you of his prayers for the realization of your hope of visiting the Holy Shrines, together with your dear husband.

With his cordial greetings to you both,

Yours in His service,

H. Rabbani

May the Almighty Spirit of Bahá'u'lláh guide and sustain you in your activities, cheer your heart, illumine your path and fulfil the dearest wish of your heart in His service,

Your true brother,

Shoghi

ॐॐ

18 July 1939

To BEULAH S. PROCTOR[19]

Dear Bahá'í Sister,

Your most welcome and encouraging letter of the 7th June reporting on your pioneer work in Halifax, Nova Scotia, has duly reached our beloved Guardian and his heart was indeed flooded with joy and gratitude at the determination, and the exemplary spirit of consecration with which you are toiling for the spread and establishment of the Cause in that remote and hitherto unexplored Canadian province, and also at the evidences of the heavenly confirmation which you are receiving in the accomplishment of such a vital and highly-meritorious task. He has noted with deep pleasure the various promising contacts you have already established, and notwithstanding the difficulties with which you will have increasingly to contend in the future, you should confidently, earnestly and resolutely continue to maintain, nay widen and enrich, such associations and contacts, and thus gradually pave the way for the formation of a study group which would eventually develop into a group of interested and confirmed believers, and possibly into a duly-constituted and properly-functioning Bahá'í Assembly in a not too distant future.

Regarding Mr. . . . : the Guardian would urge you to strive making him a firm believer, and to create in him the desire to dedicate himself heart and soul to the service of the Cause. Also with regard to your contacting the women's clubs of Nova Scotia: there would be certainly no objection to your desire to do so, but it would be preferable that you concentrate on a selected few individuals who are sincere and truly receptive and to endeavour confirming them in the Faith. Personal contacts with limited, but eager and spiritually-minded persons, are often much more effective and fruitful than addressing large audiences. In your talks and lectures you should, for the present, avoid referring to labour problems, or to any governmental scheme regarding labour issues, as such considerations might lead you into the discussion of political questions which, of course, as a believer, you should by all means strictly avoid and disregard.

As regards your daughter . . . : the Guardian will pray for her that her devotion to the Cause, and her zeal to promote its knowledge may be deepened, and that she may gradually be inspired to take an active part in teaching the Faith. He would advise you not to press her unduly, but to carefully watch over her, so that she may gradually, of her own accord, arise and lend you full support in your teaching work.

As to your wish to enter into some kind of business, so as to be independent financially, while continuing your teaching work: he highly approves of this wish you have expressed which should be indeed the ideal of every Bahá'í pioneer. Assuring you, in closing, of his prayers for the confirmation of your services, and with cordial greetings,

Yours most sincerely,
H. Rabbani

Dear and prized co-worker:
Your most welcome and inspiring letter brought immense
joy to my heart. How proud I feel of your accomplishments,
your devotion, your perseverance and determination! Perse-
vere in your historic task, be happy and grateful and never
lose heart.

Your true and grateful brother,
Shoghi

ᔐᓚ

3 August 1939

To an individual believer

Dear Bahá'í Sister,

Our beloved Guardian has received your kind and most welcome message of the 13th July, and noted its contents with feelings of utmost joy and gratitude.

He is indeed happy to hear of your good news, and grateful
that you should have written him in such moving and assuring
tone, expressing such deep longing to become of increasing service to him and to the Cause.

He profoundly appreciates these noble sentiments that so powerfully animate and sustain you in your Bahá'í life, and will assuredly pray to Bahá'u'lláh that He may, in His unfailing love and
protection, bestow upon you such measure of guidance, and such
strength of body, mind and spirit as would enable you to translate
these high aspirations of your heart into deeds of loving and loyal
service to His Faith.

Do feel happy, confident, and persevere in whatever share of
service it may be your great privilege to render the Cause at present.

Yours most sincerely,
H. Rabbani

May the Almighty bless, guide and sustain you always, and
aid you to render distinguished service to His Faith and its
institutions.

Your true brother,
Shoghi

ᔐᓚ

25 August 1939

To DORIS SKINNER[20]

Dear Bahá'í Sister,

Your delightful message of July 23rd addressed to our be-loved Guardian was most welcome indeed, and he wishes me to hasten to thank you for it, and to express his satisfaction and grati-tude at the admirable work you have been accomplishing for the Faith in Calgary during the past few months. He hopes that before long you will succeed in establishing an Assembly in that centre, and wishes you from now on to concentrate all your efforts to that end with the help of Miss Dorothy Sheets,[21] whom you have al-ready confirmed, this goal should not prove impossible of attain-ment, and it is to be hoped that as soon as the holiday season is over you will jointly endeavour to start a regular study group which will form the nucleus of the future Bahá'í Assembly of Calgary.

Your desire to also assist in spreading the Cause throughout the province, and in the prairie cities, is indeed most commend-able, and the Guardian would certainly urge you to persevere in carrying out your plans in this connection, and would also sug-gest that you endeavour to contact the Germans and Ukrainians who form the largest section of the foreign population of that re-gion.

Now regarding your questions: the Guardian has considered them carefully, and wishes me to answer them in the order in which they have been put.

- The question of whether capital punishment should be inflicted on the criminally insane is one for the Universal House of Justice to decide. Such people, however, not being responsible for their actions, will not suffer any spiritual effect from acts committed while mentally deranged. . . .

- Regarding "mercy killings" or legalized euthanasia; this is also a matter which the Universal House of Justice will have to legislate upon.

- Suicide is forbidden in the Cause. God Who is the Author of all life can alone take it away, and dispose of it in the way He deems best. Whoever commits suicide endangers his soul, and will suffer spiritually as a result in the other Worlds Beyond.

- As regards the sterilization of the mentally deficient or the physically unfit; the Teachings bear no direct reference to the subject, and it therefore devolves on the Universal House of Justice to decide and legislate on this matter.

With the assurances of the Guardian's prayers for the confirmation of your services to the Cause, and also for the spiritual enlightenment and progress of your dear mother in the World Beyond, and with very warm greetings,

Yours in His Service,
H. Rabbani

Wishing you all success in your devoted efforts to promote effectively the best and vital interests of the Faith of God and its new-born institutions,

Your true brother,
Shoghi

୬୦୦ଏ

2 March 1940

To Sutherland Maxwell[22]

GRIEVE PROFOUNDLY YET COMFORTED ABIDING REAL-IZATION BEFITTING AND SO NOBLE CAREER VALIANT EXEM-PLARY SERVICE CAUSE BAHÁ'U'LLÁH. RÚḤÍYYIH THOUGH ACUTELY CONSCIOUS IRREPARABLE LOSS REJOICES REVER-ENTLY GRATEFUL IMMORTAL CROWN DESERVEDLY WON HER ILLUSTRIOUS MOTHER.[4] ADVISE INTERMENT BUENOS AIRES. HER TOMB DESIGNED BY YOURSELF ERECTED BY ME SPOT SHE FOUGHT FELL GLORIOUSLY WILL BECOME HISTORIC CENTRE PIONEER BAHÁ'Í ACTIVITY. MOST WELCOME AR-RANGE AFFAIRS RESIDE HAIFA BE ASSURED DEEPEST LOV-ING SYMPATHY.

SHOGHI RABBANI

୬୦୦ଏ

22 April 1940

APPRECIATE MESSAGE PRAYING FRIENDS FAITHFULLY FOL-
LOW MAY MAXWELL'S⁴ NOBLE EXAMPLE LOVE.
SHOGHI RABBANI

୧∼ଏ

28 June 1941

PRAYING SUCCESS EASTERN CANADA SUMMER SESSION.
SHOGHI RABBANI

୧∼ଏ

10 July 1941

OVERJOYED FIRST CANADIAN SUMMER SESSION ASSURE AS-
SEMBLED REPRESENTATIVES DEEPEST APPRECIATION FERVENT
SPECIAL PRAYERS.
SHOGHI RABBANI

୧∼ଏ

24 September 1941

Dear Bahá'í Friends:

The Guardian has instructed me to answer your welcome letter addressed to him on the occasion of the meeting of the newly
elected Montreal Assembly, on May 12th, which he has just received.

He will indeed pray for special blessings to be vouchsafed for
your work of spreading the Faith in Montreal and surrounding
districts throughout the coming year. Montreal, being as it is the
mother Assembly of the Dominion of Canada, should receive every help and encouragement the friends can give it, that it may

grow to be at once the first and one of the largest centres of the Faith in Canada.

The marked progress the Cause has made in recent years in that country should be a source of pride and happiness to all the friends. The Guardian feels that your Assembly, with the advice and aid of the regional and the national Teaching Committees, should exert every effort to increase the number of centres in Quebec, to encourage the visits of prominent teachers, and to reach—difficult as the task may be—the French-speaking population of that Province.

The believers of Montreal have contributed many active and outstanding workers in the Faith, whether teachers, pioneers or administrators; and Shoghi Effendi assures you all that you are very close to his heart and often in his prayers.

With the assurance of his abiding love and prayers, and with warm Bahá'í greetings,

Yours in His service,

R. Rabbani

Dearly-beloved co-workers:

I was so pleased and touched to receive your most welcome message and the noble assurances it contained. You are often in my thoughts and prayers, as I attach the utmost importance to your centre, recall the part it has played in the past and cherish bright hopes for its future. The great and distinguished services which individual members of your Assembly have rendered in the past, and are still rendering at present are assets that I greatly value. The example these have set and the work they have achieved are a source of profound and enduring satisfaction. May the Beloved sustain, guide and aid you to extend rapidly the range of your services, to proclaim far and wide the truths of this glorious Revelation, and lend a mighty impetus to its onward march.

Your true and grateful brother,

Shoghi

19 October 1941

Dear Bahá'í Sister:

Your letter of September 14th has been just received, and the Guardian has instructed me to answer you on his behalf.

He has been very pleased over recent news of the progress of the teaching work in Canada, and is happy to note that you and your dear husband are again active in spreading the Cause there. He feels sure that your devotion and the added experience gained through your pioneer work in Venezuela will enable you both to contribute richly to the progress of the work in Canada.

Canada must not be allowed to lag behind in the all-important work of the Seven Year Plan. She is a vast and promising country, and is entitled to her full share of spiritual enlightenment, and the Guardian hopes that you will give as much of your time as possible to virgin territories there—aiding in opening them up and establishing nuclei of future Spiritual Assemblies.

He most deeply appreciated your self-sacrificing labours in South America, and trusts that you will win ever greater victories in service to the Faith you love so dearly and have so wholeheartedly dedicated yourself to.

Rest assured that the selfless persistence with which you are serving our beloved Faith is deeply appreciated by Shoghi Effendi, and indeed helps to lighten his burden of cares and responsibility.

He will supplicate the blessings of Bahá'u'lláh for your work, and you will both be remembered in his loving prayers.

With Bahá'í love,

Yours in His service,
R. Rabbani

Dear and valued co-worker:

I wish to assure you of my deepfelt and abiding appreciation of the noble and exemplary efforts which you and your dear husband have exerted in recent years, and of the sacrifices you have made in the path of service to our beloved Faith.

Shoghi Effendi, Guardian of the Bahá'í Faith,
taken shortly before his passing in 1957

May and William Sutherland Maxwell

Bahá'í Shrine (home of May and William Sutherland Maxwell),
Montreal, Quebec

National Convention of the Bahá'ís of the United States and
Canada, Montreal, 1927

Montreal Young People's Group, c.1929
Front row: Henry Bergson, Mary Maxwell, Glen Wade, unknown
Middle row: Ruth Lee, Rosemary Sala, Alberta Simms, Else Lohse,
Bahiyyih Lindstrom, Dorothy Wade
Back row: Eddie Elliot, Walter Lohse, Emeric Sala, Norman
MacGregor, Thomas Lee, Edward Lindstrom

Louis Bourgeois, the architect of the mother temple of the West

Siegfried (Fred) Schopflocher, c.1941

Bahá'í House of Worship,
Wilmette, Illinois

Amatu'l-Bahá Rúḥíyyih Khánum, 1958

*I will specially pray that you may continue your work in the
pioneer field in Canada, where the field is so vast and the opportunities are manifold. You are often in my thoughts and I
trust that your highest hopes may be fully realized.*

Your true and grateful brother,

Shoghi

❦

23 March 1942

To A GATHERING OF BELIEVERS IN MONTREAL

*DEEPLY APPRECIATE MESSAGE GATHERED FRIENDS PRAY-
ING ABUNDANT BLESSINGS.*

SHOGHI RABBANI

❦

12 April 1942

To AN INDIVIDUAL BELIEVER

Dear Bahá'í Sister:

Your letter of January 1st was received by the Guardian, and I
have been instructed by him to answer you.

He is delighted to hear of your pioneer activities, and hopes
that you will meet with great success and be enabled to crown
your part of the Seven Year Plan with a notable victory for that
Province in the form of a Spiritual Assembly!

Though it is premature to try and endeavour to foresee on
what basis various nations would be represented on any international council, or in any international form of government, it is
clear that from the Bahá'í standpoint it could only be carried out
on a basis of true justice; and justice does not imply one race
having a preponderating vote over some other race's representatives, and thus being in a position to dominate them.

The Guardian will pray for those friends whom you have mentioned in your letter, as well as for you, that your work—of such

great importance at this time—may be richly blessed by
Bahá'u'lláh.

With Bahá'í love,

Yours in His service,
R. Rabbani

*May the Beloved of our hearts guide and bless you always,
remove every obstacle from your path, and enable you to promote, in a most effective manner, the life-giving principles of
our glorious Faith,*

Your true brother,
Shoghi

ঙ্গৰূ

15 April 1942

To AN INDIVIDUAL BELIEVER

Dear Bahá'í Brother:

Your letter of December 14th has just arrived, and the Guardian has instructed me to answer you on his behalf.

He was most happy to hear of how enthusiastically you are
serving the Faith in Canada, and the report of the various conferences that have been held was most encouraging to him.

The Faith, at last, seems to be really becoming more widely
known and embraced in the Dominion, and the Guardian hopes
that, in spite of the difficulties that face you all, the Canadian friends
will succeed in fulfilling in its entirety the teaching part of the
Seven Year Plan in their Provinces. This is of the utmost importance, and every Canadian believer should make it the very centre
of his conscious activities, and determine to see that nothing prevents him from ensuring that the Canadian share of glory, in the
fulfilment of the Plan by the first centenary of the Faith, is not lost.

The Guardian was also very pleased to hear that your wife and
sister have both recovered health and can continue their devoted
services to the Cause.

He received many flattering reports of the last year's Ontario

Summer session, and he will certainly pray that the 1942 one will be even more successful.

He will also continue to pray for you and your dear family, as well as for the believer whom you mention, Mrs. . . . , that God may strengthen you to render great services to His Faith during the coming days.

With Bahá'í love,

Yours in His service,
R. Rabbani

May the Almighty Spirit of Bahá'u'lláh guide your steps, cheer your heart, and aid you to advance the best and vital interests of our beloved Faith and its glorious, new-born institutions,

Your true brother,
Shoghi

ৡৢ

8 May 1942

To AN INDIVIDUAL BELIEVER

Dear Bahá'í Sister:

Your letter, on behalf of the Spiritual Assembly, and dated April 18th, was received, and the Guardian has instructed me to answer it.

He was most happy to see with what zeal and determination the Montreal friends are going about planning their work, and to learn that a French Canadian believer has been confirmed through the devoted efforts of dear Lorol.[3]

He assures you, one and all, of his continued loving prayers on your behalf and his hopes for your future services.

Montreal is an old and distinguished Assembly, and he hopes she will bear rich fruits for the centenary of our Faith.

With warm Bahá'í greetings and love,

Yours in His service,
R. Rabbani

Dear and valued co-workers:

I wish to add a few words in person and express my deep and abiding appreciation of the spirit that animates you in the service of the Faith, and of the work you have already accomplished. I will continue to pray for its extension and consolidation from the depths of my heart. Persevere and rest assured.

Shoghi

ৎৡ৽

15 June 1942

To Rowland Estall[23]

Dear Bahá'í Brother:

Your letter of February 15th reached the Guardian yesterday, and he has instructed me to answer you on his behalf.

He was very happy to hear from you. He has been following your activities, through various reports, with deep interest, and the news of the formation of a Spiritual Assembly in Winnipeg this spring greatly cheered him. This is, indeed, a victory of major importance to the Seven Year Plan, and more particularly to the Faith in Canada.

The progress which the Canadian believers, so few, relatively, in numbers, have been making is truly remarkable, and the Guardian hopes that this year they will succeed in doing twice as much as last year! This year is, he feels, the most important one as upon its success and failures depends the entire Plan's success or failure. Of course, needless to say, the Guardian is not envisaging the possibility of failure at all. But the great drive forward towards our goal must be mainly carried on this year, as there will still be a great deal of consolidation work needed to round off what has already been accomplished.

He is pleased to hear that you have fully recovered your health, and he hopes that your efforts during the coming year will be even more richly blessed than in the past.

His prayers will often be offered for you, and he welcomes news of your activities.

With Bahá'í greetings,

Yours in His service,
R. Rabbani

P.S. He thanks you for the photograph you enclosed of yourself, which he was pleased to receive.

Dear and valued co-worker:

I deeply appreciate the strenuous efforts you are so devotedly exerting for the furtherance of our beloved Faith. I will continue to pray for you from the depths of my heart. Persevere in your noble efforts, and rest assured that the Beloved will richly bless your high and valued endeavours.

Your true and grateful brother,
Shoghi

ও∾ৎ

29 July 1942

To an individual believer

TOUCHED APPRECIATE MESSAGE PRAYING UNPREC-EDENTED BLESSINGS MONTREAL'S SECOND CONFERENCE.
SHOGHI RABBANI

ও∾ৎ

14 October 1942

To an individual believer

Dear Bahá'í Sister:

Your letter of August 16th has just reached the beloved Guardian, and he has instructed me to answer you on his behalf.

He was very happy to hear from you and he welcomes you into the world-wide Faith of Bahá'u'lláh, and hopes you will be able to carry its light to many other sincere and seeking souls like yourself.

The news you gave him of dear Mr. Schopflocher[5] and his wife[3] was most welcome. He is, indeed, a very devoted Bahá'í, as is Ernest Harrison[24] also, and the Guardian is happy to know you have been able to study the teachings with such fine believers as these.

He assures you that he will pray for the protection of your son, and that God may guide him to the Truth in this day as He has guided you to it.

With the assurance of his loving prayers for your future services in the Cause, and with warm Bahá'í greetings,

Yours in His service,
R. Rabbani

May the Beloved of our hearts bless richly your efforts and aid you to further the vital interests of His Faith and its institutions,

Your true brother,
Shoghi

⟨∘⟩

15 November 1942

To an individual believer

Dear Bahá'í Sister:

Your letter of September 17th has been received, and the Guardian has instructed me to answer you on his behalf.

He was sorry to hear of the serious state of health of Mrs. . . . whom you mention as being such a fine soul, and he will certainly pray for her in the Holy Shrines that she may accept this great bounty from God of the knowledge of His Manifestation, and find happiness and comfort in it.

He deeply appreciates all you and your husband are doing in the service of the Faith at this critical period in the world's history, and he hopes you will both redouble your efforts, and stimulate the other dear Canadian friends to do likewise, so that the teaching work in Canada may fulfil all its objectives under the Seven Year Plan.

The work already achieved is something to be proud of, and he feels confident the friends can, through united effort, win through to a glorious victory by 1944—our first Centennial celebration.

You may be sure you and your family are remembered in his prayers, and he feels sure your services will ever increasingly widen in scope and bring home richer harvests to the beloved Faith.

With Bahá'í love,
R. Rabbani

May the Beloved bless you, and protect you, and enable you to promote effectively the vital interests of His Faith and its God-given institutions,

Your true brother,
Shoghi

ｽﾍﾞﾛﾞ

5 May 1943

To an individual believer

Dear Bahá'í Sister:

Your warm letter was received, and, although the Guardian answered your first letter to him, it seems to have gotten lost. This last letter of yours, dated December 28th, and which I am answering on his behalf, only arrived two days ago. He hopes this time his reply will reach you safely.

He is happy to hear of your great devotion to the Cause of Bahá'u'lláh and how clearly you have grasped the fundamental truth that all the Prophets are from One Essence and one in spirit. This is one of the greatest blessings the Faith has to offer to people—the knowledge of the unity of all religions.

He will certainly pray that God may watch over your sons and bring them safely home to you. He will also pray that they may recognize the Bahá'í Teachings to be the solution to the problems of the world today.

Assuring you of his loving prayers for your services to the Cause,
Yours, with Bahá'í love,
R. Rabbani

P.S. He was pleased to know you see the dear Salas[10] and Ernest Harrison;[24] they are all truly devoted Bahá'ís.

Assuring you of my special prayers for your spiritual advancement and for the success of your efforts in the service of our beloved Faith,

Your true brother,
Shoghi

꿍

26 May 1943

To AN INDIVIDUAL BELIEVER

Dear little Bahá'í Sister:
Your little letter to the Guardian pleased him very much, and he has told me to answer you on his behalf.

He feels that Bahá'í children like you have a lot of wonderful work to do for others in the future. But you don't even have to wait until you grow up, you can help your dear Mother teach the Cause to others right now, and also tell your playmates about it.

The Guardian is going to pray that you may grow up to be a shining light in the Cause of Bahá'u'lláh.

With love to you,

In His service,
R. Rabbani

May the Beloved bless, protect and guide you and enable you to serve His Faith in the days to come,

Your true brother,
Shoghi

꿍

22 June 1943

TO AN INDIVIDUAL BELIEVER

Dear Bahá'í Sister:

Your letter dated March 10th has been received, also the photograph of your two girls which you enclosed, and the Guardian has instructed me to answer you on his behalf. He hopes the way will open for you to find and teach some receptive souls, in your neighbourhood, this blessed message. As you say, all are not yet ready for it, and though they need it their eyes are not yet open.

The beloved Guardian is very busy these days with all his worldwide correspondence and plans for the celebration of the 100th anniversary of the founding of our Faith, which will take place in May 1944.

If you can manage to attend the Bahá'í Convention in Wilmette in the Temple next May it would be a wonderful experience for you and one that would bring you great joy indeed.

The Guardian assures you he will continue to pray for the spiritual development and enlightenment of your children and for your own work in the Cause.

With Bahá'í love,
R. Rabbani

Assuring you of my special prayers for the realization of every wish you cherish in the service of the Faith and for the promotion of the interests of its institutions,

Your true brother,
Shoghi

৩৵৻৶

19 December 1943

TO AN INDIVIDUAL BELIEVER

Dear Bahá'í Sister:

The Guardian has instructed me to answer your letter dated November 11th.

He feels that, since the National Spiritual Assembly has requested you to remain away from the Bahá'í meetings for a period
of a year, you should obey them implicitly. This does not mean
spiritual death, nor that you are not a believer in the Faith.

He does not wish you to be sad, but rather to prepare yourself
to take your place again in the Bahá'í Community, and work with
all the friends in a spirit of love and harmony. Every stumbling-
block in this world can be made a stepping-stone to progress and
development.

He assures you he will pray for you in the Holy Shrines, and
for your husband, and he will also place some candles there in
your name.

With Bahá'í love,
R. Rabbani

*May the Almighty bless your efforts, and enable you to up-
hold, at all times and under all conditions, the spiritual and
administrative principles of our beloved Faith and advance its
best interests,*

Your true brother,
Shoghi

ഴ൮

30 March 1944

To AN INDIVIDUAL BELIEVER

Dear Bahá'í Sister:

Your letter of February 20th, enclosing that of your husband,
has been received, and the Guardian has instructed me to answer
it on his behalf.

He hastens to assure you that he will supplicate in the Shrines
for that spiritual insight to be given to your husband which he is
seeking with so much humility and sincerity.

The Mormons are a people with high principles and ideals,
and the step spiritually into the Cause is not as difficult for them as
for many others not possessing their faith and devotion. However,

the very zeal with which they serve their own Faith makes it difficult for them to grasp the greater vision of our Holy Cause. He hopes that Mr. . . . , so obviously a devout Christian, will, through studying the Bahá'í teachings on Christ and the prophecies in the Bible concerning His Second Coming, and through a study of the life and spirit of Bahá'u'lláh, come to see that Christ, far from being lost to Bahá'ís, is enthroned in their hearts more deeply than ever through recognizing Him in this new Manifestation.

He deeply appreciates the tireless devotion with which you are serving the Cause, and he will pray that your heart's desires may be realized and your husband feel moved, of his own free will, to join you in its service.

With warm Bahá'í love and greetings,
R. Rabbani

May the Beloved guide your steps, cheer your heart, guide your husband to embrace the truth of this Revelation, and enable you to promote its vital interests.

Your true brother,
Shoghi

ॐ

6 July 1944

To AN INDIVIDUAL BELIEVER

Dear Bahá'í Brother:

Your letter of June 6th has been received, and the Guardian has instructed me to answer it on his behalf.

Regarding your questions concerning the advisability of changing the basis of the National Assembly's election and confining it to the body of delegates or of limiting the term of office: He feels that as any such changes are of a radical nature and should therefore also apply to the National Spiritual Assemblies of other countries they are inadvisable and premature, both for this reason and because of their very nature.

What is needed is to get the Administration in its present form to run more efficiently and at the same time to build up a higher sense of responsibility among the body of the believers. They should be encouraged to think more, not only about the qualifications of members of their elected bodies, but also about such things as you mention, the law of averages, the age and indisposition of some of the members, etc.

When we look back and see what the Administration has accomplished in twenty-odd years, indeed what it has done in the last seven years, we see what strides forward have been made. Far greater tasks lie ahead; but the Guardian does not feel that the way to meet them is to change the present system but rather to perfect it by educating the believers and training them, holding more conferences, publishing more news for Bahá'ís, getting more people active.

He wants you to know that he deeply values your and your dear wife's tireless and devoted services to our beloved Cause, and he will continue to pray for you both.

With Bahá'í love,
R. Rabbani

Dear and valued co-worker:

I wish to add a few words in person and assure you of my keen and abiding appreciation of your devotion, your zeal and perseverance in the service of our beloved Faith. I greatly value your services, and above all the spirit in which you render them. May the Beloved guide every step you take, and fulfil every desire you cherish for the promotion of His glorious Faith.

Your true and grateful brother,
Shoghi

ഇം

16 October 1944

To the Bahá'ís who attended the Fourth Ontario Summer Conference

Dear Bahá'í Friends:

Your letter of August 6th with the good news it contained of the success of your conference and the large number of friends present reached the beloved Guardian, and he has instructed me to answer you on his behalf.

He is very happy to see with what awareness of their responsibilities and devotion the friends are facing this new Century we have just entered upon.

Although wonders have been achieved in the teaching field in Canada during the last seven years, great tasks still lie ahead in consolidating the new Spiritual Assemblies and forming additional ones. He hopes the Canadian Bahá'ís will forge ahead to new victories and fulfil the Master's hopes for that great Dominion.

Assuring you all of his loving prayers for the success of your devoted labours,

Yours in His service,
R. Rabbani

Dear and valued co-workers:

I was greatly cheered and heartened by your most welcome letter. I admire and feel deeply thankful for your splendid achievements. I will pray for you from the depths of my heart, and wish you to persevere in your noble task and endeavour continually to extend the range of your meritorious services,

Your true brother,
Shoghi

✂❧

13 November 1944

To an individual believer

HEART OVERFLOWING SYMPATHY YOUR SUFFERINGS SO COURAGEOUSLY ENDURED. WOULD HAVE INSTANTLY COMMUNICATED HAD I KNOWN. BOTH YOU I TASTED CUP DISILLUSIONMENT TREATMENT NEAREST RELATIVES. FEEL CLOSE TO YOU REALIZATION YOUR SORROWS MEMORY YOUR SUPERB CONTINUED IMPERISHABLE SERVICES. PRAYING FERVENTLY HOLY SHRINES DEEPEST LOVE.

SHOGHI RABBANI

✂❧

6 April 1945

TO AN INDIVIDUAL BELIEVER

Dear Bahá'í Sister:

Although you were so considerate as to ask our beloved Guardian not to take time to answer your letter of February 11th, he wishes me to nevertheless reply on his behalf and assure you that he will specially pray, for the removal of your difficulties, in the Holy Shrines, and that Bahá'u'lláh may aid you to serve His Cause and exemplify His teachings in your daily life.

The Guardian appreciates the devotion and attachment to the Faith which prompted your letter.

With loving greetings,
R. Rabbani

Assuring you of my special prayers for your spiritual advancement, and for the success of every effort you exert for the promotion of our beloved Faith,

Your true brother,
Shoghi

౭౦౿

16 May 1945

TO AN INDIVIDUAL BELIEVER

Dear Bahá'í Sister:

Your letter of March 28th has been received a few days ago, and the beloved Guardian has instructed me to answer it on his behalf, and to also thank you for the loving thoughts and messages you have sent him from time to time in your letters to me.

He deeply values the great love and devotion which you feel for our precious Faith, and he assures you he will pray for you, in the Holy Shrines, that Bahá'u'lláh may enable you to fulfil your heart's desire and attract others to His wonderful Message. In some places the people are conservative and the Cause spreads slowly at first, but you should persevere and never feel depressed.

With warm Bahá'í love,
R. Rabbani

Wishing you the utmost success in your devoted endeavours for the promotion and consolidation of our beloved Faith,
Your true brother,
Shoghi

ço∽ço

29 October 1945

To AN INDIVIDUAL BELIEVER

FERVENTLY PRAYING SUCCESS CHARLOTTETOWN.
SHOGHI RABBANI

ço∽ço

22 March 1946

To THE NATIONAL YOUTH COMMITTEE OF THE UNITED STATES AND CANADA

Dear Bahá'í Sister:

On behalf of the beloved Guardian I wish to thank you for the lovely Naw-Rúz greeting card you sent him from the Bahá'í National Youth Committee and the young believers of the United States and Canada.

He was so happy to see the young believers are celebrating our Bahá'í New Year and entering with full hearts into the new age Bahá'u'lláh has inaugurated in the world.

With best wishes for you all,
R. Rabbani

ço∽ço

24 March 1946

To EMERIC SALA[10]

Dear Bahá'í Brother,

Your most welcome letter of March 5th was received by our beloved Guardian, and he has instructed me to answer it on his behalf.

The graphic and to-the-point description you have given him of the conditions you found in Latin American Bahá'í Centres helped him very much to see the picture of the work there as a whole, and he feels your recommendations to the Inter-America Committee are excellent.

He has felt from the very beginning that these gifted, sensitive Latins, who are capable of being both spiritual and intellectual, have a great contribution to make to the future progress of the Cause everywhere, and he is very anxious that they should become strong enough to manage their own affairs.

The many valuable services you are rendering the Faith—through your book,[25] your teaching trips, and your local Bahá'í work—are very deeply appreciated by him, and he rejoices to see you and your dear wife toiling so faithfully in the service of our beloved Cause. In this connection he wishes to thank you for the copies of your book which you sent him and which he placed in various Bahá'í libraries here.

He will pray that your labours for the Faith may be ever-increasingly blessed and fruitful.

With Bahá'í love,
R. Rabbani

Dear and valued co-worker:

The services which you and your dear wife have rendered in Latin America are highly meritorious, and evoke my heartfelt admiration. I pray you may have similar opportunities in the near future, and that the Beloved may, wherever you labour, bless abundantly your notable activities and accomplishments. Persevere in your work, rest assured, and be happy.

Your true and grateful brother,
Shoghi

ভৎ৵

12 June 1946

TO THE CANADIAN TEACHING COMMITTEE

ARDENTLY PRAYING UNPRECEDENTED SUCCESS NEWLY FORMED TEACHING COMMITTEE. URGE BROADEN BASIS

PROSPECTIVE NATIONAL ASSEMBLY THROUGH MULTIPLICATION GROUPS ASSEMBLIES. ADVISE INCREASE NUMBER REGIONAL CONFERENCES STIMULATE COMMUNITY LIFE PROMOTE NATIONWIDE CO-OPERATION AROUSE INTEREST MASSES GLORIOUS REVELATION DEEPEST LOVING APPRECIATION SERVICES.

SHOGHI

24 July 1946

TO AN INDIVIDUAL BELIEVER

Dear Bahá'í Sister:

Your letter dated September 8th was most welcome, and the beloved Guardian assures you he would have answered you sooner only he has been so very busy this past year.

He followed your and your dear husband's South American tour with great interest, and was delighted at the number of centres you were able to visit; your trip will surely produce good results in the teaching field, and stimulate the pioneers and local believers to redouble their efforts.

You should never feel discouraged, for your devoted and ceaseless services are much appreciated, and have been of great help to the work in many places.

Now that Canada is so soon to have its own National Assembly, he urges you and your dear husband to concentrate your efforts on strengthening and multiplying the Canadian Assemblies. This is of the utmost importance, as a preparation for this historic step so soon to take place.

Assuring you of his loving prayers on your behalf and for the success of your labours,

Yours with warm Bahá'í love,
R. Rabbani

Assuring you of my heartfelt appreciation of your splendid services to our beloved Faith, and of my loving and ardent

prayers that you and your dear husband may be enabled to enrich the record of your notable services, and to fulfil every desire you cherish for the promotion of the Cause and its institutions,

Your true and grateful brother,
Shoghi

28 December 1946

TO AN INDIVIDUAL BELIEVER

Dear Bahá'í Sister:

Your letter (with copies of others enclosed) dated October 18th, has been received, and our beloved Guardian has instructed me to answer you on his behalf.

He fully realizes what a great shock you have sustained through the death of this son over whom your heart had yearned for so many years, especially under such tragic circumstances, and he assures you of his deep sympathy and his loving prayers for the progress and happiness of . . .'s soul. . . .

Surely the way you can now be of the greatest help to your son's soul is to serve the Cause and promote its interests. The Master has often pointed out that deeds we do for, or contributions we make to, the Cause of God in the name of a departed person, aid that person's soul in the World Beyond. This is one of the mercies of God!

Before you and your dear mother-in-law make any definite plans for a Bahá'í summer school, he feels you should consult the Assembly. In this way you will be guided to do that which is best for the beloved Faith, and will be able to find a way of serving it in the memory of your son.

He hopes you will be able to not only help guide many young people and children into the Cause, but also to assist the parents to both embrace the Message and, through its teachings, bring their children up in the spirit of the New Day.

He assures you and Mr. . . . of his loving prayers for you both, for the success of your Bahá'í work, and, especially, for . . .'s soul in the World Beyond.

With warm Bahá'í love,
R. Rabbani

May the Almighty bless richly the soul of your dear son in the world beyond, console and sustain you in your great loss, enable you to promote, in his name, the interests of the institutions of His Faith, and aid you to fulfil your heart's desire in its service,

Your true brother,
Shoghi

৵৽৻

19 February 1947

To Emeric Sala[10]

Dear Bahá'í Brother:

Your letters dated October 16th and December 19th, with enclosures, were both received, and our beloved Guardian regrets very much the unavoidable delay in answering you, caused by pressure of certain urgent matters that arose.

He feels that there must have been some misapprehension on your part of his statements regarding future Guardians: they cannot "abrogate" the interpretations of former Guardians, as this would imply not only lack of guidance but mistakes in making them; however they can elaborate and elucidate former interpretations, and can certainly abrogate some former ruling laid down as a temporary necessity by a former Guardian.

You asked his views about your statement on the Bahá'í Faith and Communism: frankly he feels that the less the friends discuss Communism, and the Faith in connection with it, the better these days, as the subject is a burning issue, and no matter how discreet we are we run the risk of being involved in this highly political issue.

He wishes you to know that he very deeply appreciates the innumerable services you and your dear wife render the Faith. Reports of your South American work have reached him, as well as your own report of your fifth western trip, and he is delighted to see the response you are getting from the public. Your book[25] has, likewise, been a very useful addition to the teaching literature of the Faith in English, and you must rejoice to see the way God is blessing your labours for His Cause.

Tremendous work still remains to be done in Canada before the approaching election of its first National Spiritual Assembly; he hopes you and Mrs. Sala will devote as much of your time to this field as you can.

Assuring you of his loving prayers on your behalf, and for the success of your services.

Yours with Bahá'í love,
R. Rabbani

P.S. Through Mr. Schopflocher[5] he recently learned of your joint gift of a property to the Cause in Canada for a Summer School. This is much appreciated, and he hopes it will develop into a fine institution in the future!

May the Beloved, Whose Cause you are serving with such zeal, devotion and perseverance, reward you for your labours, guide every step you take in the path of service, and aid you to enrich the record of your meritorious and notable accomplishments,

Your true and grateful brother,
Shoghi

ﯓ

15 March 1947

To ELSA VENTO[26]

Dear Bahá'í Sister:
Your letter of January 15th was received, and our beloved

Guardian was very happy to hear from you. He has instructed me to answer you on his behalf.

The desire you have to return to Finland and teach your sisters and other people this wonderful Message meets with his full approval, and he hopes you will make every effort to do so. This would be rendering your native land a great spiritual service of historic importance.

Finland is so far away, and so few of the Bahá'ís have been able to visit it or to speak its language, that it has been very difficult until now to teach there. What is needed are believers like yourself and Miss . . . , who speak the language and who have the longing to teach the Finnish people.

He will certainly pray that the way may open for you to return to Finland and establish the Cause there on a firm basis.

With warm Bahá'í love,
R. Rabbani

P.S. He is writing to your sister in Finland, encouraging her to teach the Cause.

May the Beloved aid you to fulfil speedily your heart's desire, and enable you, in collaboration with your sister, to promote the interests of the Faith in Finland, and lay a firm basis for its God-given institutions,

Your true and grateful brother,
Shoghi

૭૦૮

7 April 1947

To an individual believer

Dear Bahá'í Sister:

Your letter dated March 10th has been received, and our beloved Guardian has instructed me to answer it on his behalf.

He quite understands how you feel, and you must have been shocked to find something in the teachings you love so dearly which savoured of church fines! But he assures you this is due to a misapprehension caused by a very bad translation of the *Aqdas*.

The fines specified by Bahá'u'lláh are very much the same in principle as those applied by common law as a punishment for breaking the law. No one can possibly associate these necessary checks on law-breaking with a church fine of any sort.

If you study the Bahá'í teachings deeply you will see that the laws of the *Aqdas*, as they will be applied in future, are really the protective framework of the New World Order, and have nothing to do with the ecclesiastical practices of the past.

He will pray that you may become an able and gifted teacher and promoter of our beloved Faith.

With warm greetings,
R. Rabbani

Assuring you of my loving prayers for your spiritual advancement, and the success of every effort you exert for the promotion and consolidation of our beloved Faith,

Your true brother,
Shoghi

ॐ

14 April 1947

To AN INDIVIDUAL BELIEVER

Dear Bahá'í Sister:

Your letter to our beloved Guardian, dated March 17th, was received and he has instructed me to answer it on his behalf.

He is very happy to learn of your determination to enter the field of pioneer service, certainly the most thrilling and one of the worthiest branches of Bahá'í service!

As to your question regarding the Fast: if there is any doubt in the mind of a person as to whether it will really be bad for that person's health to keep it, the best doctor's advice should be obtained. But generally speaking most people can keep it, anywhere in the world, with no detriment to their health. It is very good for the health and, once one forms the habit, each year it becomes easier to keep, unless one is run down. No one is obliged to keep it if it really harms them.

He will pray that your services to our Faith may be richly blessed, and that in Moncton you may attract and teach many new souls.

With loving greetings,
R. Rabbani

May the Beloved bless your efforts in the service of our beloved Faith, and aid you to promote the best interests of its God-given institutions,

Your true brother,
Shoghi

ဗ•ယ

14 April 1947

Dear Bahá'í Friends:

Your letter of February 23rd was received by our beloved Guardian, and he has instructed me to answer it on his behalf.

He has no objection at all to copies being made of any photographs sent for *The Bahá'í World* volumes; you are free to make any copies you wish to of those at present being used for Volume X.

There is a great deal of interesting historic data preserved in old photographs of the Cause, and it would certainly be useful to use some of these in the manner you have in mind. Unfortunately at the present time it is not possible here to go through stored material, have copies made and send them on to you; the pressing work of the Cause is such as to keep him and everyone else busy all day long! But he hopes in the future this kind of work can be undertaken and such records shared with the friends.

He assures you of his interest in your work and his loving prayers on your behalf and for its success.

With Bahá'í greetings,
R. Rabbani

May the Beloved bless your meritorious efforts, guide your steps, and aid you to assist effectively in the promotion of our glorious Faith and the consolidation of its God-given institutions,

Your true brother,
Shoghi

၆

20 April 1947

To an individual believer

Dear Bahá'í Brother:

Your letter dated February 7th was received and our beloved Guardian has instructed me to answer you on his behalf.

Since you have turned to him for advice he will give it to you quite frankly: he feels that, now that Canada is so soon to have her own National Spiritual Assembly, you should remain in the Dominion and serve there. There are so few Canadian Bahá'ís, relatively speaking, and they are scattered over such a vast territory, that to lose such an active worker as yourself would constitute a weakening of their forces. Where you serve he feels is up to you to decide; no doubt in Eastern Canada the need for help is greatest, but you should make your own choice.

It is very difficult to know what choices to make in life, and they are always conditioned by our own state of spiritual advancement; what would constitute an impossible sacrifice for one soul would seem to another a very small step to take!

There is certainly no reason why you should not go through life with a companion; Bahá'u'lláh strongly upholds the institution of marriage, and it need not hinder the service of an active Bahá'í if he married the right person. He assures you he deeply values your devotion and loyalty to the Faith and your readiness to put all personal desires aside in order to serve it. You may be sure his most loving prayers will be offered for your guidance, success and your happiness.

With Bahá'í love,
R. Rabbani

May the Spirit of Bahá'u'lláh sustain, guide, and bless you at all times and under all conditions, and aid you to render inestimable services to the Faith in Canada, and lend a tremendous impetus to its growth and the multiplication and consolidation of its nascent institutions,
Your true and grateful brother,
Shoghi

༺࿇༻

6 May 1947

TO THE BAHÁ'ÍS OF CANADA

. *SHARE JOYS HOPES DEARLY BELOVED MEMBERS CANADIAN BAHÁ'Í COMMUNITY URGE REDOUBLE EFFORTS AS HOUR TRIUMPH APPROACHES LOVING FERVENT PRAYERS.*
SHOGHI

༺࿇༻

4 July 1947

TO AN INDIVIDUAL BELIEVER

Dear Bahá'í Sister:

Our beloved Guardian has received your letter to him dated April 17, and he wishes me to drop you a little line of acknowledgement as he never likes to leave the friends' letters unanswered.

He is happy to hear that your concept of the Temple's tremendous significance has augmented since reading more deeply about it. There are so many movements and people in the world working indirectly for the ultimate realization of Bahá'u'lláh's Order, but only we few believers are working directly for it; that is why we cannot afford to dissipate our limited resources and energies.

He will continue to pray for the success of your Bahá'í work.

With loving greetings,
R. Rabbani

Assuring you of my loving prayers for your spiritual advancement and the success of your efforts for the promotion of our beloved Faith,

Your true brother,
Shoghi

ços

23 August 1947

To the Charlottetown Assembly

ASSURE YOU SPECIAL FERVENT PRAYERS.

SHOGHI

ços

27 September 1947

To an individual believer

Dear Bahá'í Brother:

I have been instructed by the Guardian to answer your letter to him dated August 26th. He hopes you received the reply to your cable, and was sorry that the answer reached you at such a late date. Your letter took some time to reach him, and as you had not mentioned any date in it he did not realize an urgent reply was needed!

He is very pleased indeed to see your enthusiasm for, and devotion to, this Faith you have so recently embraced, and desire to serve so ardently. As he informed you in his cable he feels your best course is to continue your education which will not only assist your own career, but better fit you for teaching the Faith. If it were possible for you to enter university, some place where you would at the same time be able to strengthen or open up a new Bahá'í centre, he would advise you to do this.

You may be sure he will pray for the success of your work and of your services to the Cause in Canada.

With warmest greetings,
R. Rabbani

May the Beloved aid you to fulfil your heart's desire in the service of our beloved Faith, and contribute a notable share to the progress and consolidation of its new-born God-given institutions,

Your true brother,
Shoghi

୨୦୧

14 October 1947

To the Canadian National Radio Committee

Dear Bahá'í Friends:

Your letter to our beloved Guardian, dated September 13th, was received, and he has instructed me to answer it on his behalf.

He is very pleased to see you have a Canadian Radio Committee now, as this type of teaching the masses is very efficacious and reaches people who would otherwise never hear of the Faith.

Now that Canada is to have its own National Spiritual Assembly the functions of this committee will become even more important in the future, and he hopes your work will meet with great success.

His loving prayers will be offered for the advancement of your work, you may be sure,

With warmest greetings,
R. Rabbani

Assuring you of my loving and special prayers for the success of your newly initiated activity, and the realization of every hope you cherish for its expansion, consolidation and ultimate fruition,

Your true brother,
Shoghi

୨୦୧

14 October 1947

Dear Bahá'í Sister:

Your letter to our beloved Guardian, dated September 28th has been received, and he has instructed me to answer it on his behalf.

He feels, in regard to the question you asked him, that under no circumstances should such a subject be discussed in the presence of non-Bahá'ís, as it might give them the impression we are fanatics. In teaching people, when they begin to seriously study the Faith, there is no objection to impressing upon them that this Message involves great spiritual responsibility, and should not be either accepted or cast aside lightly. But we must be very gentle, tactful and patient, and not administer shocks to people.

Bahá'u'lláh teaches that the Mercy of God exceeds His Justice. Ultimately there is hope for every soul of progress and forgiveness. But at the same time to turn aside from this Cause, once we have really contacted its spirit, is a grave error and one not to be minimized. But although we Bahá'ís know this, we cannot thrust such a statement on non-Bahá'ís. We must always teach constructively, and be very sure that none of us, through disagreement among ourselves or indiscretion, cool off the souls of the seekers.

He assures you all of his loving prayers for the advancement of the Cause in Hamilton.

With warmest greetings,
R. Rabbani

Assuring you of my loving prayers for the success of your efforts for the promotion of our beloved Faith, and the realization of every hope you cherish for its advancement,

Your true brother,
Shoghi

و~ح

10 December 1947

To an individual believer

Dear Bahá'í Sister:

Your letter to our beloved Guardian, dated November 27th, has been received, and he has instructed me to answer it on his behalf.

Regarding the questions you asked: self has really two meanings, or is used in two senses, in the Bahá'í writings; one is self, the identity of the individual created by God. This is the self mentioned in such passages as "he hath known God who hath known himself", etc. The other self is the ego, the dark, animalistic heritage each one of us has, the lower nature that can develop into a monster of selfishness, brutality, lust and so on. It is this self we must struggle against, or this side of our natures, in order to strengthen and free the spirit within us and help it to attain perfection.

Self-sacrifice means to subordinate this lower nature and its desires to the more godly and noble side of our selves. Ultimately, in its highest sense, self-sacrifice means to give our will and our all to God to do with as He pleases. Then He purifies and glorifies our true self until it becomes a shining and wonderful reality.

He assures you of his loving prayers for the success of your Bahá'í services.

With warmest greetings,
R. Rabbani

Assuring you of my loving prayers for your success in the service of our beloved Faith and of its God-given institutions,
Your true brother,
Shoghi

14 December 1947

TO THE MONTREAL ASSEMBLY

GRIEVE PASSING ELIZABETH COWLES[27] PRAYING AR-DENTLY PROGRESS SOUL ABHÁ KINGDOM RECORD HER MERITORIOUS SERVICES WILL NEVER BE FORGOTTEN.
SHOGHI

The Birth of the Independent Canadian Bahá'í Community and the Five Year Plan

1948-1953

The Birth of the Independent Canadian Bahá'í Community and the Five Year Plan

13 April 1948

TO THE CANADIAN BAHÁ'Í CONVENTION

HEARTS UPLIFTED THANKSGIVING BAHÁ'U'LLÁH EPOCH-MAKING EVENT COMING AGE DEARLY BELOVED CANADIAN BAHÁ'Í COMMUNITY FORMATION FIRST NATIONAL CONVENTION CITY MONTREAL FORTHCOMING ELECTION CANADA'S NATIONAL ASSEMBLY CONSTITUTING NINTH PILLAR INSTITUTION UNIVERSAL HOUSE JUSTICE. ACKNOWLEDGE REVERENT GRATITUDE DEEPEST JOY MARVELLOUS INFLUENCE OPERATION INITIAL STAGE 'ABDU'L-BAHÁ'S DIVINE PLAN ENABLING NORTHERNMOST COMMUNITY FOLLOWERS FAITH AMERICAN CONTINENT PASS STAGE INFANCY ATTAIN STATUS ASSUME FUNCTIONS INDEPENDENT EXISTENCE WITHIN WORLD BAHÁ'Í COMMUNITY. RECALL THIS AUSPICIOUS OCCASION WITH PROFOUND EMOTION HEROIC SERVICES MOTHER COMMUNITY MAY MAXWELL[4] WHOSE LIFE DEATH FORGED UNBREAKABLE LINKS BINDING BODY CANADIAN BELIEVERS SISTER COMMUNITIES UNITED STATES LATIN AMERICA. MOVED APPEAL ASSEMBLED DELEGATES ARISE CONJUNCTION FIRST CANADIAN NATIONAL ASSEMBLY TOKEN GRATITUDE MANIFOLD BLESSINGS DIVINE PROVIDENCE INITIATE HOUR BIRTH THEIR NATIONAL ACTIVITIES FIVE YEAR PLAN DESIGNED ASSOCIATE THEM FORMALLY SYSTEMATICALLY INDEPENDENTLY SISTER COMMUNITY UNITED STATES COMMON TASK PROSECUTION WORLD ENCOMPASSING MISSION. FULFILMENT THIS COLLECTIVE TASK CONFRONTING RAPIDLY

*MATURING COMMUNITY NECESSITATES INCORPORATION CA-
NADIAN NATIONAL ASSEMBLY ESTABLISHMENT NATIONAL
BAHÁ'Í ENDOWMENTS DOUBLING NUMBER LOCAL ASSEM-
BLIES THROUGHOUT DOMINION RAISING TO ONE HUNDRED
TOTAL NUMBER LOCALITIES WHERE BAHÁ'ÍS RESIDE
THROUGHOUT PROVINCES CONSTITUTION GROUP NEW-
FOUNDLAND FORMATION NUCLEUS FAITH TERRITORY
GREENLAND SINGLED OUT SPECIAL MENTION AUTHOR DI-
VINE PLAN PARTICIPATION ESKIMOS RED INDIANS MEMBER-
SHIP SHARE ADMINISTRATIVE PRIVILEGES LOCAL INSTITU-
TIONS FAITH CANADA. FONDLY HOPE ARDENTLY PRAY CEL-
EBRATION FIRST CENTENARY BIRTH BAHÁ'U'LLÁH'S PRO-
PHETIC MISSION WILL WITNESS TRIUMPHANT CONSUMMA-
TION FIRST HISTORIC PLAN LAUNCHED CANADIAN BAHÁ'Í
COMMUNITY IN LAND WHOSE FUTURE GREATNESS GLORY
BOTH MATERIALLY SPIRITUALLY CENTRE BAHÁ'U'LLÁH'S COV-
ENANT TWICE EMPHATICALLY PROCLAIMED HIS IMMORTAL
TABLETS.*[28]

SHOGHI

౸౪

28 April 1948

To the National Spiritual Assembly

*JOYOUSLY WELCOME ASSEMBLY'S PLEDGE SUPPLICATING
BAHÁ'U'LLÁH GUIDE SUSTAIN MEMBERS BEFITTINGLY DIS-
CHARGE SACRED RESPONSIBILITIES. URGE UTMOST UNITY
ENERGETIC ACTION UNRELAXING DETERMINATION ENSURE
BRILLIANT SUCCESS INITIAL TASKS MOMENTOUS NEW PE-
RIOD CANADIAN BAHÁ'Í HISTORY.*

SHOGHI

౸౪

16 September 1948

To THE NATIONAL SPIRITUAL ASSEMBLY

CONGRATULATE COMMUNITY AS WELL AS NATIONAL REP-
RESENTATIVES SPLENDID INITIATION MOMENTOUS ENTER-
PRISES SIGNALIZING OPENING PHASE HISTORIC PLAN. OVER-
JOYED EVIDENCES MAGNIFICENT SPIRIT CONSECRATION
UNITY DETERMINATION AUGURING WELL IMMEDIATE DESTI-
NIES LAND SO RICH DIVINE PROMISES COVERING SO EX-
TENSIVE TERRITORY ENDOWED SUCH VAST POTENTIALITIES.
WELCOME ITS CONTINUED ASSOCIATION AMERICAN SIS-
TER COMMUNITY. FERVENTLY PRAYING MULTIPLICATION
RESOURCES INCREASE NUMBERS INTENSIFICATION EFFORT
ACCELERATION MOMENTUM DEPENDING CONSECRATION
DEDICATION SACRED URGENT EPOCH-MAKING TASKS CON-
FRONTING NEWBORN HIGHLY PROMISING MUCH ADMIRED
CANADIAN NATIONAL BAHÁ'Í COMMUNITY.

SHOGHI

છ્જ

15 October 1948

To THE NATIONAL SPIRITUAL ASSEMBLY

NO LETTER RECEIVED FROM ASSEMBLY FORMATION
CABLE DATE LETTERS SENT AIRMAIL COPIES.

SHOGHI RABBANI

છ્જ

4 November 1948

To THE NATIONAL SPIRITUAL ASSEMBLY

Dear Bahá'í Sister:[29]
Your letter to our beloved Guardian, dated October 6th, has
been received, and he has instructed me to answer you on his
behalf.

Regarding the matter of the young men you have raised in your letter: he feels that they should be treated like any other people seeking admittance to the Faith, and be accepted on the same basis. Our teachings, as outlined in the *Advent of Divine Justice*, on the subject of living a chaste life, should be emphasized to them just as every other applicant, but certainly no ruling what-so-ever should be laid down in this matter. The Bahá'ís have certainly not yet reached that stage of moral perfection where they are in a position to too harshly scrutinize the private lives of other souls, and each individual should be accepted on the basis of his faith, and sincere willingness to try to live up to the Divine Standards; further than this we cannot go at present. . . .

Now that your Assembly is formed, and is embarking on its independent existence as a National Body, he wishes to emphasize a point which he is constantly stressing to other National Bodies: you must avoid issuing rules and regulations. The fundamentals laid down in the Bahá'í Administration must, of course, be adhered to, but there is a tendency for Assemblies to constantly issue detailed procedures and rules to the friends, and he considers this hampers the work of the Cause, and is entirely premature. As far as is possible cases which come up should be dealt with and settled as they arise, and not a blanket ruling be laid down to cover all possible similar cases. This preserves the elasticity of the Administrative Order and prevents red tape from developing and hampering the work of the Cause. You must likewise bear in mind that you are now a wholly independent National Body, and must consider the administration of the affairs of the Faith within your jurisdiction as your separate problem. There is no more need for you to follow every single rule laid down by the American National Spiritual Assembly, than there is for the British or the Australian and New Zealand National Spiritual Assemblies to do this. Uniformity in fundamentals is essential, but not in every detail. On the contrary, diversity, the solving of the local situation in the right way, is important.

He will be very happy to receive reports of the measures you are taking to carry out your important Five Year Plan. You have the unique distinction of being the first National Body, yet formed, to be born with a Plan in its mouth! And you may be sure your fellow Bahá'ís, East and West, are watching your progress with keen interest, not unmixed with curiosity, to see how well you fare in your historic work and your newly created independence.

The Guardian has high hopes for the achievements of the Canadian Bahá'ís. Their national character, which so fortuitously combines the progressiveness and initiative of the Americans, and the stability and tenacity of the British, fits them to make great contributions to the progress of the Faith, both in Canada and throughout the world.

He urges you to keep in close touch with him, and assures you that you, and your labours, are very dear to his heart, and he is ardently praying for your success in every field of your manifold activities.

With warm Bahá'í love,
R. Rabbani

P.S. Unfortunately your letter was not received in time to cable your October 14th meeting an answer.

Dear and valued co-workers:

I hail with a joyous heart and confident spirit the truly compelling and almost simultaneous evidences of the creative, the irresistible power of the Faith of Bahá'u'lláh as witnessed by the formation of the first Canadian National Bahá'í Assembly and the inauguration of the Five Year Plan, designed to orient its members toward and canalize the energies of the entire Canadian Bahá'í Community in support of the immediate tasks lying before them. So auspicious a beginning, in the life of a community attaining adulthood, under the influence of the processes set in motion as the result of the progressive unfoldment of the Divine Plan, in a territory of such vast dimensions, blessed through both the mighty utterances, and the personal visit of the One Who fostered it from the hour of its birth, and Whose Plan enabled it to reach maturity, may well be regarded as one of the most momentous happenings immortalizing the opening years of the second Bahá'í Century.

The responsibility shouldered by an institution ranking as one of the sustaining pillars of the future Universal House of Justice is indeed staggering. The Plan entrusted to its infant hands is, in both its magnitude and implications tremendously vast. The anxieties, the strenuous exertions attendant upon the proper guidance, the effectual development and the sound consolidation of a community emerging into independent national existence, are inevitably trying. The numerical strength of that community, the immensity of the area serving as the field for the operation of its Plan, the meagerness of the resources now at its disposal, the relative inexperience of its newly-recruited members, the perils overhanging the territory in which they reside in the event of a future global conflict, the intensity of opposition which the unfoldment of its mission may provoke in the strongholds of religious orthodoxy inimical to the liberalizing influences of the Faith it represents—all these offer a challenge at once severe, inescapable and soul uplifting.

The eyes of its twin-sister community in the North American continent, which assisted it in achieving its independence, are fixed upon it, eager to behold, and ready to aid it in its march to glory. Its sister communities in Latin America, whose coming of age is as yet unattained, watch with mingled curiosity and envy, its first strides along the steep path which they themselves are soon to tread. Other sister communities in the European, African, Asiatic and Australian continents, some of venerable age, others rich in experience, and resources, still others tried and tested by the fires of persecution, observe with keen anticipation in their hearts and benediction on their lips, the manner in which this youngest recruit to their ranks will launch upon its career, the resolution with which it will face its problems, the spirit which will animate it in its battles and the stupendousness of the efforts required to win its victories.

Above and beyond them the Spirit of a Master Who nursed it in its infancy and to Whose Plan it now has consecrated its mature energies, overshadows it with that self-same solicitude that called it into existence, that stimulated His tender care in its infancy, that inspired His written promises, that prompted His lavish praise, that impelled Him to cast the radiance of His person, in the evening of His life, on its mother city,[30] and induced Him, ere His passing, to bequeath to it so rich a legacy in what may be regarded as one of the mightiest repositories of His last wishes. No one, of the galaxy of immortal heroes, now gathered to the glory of Bahá'u'lláh, can contemplate with greater delight the advances which this community has made, or intercede with greater efficacy on its behalf, than she[4] who has won the peerless title of the Mother of that community, the initial phase of whose career was signalized by the founding of the mother community in the European continent, and the conclusion of which was crowned by a death cementing the spiritual bonds now indissolubly uniting the North and South American continents.

The Five Year Plan, now set in motion, must under no circumstances be allowed to lag behind its schedule. A befitting start should be made in the execution of the Plan in all its aspects. The initial steps should be relentlessly followed by additional measures designed to hasten the incorporation of your Assembly, to accelerate the multiplication of Local Assemblies, groups and isolated centres, throughout the Provinces of the Dominion, to insure the stability of the outpost of the Faith which must be established in Newfoundland, and to incorporate a steadily growing element, representative of both the Indian and Eskimo races, into the life of the community.

Obstacles, however formidable, will have to be determinedly surmounted. Any reverses that sooner or later may be suffered should be met with stoic fortitude, and speedily offset by victories in other fields. The glorious vision now unveiled to your eyes must never be dimmed. The illuminating promises enshrined in 'Abdu'l-Bahá's Tablets should not be forgotten for a

*moment. The quality of the success already achieved by so small
a number, over so extensive a field, in so brief a period, at so
precarious an hour in the destinies of mankind, should spur
on the elected representatives of this now fully fledged community to achieve in as short a period, over still more extensive an area, and despite a severer crisis than any as yet encountered, victories more abiding in their merit and more conspicuous in their brilliance than any as yet won in the service
and for the glory of the Faith of Bahá'u'lláh.*

Your true brother,
Shoghi

ক্ষ্ণ

23 November 1948

To the National Spiritual Assembly

*DELIGHTED INCREASE MEMBERSHIP PRAYING RESPONSE
PIONEERS URGE MAINTENANCE STATUS EXISTING ASSEM-
BLIES STEADY DEVELOPMENT MULTIPLICATION GROUPS.
DETAILED LETTER DATED NOVEMBER FOURTH MAILED CABLE
RECEIPT ALSO CABLE ASSEMBLY'S TELEGRAPHIC ADDRESS
DEEPEST LOVE.*

SHOGHI RABBANI

ক্ষ্ণ

12 January 1949

To the National Spiritual Assembly

*CHEERED GRATEFUL PROUD INITIAL VICTORIES MARK-
ING UNFOLDMENT PLAN DEARLY BELOVED MUCH ADMIRED
CANADIAN BAHÁ'Í COMMUNITY. FERVENTLY PRAYING STILL
GREATER MEASURE BLESSINGS PROVIDENCE. URGE IN-
CREASED UNITY CLOSER COLLABORATION GREATER SOLI-
DARITY NOBLER SELF-SACRIFICE. DEEPEST ABIDING LOVING
APPRECIATION MIGHTY ACCOMPLISHMENTS.*

SHOGHI RABBANI

ক্ষ্ণ

16 March 1949

TO THE NATIONAL SPIRITUAL ASSEMBLY

DELIGHTED RECENT ACCOMPLISHMENTS FERVENTLY SUP-PLICATING ALMIGHTY'S BLESSINGS DELIBERATIONS ACTIVI-TIES DEEPEST LOVE.

SHOGHI RABBANI

꙰

1 April 1949

TO THE NATIONAL SPIRITUAL ASSEMBLY

CABLE NUMBER ASSEMBLIES GROUPS ISOLATED BELIEV-ERS ALSO ANTICIPATED NUMBER ASSEMBLIES COMING RIḌVÁN.

SHOGHI RABBANI

꙰

21 April 1949

TO THE NATIONAL SPIRITUAL ASSEMBLY

PAYMENT EXPENSES NATIONAL ASSEMBLY MEMBERS CON-VENTION DELEGATES LEFT DISCRETION ASSEMBLY.

SHOGHI

꙰

2 May 1949

TO THE CANADIAN BAHÁ'Í CONVENTION

ACCLAIM MAGNIFICENT VICTORY[31] UNIQUE ANNALS FAITH EAST WEST. GLORIOUS EVENTS FORESHADOWED BY 'ABDU'L-BAHÁ TABLETS DIVINE PLAN LONG LAST UNFOLDING. NA-TIONAL ELECTED REPRESENTATIVES NEWLY FLEDGED HIGHLY PROMISING RICHLY BLESSED COMMUNITY DESERVE HEARTI-EST CONGRATULATIONS. APPEAL ITS MEMBERS ARISE TOKEN GRATITUDE OUTPOURING DIVINE GRACE BESTOWED INI-TIAL STAGE ITS INDEPENDENT DEVELOPMENT VIGOROUSLY

PROSECUTE PLAN ATTAIN ALL OBJECTIVES SET IMPERISH-
ABLE EXAMPLE SISTER COMMUNITIES BAHÁ'Í WORLD. AR-
DENTLY PRAYING STILL GREATER VICTORIES.

SHOGHI

౨ーン

9 May 1949

To the National Spiritual Assembly

WELCOME ASSEMBLY'S REDEDICATION TASK SUPPLICAT-
ING ABUNDANT BLESSING TREMENDOUS GLORIOUS UNDER-
TAKING FULFILMENT HIGHEST HOPES.

SHOGHI

౨ーン

19 June 1949

To the National Spiritual Assembly

Dear Bahá'í Friends:

Your letters to our beloved Guardian, dated October 19 and December 11, 1948 and March 30, 1949, have been received, with their enclosures, as well as the material you sent under separate cover. . . .

Your Assembly has much to be congratulated upon for your victories during the past Bahá'í Year have been memorable. The passing, in both Houses, of the Bill[31] relating to the official status of your Assembly was a cause for great rejoicing, as this is the first time in Bahá'í history that any government has taken such action in relation to our Faith's status. He would like, if possible, to receive duplicates of the official *Gazette* and all publicity given this matter, as the copies you sent were placed in the Mansion at Bahjí, but he wishes to have these documents at hand in his personal files as well.

The increase in membership in the Canadian Bahá'í Community this past year was also most encouraging. It shows that there is, primarily, unity among the believers, for where this fundamental quality is lacking in a Bahá'í community any real growth is impossible. That is why the beloved Master so constantly admonished the friends to be as one soul in different bodies, for this love and unity constitutes their spiritual health and gives them the strength to overcome all obstacles in their path.

He fully realizes how great are the tasks facing your Assembly, but feels confident that the Canadian Bahá'ís will be able to accomplish them and will, indeed, set an example to their sister communities in different parts of the world. The people of that country, the national character, are such as to hold high promise for the future of the Cause there, and the great range covered by your Plan is stimulating in the extreme. To be the Trustees of such a Faith, in such a place, at such a time is a marvellous privilege, and he is looking forward to your next achievements with confidence and keen interest.

You may be sure his loving prayers are with you in all you do for the beloved Faith.

With warmest greetings,
R. Rabbani

Dear and valued co-workers:

The progress achieved in the course of the opening year of the Five Year Plan, to which the newly emerged independent Canadian Bahá'í Community is solemnly committed, is such as to excite the admiration, and merit the gratitude, of the entire Bahá'í World. A community, so small in numbers, so restricted in resources, labouring over so extensive a field, shouldering such weighty responsibilities, has passed through the initial stage of its task and discharged its duties with such distinction as to be worthy of the glowing promises and weighty utterances recorded in 'Abdu'l-Bahá's Tablets regarding the material as well as the spiritual potentialities with which that great and promising Dominion has been endowed.

Through the swift and marvellous increase in its membership; through its faithful and uncompromising adherence to both the spiritual and administrative principles of the Faith it so nobly serves; through the multiplication of its administrative centres from the Atlantic to the Pacific sea-board; through the steady consolidation of its local and national Funds designed to sustain its ever-unfolding activities; through the spirit consistently manifested by the small yet eager and valiant band of its pioneers and administrators; and more recently through the official recognition providentially accorded the body of its national elected representatives by both chambers of the Legislature in that Dominion—an act wholly unprecedented in the annals of the Faith in any country, in either East or West— this vigorous, divinely sustained, resistlessly advancing community, has not only fulfilled the expectations and hopes that greeted its birth, but set a brilliant example to its sister communities in both the Eastern and Western Hemispheres.

The task which it has so splendidly inaugurated and which is being now prosecuted with such vigour, devotion, single-mindedness, harmony and determination, is still in the initial stage of its development. The process that has stimulated the growth and increased the number of its administrative centres must be accelerated no matter how great the sacrifice involved. The development of the local and national Funds must be continuously maintained as a prelude to the establishment of local and national endowments and the ultimate erection of a House of Worship that will incarnate the soul of a flourishing nation-wide community. The initiation of a systematic and sustained campaign beyond the frontiers of that Dominion, and in obedience to the Mandate of the Author of the Divine Plan, to which it stands inescapably pledged, and aiming at the introduction of the Faith in Greenland and the conversion of the Eskimos still remains to be undertaken. The consolidation of the summer school, the gradual incorporation of firmly established, properly functioning Assemblies are, moreover, objectives that must under no circumstances be overlooked or neglected.

As the operation of the Plan gathers momentum the members of this community must evince a still greater measure of solidarity, rise to higher levels of heroism, demonstrate a greater capacity for collective achievement, and attract still more abundant blessings on the varied enterprises on which they have embarked.

I am following the unfoldment of their Plan with eager and sustained interest. My ardent prayers will surround and accompany its prosecutors at every stage of their historic undertaking. My confidence in their ultimate success is not only unshaken, but has been immensely reinforced. May He Who watches over them guide every step they take, bless every measure they adopt, remove every obstacle that impedes their onward march, and fulfil every desire they cherish for the future glory, honour and greatness of their beloved Faith in that vast and richly blessed Dominion.

Shoghi

჻

5 July 1949

TO AN INDIVIDUAL BELIEVER

Dear . . . :

Your letters to our beloved Guardian, dated April 19 and June 15, with copy of the By-Laws enclosed, and other material sent, have been received, and he has instructed me to answer you on his behalf.

He approves of the By-Laws of the Canadian National Spiritual Assembly, and is immensely pleased over this remarkable witness to our Faith's growing importance as evidenced through the passing of the Bill regarding them in both Houses at Ottawa. As he has already stated, this is a unique precedent, and one which in time to come will no doubt be of great assistance in similar cases in other countries. You must be very happy indeed to see the way your tireless efforts have been crowned with such success in this important matter.

It is these evidences of the progress of the Cause which bring the greatest joy to his heart, as he is often weary, and feels the weight of the years of Guardianship very keenly at times. The many problems which beset the Faith, especially in the Eastern countries, the actions of those who have been disloyal to the Master, the ever-increasing amount of work, weigh upon him heavily. Such news therefore, you convey from Canada, lightens his heart.

Dear . . . , he is glad to hear you are well and constantly devoting yourself to serving the Cause, and hastening the fulfilment of the Five Year Plan, in Canada. There is much to be done, but he feels the Canadian National Spiritual Assembly is alert and devoted, and intent upon reaching all the goals set in good time. The spread of the Cause there is truly remarkable and promising. After all the years when the Faith seemed to barely move forward, it is now leaping ahead in that Dominion, which shows the patiently laid foundation was well laid, and the superstructure can now rise rapidly.

His loving thoughts are often with you, you may be sure.

With Bahá'í love,
Rúḥíyyih

Dear and valued co-worker:

Your recent and splendid accomplishments in connection with the incorporation of the Canadian National Assembly and the formulation of its By-laws are services of which I feel truly proud, and for which I will always feel grateful. You have indeed enriched the long and splendid record of your services to our beloved Cause. The Beloved will surely reward you abundantly for all that you have achieved. I will continue to remember you in my prayers, and will supplicate for you the Master's richest blessings.

Your true and grateful brother,
Shoghi

5 August 1949

To INDIVIDUAL BELIEVERS

Dear Bahá'í Friends:

Your letter of June 3 has been received, as well as the prospectus about your summer camp, and our beloved Guardian has instructed me to answer you on his behalf.

He wishes you and your son every success in this new undertaking, and hopes it will be a place where young minds can be guided into the right path—for they sorely need it in an age when the parents themselves are often confused, and can provide no moral inspiration for their children, and no proper example.

The way the work in Canada is progressing encourages him very much, and he appreciates very much the loyal and devoted services you are constantly rendering the Cause there.

With Bahá'í love,
R. Rabbani

Assuring you of my loving and fervent prayers for your welfare and spiritual advancement, and the realization of every wish you cherish, and the success of every effort you exert, for the promotion of our beloved Faith and the consolidation of its newly-born Institutions in that vast and promising country,

Your true brother,
Shoghi

৽৵

5 August 1949

To WINNIFRED HARVEY[32]

Dear Bahá'í Sister:

Your letter of June 28, 1949, was received, and our beloved Guardian has instructed me to answer you on his behalf.

In regard to your going to Newfoundland: he feels that since someone else is willing and eager to proceed there, and you would

lose a great deal by giving up your present employment, it is better
for you to postpone going there and in the mean time try and see
if the government would not be able to give you a job there in its
service, and by which you would not forfeit your pension. Also,
you might be able to arrange to spend your vacations there and
thus directly help the work.

The work you have done in Ottawa is very deeply appreciated
by the Guardian, and he feels sure that wherever you are, you will
constantly be supporting and expanding the work of the Faith.

With Bahá'í love,

R. Rabbani

*Assuring you of my loving prayers for your welfare, suc-
cess and spiritual advancement, and the realization of every
hope you cherish for the promotion of the interests of our beloved Faith in Canada, and particularly in Newfoundland,*

Your true and grateful brother,

Shoghi

〜

22 August 1949

To the National Spiritual Assembly

CABLE WHETHER LETTER TO ASSEMBLY REACHED YOU.

SHOGHI

〜

23 August 1949

To the National Spiritual Assembly

*DELIGHTED RECENT ACHIEVEMENTS URGE DIRECT SPE-
CIAL ATTENTION VITAL URGENT NEEDS GREENLAND AND
INDIANS ARDENTLY SUPPLICATING BLESSINGS MANIFOLD
TASKS CONFRONTING YOUNG VALIANT PROMISING COMMU-
NITY.*

SHOGHI

〜

4 September 1949

To an individual believer

Dear Spiritual Brother:

Your letter dated June 13 has been received by the Guardian, and he has instructed me to answer you on his behalf, and to thank you for the interesting material you forwarded with it.

He can only offer you, sincerely, his advice, which is to overcome whatever obstacles are hindering you from active membership in the Bahá'í Community. Man-made things are one thing, and God-given things another. It is not spiritually healthy to recognize the Revelation of God for this age—or at any period in history to recognize a Revelation sent by God for our good and development—and not embrace it. There is no middle course open for the soul who has found the Eternal Beloved. He must serve Him, or he will grow cold and spiritually confused.

As you obviously seem to have taken these teachings to heart he feels you should now become active in the service of the Cause.

He will pray for your progress and happiness and that you may be able to take this next step on your spiritual journey through life.

With kind regards,
R. Rabbani, Secretary

ৡৰৎ

17 September 1949

To the National Spiritual Assembly

ASSURE PIONEERS TRAVELLING TEACHERS FERVENT PRAYERS ACCOMPANYING THEM HIGHLY GRATIFIED ASSEMBLY'S DECISION MERITORIOUS LABOURS CONTINUALLY SUPPLICATING RICHEST BLESSINGS MAGNIFICENT HISTORIC ENDEAVOURS EVENTUAL GLORIOUS VICTORY.

SHOGHI

ৡৰৎ

24 September 1949

Dear Bahá'í Brother:

Your welcome letter of August 22 has been received, and our beloved Guardian has instructed me to answer you on his behalf.

He was very happy to hear the good news you conveyed in your letter, especially about the prospect of being able to arrange a pioneer for Greenland, as he attaches the greatest importance to this work, a work he feels which would particularly rejoice 'Abdu'l-Bahá's heart. He hopes the Canadian National Spiritual Assembly will be able to follow up this possibility and crown it with success.

You are welcome to write to him, but please do not feel he does not appreciate it if his answer is not always prompt.

Your trip will no doubt be of great interest to the friends in Canada and stimulate them, when they hear of the solid accomplishments of the European friends, in their own labours to fulfil their Plan.

He will certainly pray for your dear family, and your success in every way. Your constant services are deeply appreciated, you may be sure, by him.

With Bahá'í love,
R. Rabbani

Dear and valued co-worker:

I was so pleased to receive your letter and to learn of your active participation in the proceedings of the European Conference. Your meritorious activities and services in Canada are deeply appreciated, and I will supplicate the Beloved to bless continually your efforts, guide every step you take, remove all obstacles from your path, and enable you to win splendid victories for the newly born institutions of our beloved Faith. Persevere, rest assured and be happy.

Your true and grateful brother,
Shoghi

30 September 1949

TO AN INDIVIDUAL BELIEVER

Dear Bahá'í Sister:

Your letter to our beloved Guardian, dated August 16, reached him and he has instructed me to answer it on his behalf.

He was grieved to hear of some of the things you describe. It shows great spiritual immaturity on the part of some of the Bahá'ís and an astonishing lack of understanding and study of the teachings. To live up to our Faith's moral teachings is a task far harder than to live up to those noble principles the Moral Re-Armament inculcates, fine and encompassing as they are! Every other word of Bahá'u'lláh's and 'Abdu'l-Bahá's writings is a preachment on moral and ethical conduct; all else is the form, the chalice, into which the pure spirit must be poured; without the spirit and the action which must demonstrate it, it is a lifeless form.

He judges, from what you say, that the friends have not or at least many of them have not, been properly taught in the beginning.

There is certainly no objection to stressing the "four standards" of the Moral Re-Armament—though any teaching of our precious Faith would go much more deeply into these subjects and add more to them.

When we realize that Bahá'u'lláh says adultery retards the progress of the soul in the afterlife—so grievous is it—and that drinking destroys the mind, and not to so much as approach it, we see how clear are our teachings on these subjects.

You must not make the great mistake of judging our Faith by one community which obviously needs to study and obey the Bahá'í teachings. Human frailties and peculiarities can be a great test. But the only way, or perhaps I should say the first and best way, to remedy such situations, is to oneself do what is right. One soul can be the cause of the spiritual illumination of a continent. Now that you have seen, and remedied, a great fault in your own life, now that you see more clearly what is lacking in your own community, there is nothing to prevent you from arising and showing such an example, such a love and spirit of service, as to enkindle the hearts of your fellow Bahá'ís.

He urges you to study deeply the teachings, teach others, study with those Bahá'ís who are anxious to do so, the deeper teachings of our Faith, and through example, effort and prayer, bring about a change.

With Bahá'í love,
R. Rabbani

P.S. He feels your experience at the Temple should be regarded as in part an emotional reaction produced by disappointment and the fact you were still exalted by your happy days at the Moral Re-Armament camp. No doubt, if you visit the Temple under different circumstances, you will feel there an entirely different atmosphere—the one you expected to find, and which does exist.

May the Almighty guide, bless and sustain you, remove all obstacles from your path, and enable you to serve, effectively and at all times, the vital interests of His Faith and of its institutions,

Your true brother,
Shoghi

༄

20 October 1949

To an individual believer

Dear Bahá'í Sister:

Your letter dated August 10 has been received by our beloved Guardian, and he has instructed me to answer you on his behalf. He regrets the delay, but he has been very busy of late.

In regard to the question you asked him: he feels that if this annuity is paid to you by the Government direct, as a recompense for services you rendered, and in return for contributions you yourself made towards receiving it, there is no objection to your accepting it. But, if it is being given to you under the apprehension you are still a member of the church, he feels that is not proper, as, of course, you no longer are a church adherent.

He will certainly pray for the progress of the work in Regina, and he deeply appreciates the many devoted services you render our glorious Faith.

With warm Bahá'í love,
R. Rabbani

May the Almighty guide and sustain you in your devoted endeavours for the advancement of our beloved Faith, enable you to promote effectively the best interests of its nascent institutions, and contribute, at all times, to their multiplication and consolidation,

Your true brother,
Shoghi

ക‍ര

26 October 1949

To AN INDIVIDUAL BELIEVER

Dear Bahá'í Brother:

Your letter of September 21 was received, and our beloved Guardian is happy to see you are now settled down and that your dear mother and the Salas[10]—such devoted and fine believers— gave you assistance when you needed it.

No doubt your presence in Canada will be an asset to the work there, as it was to the progress of the European work, which you served so devotedly, and he will pray that you may soon be re-united with your family.

With warmest greetings,
R. Rabbani

Assuring you of my deep and abiding appreciation of your past services to the Faith, and of my ardent and loving prayers

*for the success of every effort you exert for its promotion in
the days to come,*

Your true and grateful brother,
Shoghi

ৼৄ

13 November 1949

To AN INDIVIDUAL BELIEVER

Dear Bahá'í Sister:

Your letter, dated October 28, with photo of your sweet child
enclosed, was received, and our beloved Guardian has instructed
me to answer it on his behalf.

He is very busy; but he assures you he thinks it no sacrilege
for a Bahá'í baby to lisp out the names dearest to our hearts! May
she grow up to be a radiant soul! He will pray for her in the Holy
Shrines,

With Bahá'í love,
R. Rabbani

*Assuring you of my prayers for you and for your progress
and spiritual advancement,*

Your true brother,
Shoghi

ৼৄ

24 November 1949

To AN INDIVIDUAL BELIEVER

Dear Bahá'í Sister:

Your letter of November 11 has been received by our beloved
Guardian, and he has instructed me to answer it on his behalf.

If there is any such movement, such as the one your friend
believes exists, he is not aware of it. He does not know if there is
any foundation of truth in this matter or not.

However, he feels that the Bahá'ís have a Plan, a solution to
the world's problems given by the Prophet of God for this day.

Their best way of serving the world is through the positive and constructive medium of the Cause, and not though the negative approach of fear of any one group. We have not the power—in the material sense of that word—to do any good in combatting many of the evils in the world today, economic or political or social, but we can do a unique service through our Bahá'í work, for this way we release the power of God, which is the only Force that can redeem men and carry us forward to an ultimate victory over the evil of today. He therefore urges you to devote your mind to peacefully serving the Cause and not worry over whether such a destructive group does or does not exist.

With Bahá'í love,
R. Rabbani

May the Almighty sustain, guide and bless you always, remove all obstacles from your path, and enable you to win great and memorable victories for His Faith and its institutions.

Your true brother,
Shoghi

ی‌ه‌ش

18 December 1949

To the National Spiritual Assembly

DELIGHTED NEWS PROGRESS FAITH ARDENT LOVING PRAYERS SURROUNDING YOU ALWAYS.

SHOGHI

ی‌ه‌ش

19 March 1950

To individual believers

Dear Bahá'í Friends:

As our beloved Guardian is very busy and over-worked at present this is just a little note on his behalf to tell you your letter of October 28 was received.

He will pray for you both and particularly Mr. . . .'s health.
With warm greetings,
R. Rabbani

May the Beloved bless your efforts, guide and sustain you always, and enable you to promote the vital interests of His Faith,

Your true brother,
Shoghi

ɷᴥ

4 April 1950

To the National Spiritual Assembly

CABLE WHETHER ANY PIONEER ENTERED GREENLAND. IF NOT WHEN.

SHOGHI

ɷᴥ

9 April 1950

To the National Spiritual Assembly

PREPARE PROMPTLY MAP CANADA SHOWING ASSEMBLIES GROUPS ISOLATED CENTRES AIRMAIL HAIFA.

SHOGHI

ɷᴥ

1 May 1950

To the National Convention

ASSURE ASSEMBLED DELEGATES VISITORS LOVING REMEMBRANCE SHRINES ARDENTLY PRAYING BLESSINGS DELIBERATIONS. MAY ENTIRE COMMUNITY BE VOUCHSAFED DIVINE STRENGTH DISCHARGE BEFITTINGLY SACRED DUTIES PROSECUTE VIGOROUSLY PLAN LEND TREMENDOUS

IMPETUS PROGRESS FAITH CONSOLIDATE MAGNIFICENT HIS-
TORIC ACHIEVEMENTS.

SHOGHI

ᔫᄰᔆ

23 June 1950

To the National Spiritual Assembly

Dear Bahá'í Friends:
Your letters dated June 21, October 3, December 20, 1949,
and February 15, April 10, and May 14, 1950 as well as various
other material, have been received by our beloved Guardian, and
he has instructed me to answer you on his behalf.

He feels sure you will understand the reason for the delay in
answering your letters—and, indeed, all the other National Spiritual Assemblies' letters—when he explains that not only has this
been a terrific winter of work in connection with the construction
of the Shrine, but since the beginning of April my dear father, Mr.
Maxwell,[22] has been dangerously and desperately ill. The anxiety
this caused us all, and the constant coming and going of doctors,
nurses, and two periods in hospital, has necessitated putting aside
all correspondence for months. Now, however, thank God, Mr.
Maxwell is slowly improving, and the threads of normal existence
can be taken up again by us all.

The Guardian was very happy to note the community increased
this year by sixty-six. He was also delighted to see your Assembly
arranged for all delegates to be present. This is very important,
especially during this period when full consultation and co-operation is necessary amongst all the far-flung Canadian Assemblies and groups, as well as isolated believers, in order to ensure
the success of your first and so important Plan.

He approves of the measures you have inaugurated for intensive teaching during the coming year, and trusts they will meet
with great success.

The British victories, in the face of great obstacles, and the
consistent success across the border in the United States, must be
at once an inspiration and a challenge to the Canadian friends.

There is no doubt they can succeed if the entire Community applies itself eagerly and confidently to its task.

The Guardian is immensely pleased over the settlement of pioneers[33] in Newfoundland; this has accomplished one of the specific desires of the beloved Master, and will redound to the glory of the Canadian Bahá'ís.

The next, most important task is to get Miss Gates[34] into Greenland. This is fraught with many difficulties, but he urges your Assembly to persevere and exert its utmost to remove every obstacle. He will specially pray that a way may open for her to enter that country.

Regarding your question about contributions: it is up to the individual to decide; if he wishes to devote a sum to a specific purpose, he is free to do so; but the friends should recognize the fact that too much labelling of contributions will tie the hands of the Assembly and prevent it from meeting its many obligations in various fields of Bahá'í activity.

Concerning the points your Assembly raised in the letter of December 20, 1949:

1. The Guardian considers this a purely secondary question of administrative procedure which your Assembly can decide upon for itself.[35] He is very anxious that no new rules and regulations should be introduced. As far as possible each National Spiritual Assembly should decide secondary matters for itself, and not try to lay down a rule general in application.

2. No fixed rule should be laid down about this either.[36]

3. Bahá'u'lláh gives no right of appeal to the law that both parents must give permission to the marriage, if they are living. Bahá'í marriages should be referred to Assemblies to officiate; where there is no Assembly to officiate your body is free to decide what procedure should be followed. Whether it is the chairman or secretary or some other person who actually conducts the marriage is, likewise, a matter for your body to decide.

The Guardian feels that next Convention you should permit only Assemblies to send delegates. This will encourage the various Provinces to ensure they do have an Assembly and consequently a delegate, or delegates.

The Guardian has not found it desirable, for various reasons, to send a recorded message to any Convention.

The work being done by various Bahá'ís, including our dear Indian believer[37] who returned from the United States in order to pioneer amongst his own people, in teaching the Canadian Indians, is one of the most important fields of activity under your jurisdiction. The Guardian hopes that ere long many of these original Canadians will take an active part in Bahá'í affairs and arise to redeem their brethren from the obscurity and despondency into which they have fallen.

The desire of your Assembly to remain in the closest touch with the Guardian pleases him very much—he assures you that the desire is mutual!

With the assurance of his loving prayers for you all,

Yours in His service,

R. Rabbani

P.S. The maps you forwarded were of great interest, and he thanks you for them. He intends to have one of them published in the next edition of *Bahá'í World*.

Dear and valued co-workers:

The progress achieved in various fields by the members of the Canadian Bahá'í Community under the direction of its national elected representatives, since the inception of the Five Year Plan, merits the highest praise, and augurs well for its success in the years that lie immediately ahead. The spontaneity with which the members of this community, on the morrow of its having attained an independent national existence, have arisen to execute the Plan designed for the furtherance of its interests and the consolidation of its newly-born institutions, the zeal and resolution which have characterized the prosecution of the task entrusted to their care, the notable success they have already achieved in the initial stages of their enterprise, have served to heighten my feelings of admiration for those who have directed its course and participated in its unfoldment, and to evoke the unstinted praise of all sister communities in both the East and the West.

Though much has been achieved in the course of the two years that have elapsed since the formulation of the Plan, the objectives that the members of this struggling, youthful and valiant community have set themselves to attain are still far from being fulfilled. Though the process of the multiplication of Bahá'í centres, over the length and breadth of so vast a territory, has been, steadily and speedily, gathering momentum, the number of groups that have achieved Assembly status is still relatively insignificant, while the pioneer activity designed to awaken and stimulate the interest of the Eskimos in the Faith and enlist their support may hardly be said to have been vigorously and adequately launched. The call to which this newly-fledged community has been summoned is admittedly urgent and challenging. The character of the tasks allotted to it is, in many respects, unique. The resources at its disposal for the discharge of its peculiar responsibilities are no doubt as yet inadequate. The obstacles that stand in its way and obstruct its path seem almost insurmountable. Its membership, when viewed in relation to the range over which it operates, is no doubt wholly inadequate. Yet the spirit which has consistently animated the members of the entire community, and the energy and determination which have distinguished their elected representatives in the discharge of their sacred duties, are such as to fortify the hopes which I, as well as their fellow-workers in both hemispheres, have cherished in our hearts, since the inauguration of their first collective enterprise in a land so rich in promise, so vast in its potentialities, and so honoured by the visit of the Centre of the Covenant Himself as well as by the glowing references made to it by Him in His immortal Tablets.

As the centenary of the birth of Bahá'u'lláh's prophetic Mission approaches, as the first historic Plan, signalizing the birth and rise of a highly privileged community, the sole partner of its great sister community in the South in the prosecution of 'Abdu'l-Bahá's Divine Plan, gathers momentum and enters the concluding stages in its evolution, a dedication even more conspicuous than that already manifested in the hour of the launching of the Plan must needs be displayed by all those who are called upon to participate in its prosecution. A sterner resolve, a nobler heroism, a greater unanimity in sacrifice, a further intensification of effort must be manifested, as the first stage in the evolution of the mission of the Canadian Bahá'í Community draws to a close, and paves the way for the inauguration of still more splendid enterprises along the path laid down for them by the unerring hand of the Author of the Divine Plan.

That this community will never relax in its high endeavours, that the vision of its glorious mission will not be suffered to be dimmed, that obstacles, however formidable, will neither dampen its zeal or deflect it from its purpose, is my confident hope and earnest prayer. He Who watches over its destinies, from Whose pen testimonies so significant and soul thrilling have flowed, will no doubt continue to direct its steps, to shower upon it His loving bounties, to surround it with His constant care, and to enable it to scale loftier heights on its ascent towards the summit of its destiny.

With a heart brimful with gratitude for all that this community has so far achieved, and throbbing with hope for the future exploits that will distinguish its record of stewardship to the Faith of Bahá'u'lláh, I pray that by its acts, this community will prove itself worthy of the trust confided to its care, and the station to which it has been called,

Your true and grateful brother,
Shoghi

☙❧

17 July 1950

Dear Bahá'í Brother:
Your letter of June 24, with the interesting enclosure, was received, and our beloved Guardian was delighted to hear from you,
as he followed with interest your trips abroad and your teaching
activities.

Although it is a considerable disappointment to have all doors
seemingly closed in the face of Nancy Gates,[34] it is wonderful news
you give him that Mr. Fuller[38] will be in Greenland for nine months!
God seems to have arranged for one believer to be on the spot
until your Assembly can get a real pioneer there.

It would be a great help if Mrs. Jensen of Copenhagen could
enlist the sympathy of her sister, and perhaps even visit her there,
and thus procure an opening for some believer from Denmark to
get a job in Greenland?

The Guardian very deeply appreciates the services you are rendering the Cause, and have rendered it in the past. You may be
sure he will support you with his loving prayers.

With Bahá'í love,
R. Rabbani

*May the Almighty bless, sustain and guide you always, re-
ward you abundantly for your meritorious labours, remove
every obstacle that hinders the progress of your work, and graciously assist you to promote effectively the best interests of
His glorious Faith,*

Your true brother,
Shoghi

ର୍ଚ୍ଚ

3 September 1950

*DELIGHTED MAGNIFICENT NEWS WELCOME EVIDENCES
ENERGETIC EFFORTS NOBLE ENDEAVOURS HIGH PURPOSE*

APPROACHING VICTORY ARDENTLY SUPPLICATING BOUNTI-
FUL BLESSINGS FULFILMENT CHERISHED HOPES DEEPEST
LOVING GRATITUDE ASSEMBLY'S INCESSANT EXEMPLARY
LABOURS.

SHOGHI

ཀྱ

11 September 1950

To the National Spiritual Assembly

Dear Bahá'í Sister:

Under separate cover the beloved Guardian is mailing you two photographic enlargements of the finished arcade of the Báb's Shrine.

He wishes you to please have these circulated as far as possible amongst the different centres, so the friends can enjoy seeing the finished beauty of the arcade, and afterwards hang them wherever the Bahá'ís will visit most and be able to enjoy them.

Please also inform the believers that the film of one view has been sent to the American National Spiritual Assembly and copies may be ordered from it.

Also be so kind as to acknowledge at once the safe arrival of these pictures.

With Bahá'í love,
R. Rabbani

ཀྱ

30 September 1950

To an individual believer

Dear Bahá'í Sister:

This is just a short note in reply to your letter of June 17 to our beloved Guardian, as he is so overworked and exhausted that he can barely keep up with his mail. In fact it begins to look as if he could no longer do so!

He thanks you for the book you are sending him. He sees no reason why you should not tell the Bahá'ís that cancer seems to be successfully treated by this method sometimes. But as we are a religion and not qualified to pass on scientific matters we cannot sponsor different treatments. We are certainly free to pass on what we have found beneficial to others.

With Bahá'í love,
R. Rabbani

May the Beloved bless, guide and sustain you, and enable you to promote the vital interests of His Faith,

Your true brother,
Shoghi

ဖြစ်

30 September 1950

To THE BELIEVERS PRESENT AT THE 11TH ONTARIO SUMMER CONFERENCE

Dear Bahá'í Friends:

Your message dated August 18 has been received, and our beloved Guardian has instructed me to answer you on his behalf.

He was delighted to see so many friends had been present, and to witness the growth in this annual gathering, so useful for the teaching work and for promoting closer co-operation amongst the friends.

He assures you of his prayers for the success of your Bahá'í labours, and for the speedy realization of more of the goals set forth in your Five Year Plan.

With Bahá'í love,
R. Rabbani

Dear and valued co-workers:

I was so pleased and cheered to learn of the progress of your highly meritorious labours, and feel deeply grateful for the sentiments you have expressed. I wish to assure you of my special prayers for the steady extension of your activities to which I attach great importance, and for the future of which I cherish the brightest hopes. May the Beloved bless bountifully

Bahá'ís of Montreal, Quebec, c.1930

First Bahá'í Spiritual Assembly in the Maritimes,
Moncton, New Brunswick, 1938
Seated: J. H. King, Irving Geary, William Byrne
Standing: Alma Fairweather, Agnes King, Berford Stevens,
Ruth Wilson, Mark McEwen, Grace Geary

First Spiritual Assembly of the Bahá'ís of Winnipeg, Manitoba, 1941
Seated: Stella Pollexfen, Lillian Tomlinson, Sylvia King, Sigrun Lindal
Standing: Ernest Court, Helen Poissant, Rowland Estall,
Beth Brookes, Ernest Marsh

Lorol Schopflocher

Beulah Proctor
Halifax, Nova Scotia, 1941

Participants at the Bahá'í summer session held at Rice Lake,
Ontario, 1941

Participants at a Bahá'í summer conference at the Schopflocher
home in Montreal, Quebec, 1942

Edythe MacArthur and friend
at Rice Lake, Ontario, 1944

Howard Colby Ives and
Mabel Rice-Wray Ives

Eddie Elliot, first black
Bahá'í in Canada, c.1930

First Canadian Teaching Committee of the National Spiritual
Assembly of the Bahá'ís of the United States and Canada, 1946
Seated: Laura Davis, Doris Richardson
Standing: Siegfried Schopflocher, John A. Robarts, Victor Davis, Rowland
Estall, Emeric Sala

First Canadian Bahá'í National Convention of the Bahá'ís of Canada,
pictured behind the Maxwell home, Montreal, Quebec, 1948

First National Spiritual Assembly of the Bahá'ís of Canada, 1948
Front: Rosemary Sala, Fred Schopflocher, Laura Davis, Ross Woodman,
John A. Robarts
Back: Emeric Sala, Rowland Estall, Doris Richardson, Lloyd Gardner

Laura Davis, Secretary of the first
National Spiritual Assembly of
the Bahá'ís of Canada

Ola Pawlowska

First Spiritual Assembly of the Bahá'ís of Ottawa, Ontario, 1948
Seated: Francoise Rouleau, Katharine Ferguson, Winnifred Harvey, Gladys Young
Standing: Charles Murray, Marion Frederick, Ken MacLaren, Edna Hughes, Irving Frederick (Photographer: William Lingard, Ottawa)

First Spiritual Assembly of the Bahá'ís of Calgary, Alberta, 1949
Front: Jerry Stachow, Noel Wuttunee
Back: Millie Ogston, Doris Skinner, Edythe MacArthur, Greta Christopherson, unknown, Dorothy Sheets
Not shown: Douglas Wilson (photographer)

Spiritual Assembly of the Bahá'ís of Charlottetown,
Prince Edward Island, 1949
Front: Christine McKay, Edna Hollowell, Irving Geary,
Daisy Lyle, Grace Geary
Back: Jameson Bond, Marjory Patterson, Doris McKay,
Willard McKay

Spiritual Assembly of the Bahá'ís of Toronto, Ontario, c.1949
From left: Virginia Young, Charles Roberts, George Keith-Beattie, Victor
Davis, Laura Davis, Lloyd Gardner, Mabel Aslett, Inez Hayes, Peggy Ross

Spiritual Assembly of the Bahá'ís of Hamilton, Ontario, c.1949
Seated: Dorothy Clarke Boys Smith, Hazel Cuttriss,
Frances Young, Amelia Clarke
Standing: William MacGregor, Gertrude Barr, Amy Putnam,
Nancy Campbell, Arthur Lehman

Bahá'í Conference, Victoria, British Columbia, 1949

Marion Jack in Bulgaria

John A. and Audrey Robarts and
and children Nina, Patrick, Gerald
and Aldham, c.1950
(courtesy of Nina Robarts Tinnion)

Jameson and Gale Bond, 1953

Emeric and Rosemary Sala in Zululand, c.1954

Shrine of the Báb,
Haifa, Israel, c.1954

your high endeavours and assist you to further effectively the
vital and manifold interests of His Faith,

Your true and grateful brother,
Shoghi

ᦡᦡ

4 October 1950

TO THE GREENLAND TEACHING COMMITTEE

Dear Bahá'í Brother:

Your letter of July 14 has been received, and our beloved Guardian has instructed me to answer you on his behalf. As he is very busy and overtired he wishes you to please consider this as an appendix to the letter recently mailed you, as that makes it easier for him.

He feels your Assembly's best hope for Greenland seems to be the possibility of getting a Danish Bahá'í to go there as your deputy. If some believer from Denmark could get employment, or at least permission to proceed there, the details could no doubt be worked out.

Likewise, any Canadian Bahá'í who could qualify for scientific work there should make every effort to get in.

He is pleased to hear that at least Mr. Bond[39] and Mr. Fuller[38] will be there temporarily, and they should investigate all possibilities and report to your Assembly.

He will continue to pray that the way may open for real pioneer work to be undertaken there.

With Bahá'í love,
R. Rabbani

With the assurance of my fervent and loving prayers for
your success and the realization of every hope you cherish for
the promotion of our beloved Faith,

Your true brother,
Shoghi

ᦡᦡ

30 October 1950

Dear Bahá'í Friends:

Our beloved Guardian was very happy to receive your letter of September 10, which unfortunately took some time to reach him, or he would have answered sooner.

He is delighted over the success you have met with in your teaching efforts there, and very deeply appreciates the sacrifices you and your dear wife have made in order to render our Faith, and your people, this valuable service.

He does not feel it is right for you and your family to impoverish yourselves further in order to remain on the Reservation; on the other hand your being there and living amongst the people is undoubtedly the best way to teach them. He, therefore, suggests you present your problem and your own suggestions to the National Spiritual Assembly of Canada, and seek their advice and help.

He will pray that a way may open for you to earn your living properly, and also continue among the Indians.

He sends you and your family his love.

In His service,
R. Rabbani

With the assurance of my abiding and deepest appreciation of your services to our beloved Faith, of my heartfelt admiration for the spirit that animates you, and of my ardent prayers for the success of every effort you exert for its promotion and consolidation,

Your true and grateful brother,
Shoghi

꙳

2 November 1950

Dear Bahá'í Sister:

The beloved Guardian has mailed your Assembly, as a gift, two enlargements of the Báb's Shrine which he wishes to be shown widely to the believers and then hung where as many as possible will be able to see them.

Whenever these photos reach you please acknowledge receipt by cable.

He has sent two negatives to the American National Spiritual Assembly, and copies of these pictures can be purchased from them if the friends desire to order any.

With Bahá'í love,
R. Rabbani

P.S. I wrote you all this before but fear the letter may have been lost, as one to Mr. Holley,[7] mailed at the same time, was lost.

৽৽৽

January 1951

Dear Fred:[5]

Your letter of September 13 has reached the beloved Guardian, as well as the contribution made by the National Spiritual Assembly of Canada and some of the friends towards the construction of the Báb's Shrine, a receipt for which I am enclosing.

He is pleased to accept this loving donation for an enterprise so dear to all our hearts—and one which is fulfilling one of the Master's cherished plans.

There are so many obstacles to be overcome and so much red tape to be waded through, but he feels no time must be lost, and has just had the contract signed in Italy for the stone work for the octagon. God has opened all doors so far—he feels sure He will continue to do so.

With warmest loving greetings to you.
Rúḥíyyih

May the Almighty bless you and your dear and devoted co-workers, whose labours I deeply appreciate, whose contributions I greatly value, and whose spirit I truly admire. I will supplicate ardently on your behalf, that the Beloved may reward you abundantly, and enable you to win great and memorable victories in His service.

Your true brother,
Shoghi

ৎৣৣৄ

1 March 1951

To the National Spiritual Assembly

Dear Bahá'í Friends:

Your letters dated June 20th, September 8th and October 12th, 1950, and February 7th, 1951, with enclosures, have been received; and our beloved Guardian has instructed me to answer you on his behalf. He has also received the material sent under separate cover, for which he thanks you.

Although he is finding it so difficult to keep up with his correspondence, owing to the increase of work here at the International Centre, he follows with interest the progress being made by the believers in Canada; and is delighted to see how your Assembly is growing in maturity and capacity to handle the problems which invariably arise in connection with administering the affairs of the Faith in such a vast area as the Dominion of Canada.

He was very happy to know that the work in connection with the Indians and the Eskimos is receiving special attention; and he would like your Assembly to please express to Miss Nan Brandle[40] his deep appreciation of the unique service she is rendering the Cause, and of the exemplary spirit which is animating her. He hopes other believers will follow in her footsteps, and arise to do work in this very important field of Bahá'í activity.

He was also pleased to see that your Assembly had increased the annual budget, as this expresses the determination of the Canadian believers to expand their activities and carry on their work on a larger scale than ever before.

He was also very pleased to see that Mr. Bond[39] had gone north and had been able to contact the Arctic Eskimos. He hopes that the way will open for this devoted believer to establish a more permanent contact in that area in some field of government work.

He considers the policy of your Assembly of helping delegates from distant points to attend the Convention, an excellent one, as the attendance of these delegates enables them to carry back a very real awareness of the work in hand and the needs of the hour, to their local Communities.

The Guardian feels that, although the Canadian Bahá'ís are making excellent progress in consolidating their National Assembly and its subsidiary committees, in holding Conferences and Summer Schools, in sending forth travelling teachers, and in contacting the important minority groups, the Eskimos and Indians, that they are not making sufficient progress in the all-important field of pioneer activity. If they are to succeed in accomplishing their plan, a far greater number of Canadian Bahá'ís will have to arise and go into the pioneer field. He feels sure that they can do this, as they have already had the stirring example of how much was done in the British Isles by a Community of about their size. In comparing the problem which faced the British Bahá'ís under their Six Year Plan, and that which faces the Canadian Bahá'ís under their Five Year Plan, the friends should bear in mind that they were spared the severest ordeals of the war, the extreme restrictions and rationing which the British believers had to put up with. If the British Bahá'ís, with all their handicaps and suffering real physical and nervous exhaustion from the long war years, could accomplish so much, then surely the Canadian Bahá'ís, who were spared these conditions, are in a much better state to carry on and prosecute their tasks. What was done at the very breaking point in England, Ireland, Scotland and Wales could be done—must be done—by the Canadian believers, with much less effort. Although sacrifice is required, he feels sure that the friends are ready and willing to make the necessary sacrifice, and arise to ensure that the very first Plan, the very first organized work undertaken by them as an independent national Bahá'í Community, will be carried forward and victory ensured by the appointed time.

He assures all the members of your Assembly, and through you, the Community that you serve and represent, that your work is very dear to his heart, and that you are often remembered in his prayers. He is waiting to receive the good news that many more objectives have been achieved during this coming Bahá'í year.

With warmest Bahá'í love,
R. Rabbani

P.S. The Guardian has no objection to your publishing the excerpt from his letter dated August 25, 1939.

Dear and valued co-workers:

The energy, fidelity and courage, with which the Canadian Bahá'í Community has, in the course of this past year, faced its problems, discharged its duties and expanded the scope of its teaching and administrative activities merit the highest praise, and have greatly raised my hopes for the eventual consummation of the Plan which its members are so steadfastly prosecuting. Though unable, owing to a chain of circumstances beyond my control, to address them more frequently and convey to them my feelings of gratitude and admiration for their recent achievements, I have followed closely the course of their manifold activities, perused, with care and interest, the various publications which testify to their unremitting labours, and remembered them in my prayers in the Holy Shrines.

This community, though still in its infancy, is manifesting, in the course of the first years of its existence as an independent administrative entity, a virility, a steadfastness of purpose, a dedication to the Cause it serves, an organizing ability in the administration of its affairs that augur well for the glorious destiny disclosed by the Pen of the Author of the Divine Plan in His epoch-making Tablets. Already in the early stages of its life, when its administrative machinery was still merged with the institutions evolved by the followers of the

Faith residing in the Great Republic of the West, its fame, through a series of memorable events and noble exploits that have greatly enriched the annals of the Cause of God, had spread far and wide and the shadow of its future glory had run before it to the remotest corners of the Bahá'í World. For was it not 'Abdu'l-Bahá's own pen which, as far back as the dark years of the first World War, had forecast the splendour of the memorable achievements which, spiritually and materially, would distinguish and illuminate its annals in the years to come? "The future of the Dominion of Canada . . . is very great and the events connected with it infinitely glorious . . . Again I repeat that the future of Canada is very great, whether from a material or a spiritual standpoint."[28]

It was a Canadian,[41] of French extraction, who through his vision and skill was instrumental in conceiving the design, and delineating the features, of the first Ma_sh_riqu'l-A_dh_kár of the West, marking the first attempt, however rudimentary, to express the beauty which Bahá'í art will, in its plenitude, unfold to the eyes of the world. It was a Canadian woman,[42] one of the noblest in the ranks of Bahá'í pioneers, who alone and single-handed, forsook her home, settled among an alien people, braved with a leonine spirit the risks and dangers of the world conflict that raged around her, and who now, at an advanced age and suffering from infirmities, is still holding the Fort and is setting an example, worthy of emulation by all her fellow pioneers of both the East and the West. It was a member[15] of that same community who won the immortal distinction of being called upon to be my helpmate, my shield in warding off the darts of Covenant-breakers and my tireless collaborator in the arduous tasks I shoulder. It was a Canadian subject,[4] the spiritual mother of that same community, who, though fully aware of the risks of the voyage she was undertaking, journeyed as far as the capital of Argentina to serve a Cause that had honoured her so uniquely, and there laid down her life and won the everlasting crown of martyrdom. It was, moreover, a Canadian[22] who more recently achieved the immortal renown of designing the exquisite shell destined to envelop, preserve and embellish the holy and priceless structure enshrining the dust of the Beloved Founder of our Faith.

A community which, in the course of less than fifty years, has to its credit such an imperishable record of international service, and standing now on the threshold of a new epoch in its evolution, recognized as a self-governing member of the family of Bahá'í national communities, functioning according to a Plan of its own conceived for its orderly and efficient development, must, if it is to maintain the standard of excellence it has already attained, display on a still wider front, and continue to demonstrate, a no less profound spirit of dedication, as it forges ahead, in the years to come, along the road laid down for it by the Centre of the Covenant Himself in His historic Tablets.

As co-partner with the American Bahá'í community in the execution of the Divine Plan, it must evince in both the administrative and pioneer fields, a heroism that may be truly worthy of its high calling. In the remote and inhospitable regions of the North, amidst the Eskimos of Greenland and the Indians of the Dominion of Canada; throughout the Provinces of a far flung territory where newly fledged Assemblies, and nuclei of future Bahá'í institutions in the form of groups and isolated centres, lie scattered; in its relationships and negotiations with the local, provincial and national representatives of civil authority in issues affecting matters of personal status and the independence of the Faith and the establishment of its endowments; in its contact with the masses and in its effort to publicize the Faith, enhance its prestige and disseminate its literature, this community, so young, so vibrant with life, so laden with blessings, so rich in promise, must rise to such heights and achieve such fame as shall eclipse the radiance of its past administrative and pioneer achievements.

Then and only then will this community acquire the spiritual potentialities that will enable it to discharge, as befits a co-heir of the Tablets of the Divine Plan, the tremendous re-

sponsibilities, and fulfil the functions, devolving upon it be-
yond the oceans, and in all the continents of the globe.

May this community, the leaven placed by the hands of
Providence in the midst of a people belonging to a nation, like-
wise young, dynamic, richly endowed with material resources,
and assured of a great material prosperity by 'Abdu'l-Bahá,
play its part not only in lending a notable impetus to the world-
wide propagation of the Faith it has espoused, but contribute,
as its resources multiply and as it gains in stature, to the spiri-
tualization and material progress of the nation of which it
forms so vital a part.

Shoghi

❧

29 April 1951

TO THE NATIONAL CONVENTION

ASSURE DELEGATES FOURTH ANNUAL CONVENTION
HEARTFELT APPRECIATION NOBLE SENTIMENTS LOVING RE-
MEMBRANCE SHRINES. APPEAL CONCENTRATION EFFORTS
RESOURCES UNPRECEDENTED INCREASE PIONEERS STEADY
MULTIPLICATION CENTRES SETTLEMENT GREENLAND VIGOR-
OUS PROSECUTION WORK INITIATED ESKIMOS RED INDIANS.
SHARE HOPE PRAYER HOLY PRECIOUS RELIC MAY ENDOW
ENTIRE COMMUNITY LENGTH BREADTH VAST DOMINION
POTENTIALITIES ENABLE MEMBERS LEND COLLECTIVE TRE-
MENDOUS IMPETUS TASK CONFRONTING THEM ASSIST THEM
ATTAIN OBJECTIVES FIRST HISTORIC PLAN LAUNCHED NEWLY
EMERGED RAPIDLY CONSOLIDATING HIGHLY PROMISING
MUCH LOVED NATIONAL CANADIAN BAHÁ'Í COMMUNITY.

SHOGHI

❧

4 May 1951

DELIGHTED SUCCESS CONVENTION CONFERENCE ASSURE NEWLY ELECTED ASSEMBLY FERVENT PRAYERS EFFECTIVE RAPID PROMOTION PLAN DEEPEST LOVE.

SHOGHI

৵৹৵

27 July 1951

To John A. Robarts[18]

Dear Bahá'í Brother:

Your letter of May 21 has been received, and our beloved Guardian has instructed me to answer you on his behalf, and to also forward to you the enclosed receipt for your generous and loving contribution towards the building of the Holy Shrine.

He has been in touch with Mr. Bischoff,[43] and was overjoyed to see such a fine, conscientious soul was going to Greenland as a pioneer. Let us hope he will get results, as no doubt his task will require great tact.

The Guardian hopes the Canadian friends will, stimulated by the progress in Bahá'í work over the entire globe, arise with more determination to achieve their own Plan. They are too old and important a community to countenance failure!

He sends his loving greetings to you and your dear family,

With Bahá'í love,

R. Rabbani

With the assurance of my abiding appreciation of your generous contribution, my gratitude for your splendid and meritorious services, and my fervent and loving prayers for the success of every effort you exert for the promotion and consolidation of our beloved Faith,

Your true brother,

Shoghi

৵৹৵

30 October 1951

Dear Bahá'í Friends:

Your letters of March 29 and July 22 have been received, with enclosures, and the beloved Guardian has instructed me to answer you on his behalf.

Regarding the question of Mr. and Mrs. . . . : the Administrative Order is not a governmental or civic body, it is to regulate and guide the internal affairs of the Bahá'í community; consequently it works according to its own procedure, best suited to its needs. A Bahá'í who does more than visit temporarily a Community is considered for our administrative purposes as a resident and can vote and serve accordingly. Students in foreign lands, most obviously not residents, are registered as local Bahá'ís, and therefore entitled to do their share of work and play their part in the local Community life. This should be pointed out to . . . who seem to be confusing our internal administration with external practices which have no relation to it. As regards their personal attitudes the Guardian, remembering what a devoted worker . . . has been in the past, is very sorry to see she is no longer active. He does not feel this will lead to either her happiness or that of . . . ; for, whenever we compromise with what is noblest and best in ourselves, we are the losers invariably.

The Guardian was delighted to hear the friends are at last responding to the urgent needs of the Plan and going forth as pioneers. Plans are concrete things, and not mere honours, and victories—like all other achievements in life—must be purchased at the cost of persistent effort! He feels sure the Canadian Bahá'ís, perhaps slow to get under way, will display the counterpart of this British characteristic, and cling like bull dogs to their tasks, once they do get under way.

The departure of Mr. Bond[39] for the Arctic made the Guardian very happy; this, as well as the sailing of Mr. Bischoff[43] for Greenland, marks the opening stage of the campaign to carry the Faith to the Eskimos, a plan set forth by 'Abdu'l-Bahá and very dear to His heart.

Encouraging as these steps are, they do not take care of the main body of the work—the establishment of new Assemblies and groups. In order to accomplish this the entire Canadian Community will have to rise to a new level of activity, consciousness, and sacrifice, just as did the British Bahá'í Community during their Six Year Plan. Their success is perhaps one of the most remarkable ever achieved in the Bahá'í world because they were few in number, run down in health from the long years of suffering during the war, and poor in financial resources. Their determination, dedication and moral stamina, however, carried them through, and Bahá'u'lláh gave them the victory. He will give the same victory to everyone who shows the same characteristics. Success breeds success, and this same Community, now rightfully proud and conscious of its importance, is carrying on its African work in a brilliant manner. The Canadian Bahá'ís, more prosperous, less restricted, and equally capable, can accomplish just as much if they unitedly determine to do so.

The response made by the Canadian friends to the Guardian's appeal for support of the Shrine work has touched him very much. He wishes to thank all those who contributed for their loving generosity, and to assure them that their co-operation in this wonderful task has added to the spiritual beauty of an Edifice already so Holy and so beloved by all the believers the world over.

He wishes you all every success in the discharge of your arduous duties, and is praying for a marked quickening in the pace of the Five Year Plan.

With Bahá'í love,
R. Rabbani

P.S. The Guardian has received no copy of his last letter to you, sent last spring, and thinks perhaps the material was lost. Will you please send him a copy in whatever form it was circulated amongst the believers?

Dear and valued co-workers:
The Plan on which the attention of the Canadian Bahá'í

Community is focused, and upon the success of which must depend its immediate destinies, is now entering a critical stage, demanding increasing vigilance on the part of all its members, utter consecration to the Plan's objectives, and a determined inflexible resolve to carry it to a successful conclusion.

Little over a year separates this valiant community, still in the earliest stage of its independent existence, from the fateful hour that will mark the termination of the first collective enterprise undertaken in its history. The vastness of the field in which its infant strength is being tested is indeed staggering. The resources it can command are severely limited. The number of active participators, whether as pioneers or administrators, is admittedly small. The experience of the vast majority of its supporters is inadequate to the tremendous obligations it has assumed. The obstacles confronting it whether in Greenland, or among the Indians and the Eskimos of the extreme North, are truly formidable. Yet the potency infused into this community, through the Revelation of 'Abdu'l-Bahá's Divine Plan, and the spiritual capacity engendered in its earliest members through His visit to their native land—distinctions which it fully shares with its sister community in the Great Republic of the West—empower it to discharge—if it but rise to the occasion—all the responsibilities it has undertaken and consummate the task to which it stands pledged.

The eyes of the Bahá'í world are expectantly turned towards this newly erected pillar, designed to sustain in conjunction with other National Assemblies the weight of the Supreme Legislative Body of the World Order of Bahá'u'lláh. Sister communities in both the East and the West, less privileged than it and deprived of the primacy with which the twin Bahá'í national communities labouring in the North American continent have been invested by the unerring Pen of the Centre of Bahá'u'lláh's Covenant, yet able to achieve, under circumstances no less challenging, a success wholly out of proportion to their numbers, are eagerly awaiting the outcome of this initial crusade embarked upon by this blessed, this envied com-

*munity in conformity with the Mandate issued by 'Abdu'l-Bahá
in His immortal Tablets.[28] He Himself Who nourished and
watched over it with such loving care from the earliest days of
its inception, Who, in unmistakable language and on more
than one occasion, foreshadowed its glorious future, both
materially and spiritually, is from His station on high, gazing
down upon the youthful efforts exerted by a community so
dear to His heart, so newly launched upon a course which He
Himself has charted.*

*This final phase of the first Plan, undertaken by a newly
fledged, repeatedly blessed community, as it speeds to a close,
must witness an upsurge of spirit, of courage and determination, a display of activity, a demonstration of self-sacrifice
and of solidarity such as to eclipse its brightest achievements
in the past. The highly meritorious tasks initiated in both
Greenland and Newfoundland need not be enlarged at the
present hour, but should, under no circumstances, be allowed
to suffer any setback. The work started among the Eskimos
and Indians should be maintained at its present level, and
should not be permitted to decline. An extraordinary concentration of effort, systematic, determined and sustained, is however required throughout all the nine provinces of the Dominion, aiming at an unprecedented flow of contributions by the
entire body of the believers, each according to his or her means,
into the National Treasury; a marked increase in the number
of pioneers; a much greater dispersion; a higher degree of aus-
terity; a still nobler display of consecration—all of which must
result in a speedy multiplication of Assemblies and groups,
which constitutes the core of the Plan, and on which hinges its
fortunes.*

*The fleeting months ahead will be truly decisive. Upon the
success of the present Plan must depend, not only the joint
tribute to be paid by the Canadian Bahá'í Community to the
memory of the Founder of the Faith on the occasion of the
centenary of the Birth of His Revelation, but also the rapid
unfoldment of subsequent stages of the Mission which the Tab-*

lets of 'Abdu'l-Bahá so clearly and emphatically entitle it to fulfil.

The opportunity given to this Community is precious, unutterably precious. The fate of this first historic Plan now hangs in the balance. The present chance, if lost, cannot be retrieved. The issues on which hinge the successful prosecution of the Plan are so weighty that none can assess them at present. The needs of a sorely-stricken society, groping in its distress for God's redemptive Message, are growing more acute with every passing hour. The Canadian Bahá'í Community, newly emerged as an independent member of the Bahá'í World Community, so richly blessed through its elevation to the rank of a chosen prosecutor of a Divine Plan, unique, in many respects, among its sister communities in both Hemispheres in the manifold blessings bestowed upon it, can neither afford to flinch for a moment or hesitate in the discharge of its sacred duty. Every effort exerted by this community, during these fate-laden months, every sacrifice willingly endured by its members, will, if they but persevere, be richly blessed by Him Who brought it into being, Who nursed it through His love, Who conferred upon it so distinguished a Mission, Who made such magnificent promises regarding its future, and Who will continue to sustain it through His unfailing, His abounding grace and favour.

May this Community, ever aware of the position it occupies, and of the bright prospects unfolding before it, brace itself for one, last, supreme effort, and ensure, while there is yet time, the complete and total success of the enterprise to which it stands committed.

Shoghi

ೞ⌇

31 October 1951

To INDIVIDUAL BELIEVERS

Dear Bahá'í Friends:

Our beloved Guardian thanks you very much for the loving contribution you forwarded for the Shrine, in your letter of September 9, from you and your dear children. I am enclosing his receipt herewith.

He is delighted to see you are settled in such a virgin region (from our Bahá'í standpoint), and, although the teaching work will no doubt go very slowly at first, the effects of your labours will sooner or later be felt and be fruitful.

He will pray that the way may open for receptive souls to be found, especially among the Indians, and that you may soon claim at least one Bahá'í.

He sends you his loving greetings, and urges you to never feel discouraged.

With Bahá'í love,
R. Rabbani

Assuring you of my deep appreciation of your contribution, and of my fervent prayers on your behalf,

Your true brother,
Shoghi

ঙ৽৵

25 November 1951

To THE NATIONAL SPIRITUAL ASSEMBLY

CHARLOTTETOWN ESSENTIAL MONCTON SHOULD WAIT NEXT YEAR. PRAYING SUCCESS CONFERENCE DEEPEST LOVE.

SHOGHI

ঙ৽৵

25 December 1951

To INDIVIDUAL BELIEVERS

Dear Bahá'í Friends:

Our beloved Guardian has instructed me to acknowledge on his behalf your letter of November 11th, together with the loving contribution you have enclosed for the Shrine of the Báb. You will find a receipt attached.

The work on the Shrine is steadily progressing; and this holy enterprise is serving to draw the believers all over the world closer to the heart and centre of their Faith.

The Guardian assures you he will pray for the assistance of the devoted Canadian friends in achieving their goal, which includes a strong Halifax Assembly.

He trusts the Canadian Bahá'í Convention, which will be held in Halifax in April, will prove to be a great success and a mighty force to stimulate all the Bahá'ís to redouble their efforts.

With warm Bahá'í love,
R. Rabbani

Assuring you of my deep appreciation of your contribution and of my loving prayers on your behalf,

Your true brother,
Shoghi

৽৹৻

3 March 1952

To an individual believer

Dear Bahá'í Sister:

Your letter of February 14th has reached the beloved Guardian through the kindness of our dear Bahá'í brother, Mr. Schopflocher;[5] and he has instructed me to answer you on his behalf.

He hopes that you will be able to render the Cause increasingly valuable services; and feels sure that, with your love for it and devotion to it, you will be able to accomplish great things.

With warmest Bahá'í love,
R. Rabbani

Assuring you of my loving prayers for your success and spiritual advancement,

Your true brother,
Shoghi

৽৹৻

14 April 1952

Dear Bahá'í Sister:

Your letter of February 28th has been received by our beloved Guardian, and he has directed me to answer you on his behalf.

Your newspaper clipping book for the year 107 just arrived; and he will place it in the Mansion of Bahá'u'lláh, in the Reading Room.

He thinks the way the book is gotten up is quite satisfactory, but hopes that it does not cost you too much to go into such a presentable binding!

The services of your Committee are very deeply appreciated; and he hopes that you will ever increasingly be able to bring the Faith before the public in Canada.

With warm Bahá'í greetings,
R. Rabbani

May the Almighty bless you and your dear co-workers, and enable you to lend a great impetus to the progress of the Faith and the consolidation of its institutions,

Your true brother,
Shoghi

୭୬

27 April 1952

DELEGATES LOVINGLY REMEMBERED SHRINES PRO-FOUNDLY APPRECIATE REDEDICATION SACRED TASKS PRAYING FERVENTLY ATTAINMENT GOALS URGE CONCENTRATE OBJECTIVES MULTIPLICATION CONSOLIDATION ASSEMBLIES ESSENTIAL FOUNDATION EXPANSION FULFILMENT FUTURE MISSION BEYOND CONFINES DOMINION EXECUTION 'ABDUL-BAHÁ'S PLAN DEEPEST LOVE.

SHOGHI

୭୬

28 April 1952

To THE NATIONAL SPIRITUAL ASSEMBLY

FERVENTLY PRAYING SUCCESS NEWLY ELECTED ASSEM-BLY.

SHOGHI

❧

14 May 1952

To THE NATIONAL SPIRITUAL ASSEMBLY

WHETHER BEAULAC[44] BE MAINTAINED OR NOT LEFT ASSEMBLY'S DISCRETION. CONSIDER MATTER OBJECTIVELY. ARRANGING SEND TWO THOUSAND POUNDS MY CONTRIBU-TION FUTURE ḤAẒÍRA URGE ENERGETIC EFFORTS DEEPEST LOVE.

SHOGHI

❧

20 May 1952

To AN INDIVIDUAL BELIEVER

Dear Bahá'í Sister:

Your letter of May 4th has been received, and the beloved Guardian has instructed me to answer you on his behalf.

He deeply appreciates your great devotion to the Faith. The Guardian was happy to learn of the success you are having in your teaching work, especially with the Jewish people. He wishes me to assure you that he will pray for those whom you have succeeded in attracting to the Cause of Bahá'u'lláh, and that your own efforts may be richly blessed.

With warm Bahá'í greetings,
R. Rabbani

Assuring you of my loving prayers for your success and spiritual advancement,

Your true brother,
Shoghi

❧

20 May 1952

To an individual believer

Dear Bahá'í Brother:

Your letter of May 2nd has been received, and the beloved Guardian has instructed me to answer you on his behalf.

The Guardian has cabled the Canadian National Assembly regarding the Beaulac Summer School,[44] and feels sure that they will come as a Body to a wise decision. . . .

However, the most important thing is that the Bahá'í Summer Schools should serve the maximum number of friends in as efficient and economic a way as possible. Decisions regarding such institutions must be referred to the National Body; and, as you are a member of that Body, he feels sure that you will add your deliberations to those of your fellow-members, and come to the right decision.

You and your dear wife's services to the Cause are very deeply appreciated, you may be sure.

With Bahá'í love,
R. Rabbani

May the Beloved bless, guide and sustain you always, aid you to promote, at all times, the vital interests of His Faith, and lend a great impetus to the consolidation of its institutions,

Your true brother,
Shoghi

৽৽৽

8 June 1952

To the National Spiritual Assembly

Dear Bahá'í Friends:

Your letters dated October 9, 1951, signed by John A. Robarts,[18] November 28, 1951, February 15, March 17 and April 19, 1952, signed by Laura R. Davis[29] and May 15, 1952 signed by Ross Woodman,[45] with their various enclosures, have been received, and the beloved Guardian has requested me to answer you on his behalf.

He was very happy to hear that the Convention had been such a success, and above all, that the delegates had realized how urgent are the teaching tasks still facing the Canadian Community. He hopes that they will carry back to their local Communities a sense of this urgency, and stimulate the friends to make a heroic last effort and succeed. They say success breeds success; and there can be no doubt that, upon the accomplishment of the present goals must depend the work in the immediate future—both the degree of spiritual help that will be vouchsafed by God, and the number of tasks that will be entrusted to the Canadian Bahá'ís. He feels sure that if the believers become sufficiently aroused to an awareness of the critical nature of the coming months, they will take the necessary action, however great the sacrifice involved.

As he cabled you, he feels that Charlottetown, representing as it does one of the Canadian provinces, must be maintained at any cost.

In regard to the question you asked about the holding of the Canadian Convention in Wilmette, this would not be possible, as the National Body must hold its Convention in its own country. He suggests, however, that you make an effort to coordinate the dates in such a way that the friends can later proceed to Wilmette for the Intercontinental Teaching Conference and the dedication of the Temple. As long as it is held within the Riḍván period, the dates can be arranged any way that suits your convenience, and of course the Convention can be convened any place in Canada your Assembly decides upon, even on the American frontier at a point en route to Chicago.

The Guardian was most happy to hear of the excellent work some of the Bahá'ís are doing with the Eskimos and the Indians, and considers their spirit most exemplary. They are rendering a far greater service than they, themselves, are aware of, the fruits of which will be seen, not only in Canada, but because of their repercussions, in other countries where primitive populations must be taught.

He feels that the opening for a Canadian believer to visit the Governor of Greenland and his wife is extremely important.

The personality of the Bahá'í who accepts this invitation should be carefully considered, because to be a guest of people in a different climate and environment, of a different nationality and speaking a different language, so far away, might be a little trying, and of course the impression that this Bahá'í creates will be of infinite importance to the Faith in its future development in Greenland. Whether . . . makes the sacrifice and goes, or some other individual is chosen, he urges your Assembly to above all consider this matter tactfully and from the human standpoint, rather than the religious one, if one can put it that way.

He sees no objection to circulating the Tablet and the Prayer translated by Dr. Ali Kuli Khan.[46] The word that you marked in red is "Ark".

Your Assembly must decide, as the Guardian already told dear Mr. Schopflocher[5] when he was here, upon the advisability of maintaining the Laurentian School,[44] in an objective spirit. The Guardian can only outline to you the principle, which is that Bahá'í funds should not be invested in building up a place that has dear associations for a number of the friends, but is not going to really serve a large group of the believers. We are all familiar with the tremendous sums that have gone into the upkeep of Green Acre over the years, without so far bringing returns commensurate with the investment of our limited Bahá'í monies. However Green Acre, through its close association with the Master, undoubtedly has historic importance, and for this reason cannot be abandoned.

The Guardian's point is that National Bodies when creating national institutions, should use sound judgement, because of the financial investment involved. This is only reasonable.

Your Assembly must therefore decide what to do about the Laurentian School, and you are free to make your own decisions.

He would be very happy to have the National Assembly maintain the grave of dear Sutherland Maxwell.[22] His association, not only with Canada and the inception of the Faith there, but with the World Centre and the Shrine of the Báb, naturally endears him to all the friends, and his grave should be a national memorial. When the time comes to erect the tomb-stone, the question of receiving contributions from your Body can be considered.

He feels that the Canadian Community, old in the Northern Hemisphere, but young in its independence, is showing great promise, and he is proud of it and of the spirit that animates both its National Assembly and its members. He also feels confident it will distinguish itself, not only during the coming year, but during the next ten years before our Most Great Jubilee falls due in 1963.

With warm Bahá'í love,
R. Rabbani

P.S.—Regarding your question concerning St. John's, Newfoundland and the believers living outside the town limits: no exception to the general rule can be made in this case.

Dear and valued co-workers:

The Plan, with which the immediate destinies of the valiant, newly emerged, independent, highly promising Canadian Bahá'í Community are linked is, as it approaches its closing stage, passing through a very critical period in its unfoldment. Proclaiming as it does the formal association of the second Bahá'í community to attain an independent status in the Western Hemisphere with its sister communities who, in various parts of the Bahá'í world, are prosecuting specific Plans designed to foster their organic development, signalizing the alignment of this community as the sole ally of the Chief Executors of 'Abdu'l-Bahá's Master Plan, this collective fate-laden enterprise upon which this youthful and virile member of the world Bahá'í Family has so whole-heartedly and enthusiastically launched—an enterprise on the successful consummation of which the effective initiation of its glorious mission, far beyond the borders of the Dominion of Canada, must ultimately depend—such an enterprise, however vast the field in which it operates, and no matter how circumscribed the resources of the small band of stalwart pioneers engaged in its prosecution—*must, under no circumstances, be allowed to register a failure.*

In Newfoundland, in Greenland, among the Eskimos and Indians, through the incorporation of its National Assembly, the immediate objectives have been practically attained. The attention of the entire community must, in the remaining months ahead, be focused on the dire necessity of multiplying, at whatever cost, the number of pioneers, the rapid formation of groups, and the conversion of groups into Assemblies, so that the complete and total success of the Plan may be assured, and a triumphant community may step forward, confident and unencumbered by any liabilities, into a vast arena of service, prosecute a still more glorious mission, and win still mightier victories.

While the energy of this community is being expended on the conduct of this fateful undertaking, marking the baptism of this community, a collateral effort must, owing to unforeseen circumstances, be exerted for the establishment of an institution which, though not an integral part of the Plan formulated for that community, is nonetheless regarded as indispensable owing to its emergence into an independent existence, and the necessity of its following the lead of its sistercommunities in East and West, which have, at various stages in their development, adopted this vital measure for the consolidation of their national institutions and the raising of the prestige of the Faith in their respective countries. The selection of the city to serve as the seat of the national Ḥaẓíratu'l-Quds in the Dominion of Canada; the purchase of either a plot to serve as a site for the construction of this Edifice, or, preferably, of a building to serve as a provisional national administrative headquarters for a rising, steadily expanding community; the association of all other National Assemblies throughout the Bahá'í world in contributing towards this highly meritorious enterprise; my own association with the Bahá'ís the world over in providing for the early emergence of such a Centre towards which the manifold activities initiated through-

out the length and breadth of a vast Dominion must converge, and from which the impulses generated by a rapidly evolving, divinely appointed Administrative Order must radiate—these constitute the imperative needs of the present hour. The consummation of this added undertaking, the prompt discharge of this additional responsibility will, no doubt, constitute a befitting contribution by one of the youngest national communities in the Bahá'í world to the world-wide celebrations that are to commemorate the centenary of the birth of Bahá'u'lláh's Mission, and which will parallel the termination of the fifty-year-old enterprise of the first Mashriqu'l-Adhkár of the West and its official opening for public Bahá'í worship.

In conjunction with the various National Administrative Headquarters purchased or constructed, in the course of the last three decades, in five continents of the globe, and for the most part in the capital cities of several countries in the Eastern Hemisphere, this latest Edifice in the chain of Bahá'í national institutions linking five continents will, no doubt, serve to enhance the growing prestige of a world-wide Faith and consolidate the foundations of its administrative Structure. From far-off Sydney, on the shores of the South Pacific Ocean, and successively through New Delhi in the heart of the Indian subcontinent, Tihrán, the capital of Bahá'u'lláh's native land, Baghdád, the 'Iráqí capital enshrining His most holy House, Cairo, the Egyptian capital, the admitted centre of both the Arab and Muslim worlds, the city of Frankfurt in the heart of both Germany and of the European continent, and as far as the heart of the North American continent and in the neighborhood of the first Bahá'í centre established in the Western Hemisphere, this chain of Bahá'í bastions of a world-encircling Order, must be further extended through an additional link to be forged in the northern part of the Western Hemisphere, and its subsequent prolongation into Latin America as far as the Republics of South America.

One more word in conclusion. The passing, at this juncture, of one who, through a long career of distinguished ser-

vice to the Cause of Bahá'u'lláh, not only since the birth of this community but in more recent years in the heart and centre of the Bahá'í world, has left an indelible mark on the annals of the Faith, has evoked not only the deepest sorrow but the utmost regret at a time when this community is beginning to reap at long last the first fruits of its stewardship to the Cause of God, and the whole Bahá'í world is on the eve of celebrating one of its greatest Jubilees. By reason of his own saintly life, his self-effacement, gentleness, loving kindness and nobility of soul; by virtue of his remarkable endowments which he so devotedly consecrated to both the embellishment of the slopes of God's holy mountain and the creation of a befitting design for the second most holy Bahá'í Edifice embosomed in its very heart; and because of his kinship, on the one hand, with a wife[4] whom posterity will regard, not only as the mother both of the Canadian Bahá'í Community and of the first Bahá'í centre established on the European continent but also as one of the foremost pioneers and martyrs of the Faith, and, on the other with a daughter,[15] whose unfailing support to me as my helpmate, in the darkest days of my life, has earned her the title already conferred on her father—Sutherland Maxwell[22] has left a legacy, and achieved a position excelled by only a few among the supporters of the Faith of Bahá'u'lláh throughout the eleven decades of its existence.

Inspired by the example and the accomplishments of those of its members who have distinguished themselves in the Holy Land, on the European continent and in both the northern and southern continents of the Western Hemisphere, this community must forge on, with added determination, with increasing dedication, with thanksgiving and redoubled zeal, on the road leading it to a still more glorious destiny in the years immediately ahead. That it may press forward, conquer still greater heights, plumb greater depths of consecration, spread wider and wider the fame of the Cause of God is the cherished desire of my heart and the object of my constant supplication.

Shoghi

৩৵৵

15 June 1952

To THE NATIONAL SPIRITUAL ASSEMBLY

Dear Bahá'í Friends:

The beloved Guardian has instructed me to write you in his behalf, to request that the information relating to Canada and its activities, contained in the booklet *The Bahá'í Faith: Information Statistical and Comparative* be brought up to date as of May 1, 1952, and sent to him here by the first possible air mail post.

One of the features of the Holy Year will be the re-issuance of this important book; inasmuch as the Holy Year is fast approaching, the Guardian wishes the information as quickly as possible.

Briefly, the information which your National Spiritual Assembly is to provide, brought up to date as of May 1, 1952, is as follows:

Incorporated Local Spiritual Assemblies.

Localities where Bahá'ís reside in Canada, showing various Provincial divisions, such as is done in page 24 of the present book.

Any information not immediately available should be handled by telegraph, but such information as is available should not be delayed for any one or two delinquents. You can appreciate that if the booklet is to be published early in the Holy Year, the information should reach the Guardian at a very early date.

The Guardian sends his loving greetings to the National Assembly, and its devoted members.

Faithfully yours,
Leroy C. Ioas

༄

18 June 1952

To AN INDIVIDUAL BELIEVER

Dear Bahá'í Brother:

Your loving letter of Azamat 14, 109, has been received by the beloved Guardian, and he has asked me to acknowledge it on his behalf.

Your contribution and the one made through you to the Shrine of the Báb are deeply appreciated by him. Enclosed are the two receipts which you request.

The Guardian sends loving greetings to the members of the Toronto Assembly and Community.

The teaching activities in Canada are of the greatest importance, particularly in and around Toronto. The Guardian therefore hopes that all of the friends will devote their energies to the diffusion of the Faith.

The work on the glorious Shrine of the Báb is proceeding. The stone work on the drum is being put in place. The Guardian is very hopeful that this work may continue uninterruptedly until the entire building is completed.

With loving Bahá'í greetings, I am,
Leroy Ioas

۹۰و۹

28 July 1952

To the Treasurer of the National Spiritual Assembly

Dear Bahá'í Friends:

Your loving letter of July 14th has been received by the beloved Guardian, and he has asked me to acknowledge it in his behalf.

The contributions which have been made to the Shrine of the Báb are deeply appreciated by him. Receipts are enclosed herewith, which he would appreciate your giving to the contributors.

The Guardian is very deeply impressed with the wonderful work being done by the Canadian Bahá'ís. With their limited numbers and resources, they are rendering unique and outstanding services. Certainly they will be richly blessed and confirmed by the Master.

He is hoping that additional victories will be gained by the Canadian Bahá'ís during the present year, so as to lay the proper foundation for the great Teaching Crusade of the next ten years, and the important part that Canada must play in this world undertaking.

The work on the drum of the Shrine is proceeding rapidly now, and its beauty is more evident as the work progresses. The beloved Guardian is very hopeful that the work can continue on the Shrine uninterruptedly until both the drum and the dome have been finished.

With warm Bahá'í greetings,
Leroy Ioas

ဖ–၁

2 August 1952

To Greta Jankko[47]

Dear Bahá'í Sister:

Your loving letter of July 18th has been received by the beloved Guardian, and he has asked me to acknowledge it in his behalf.

Your contribution to the Shrine of the Báb is very deeply appreciated. Receipt is enclosed herewith.

The Guardian is very happy indeed to learn that, since becoming a Bahá'í, you are very anxious to serve the Faith. It would be very wonderful if you could undertake the translation of one or two pamphlets into Finnish after consultation with the European Teaching Committee, and carry on correspondence with any friends you might have in Finland concerning the Bahá'í Teachings.

There is a small beginning in Helsinki. The Guardian is very anxious that the Faith be spread in your land.

He will pray for your guidance and success.

You will be interested to know that work on the Shrine of the Báb is going forward quite rapidly at this time. The drum is taking shape, and adds to the beauty of the building. The beloved Guardian hopes the work may continue until it is entirely completed.

With loving greetings, I am,
Leroy Ioas

ဖ–၁

5 August 1952

To the National Teaching Committee

Dear Bahá'í Sister:

Your letter, on behalf of the National Teaching Committee, dated June 27, has been received, and the beloved Guardian has instructed me to answer it on his behalf.

It would seem as if the Canadian Community strongly resembles the British Community, very slow to move, but indomitable once it gets under way. But, whereas the work in Britain lay dormant for about forty years, the Canadian friends have only shown a relatively slight inertia for four years. He feels sure they will overcome it, and when they do, they will undoubtedly be launched down a path along which they will travel with ever greater momentum and glory.

Their consciousness of full national responsibility is still so fresh in their minds that they seem not yet fully aware of the fact that all their affairs and their destiny are now in their own hands exclusively; there is no one to fall back on and do it for them!

However, they can boast a great deal more experience, forming as they did until recently, an integral part of the American Bahá'í Community in existence since 1894, than their sister-communities in Latin America, who have chosen for themselves recently two plans, much more difficult of accomplishment than the remaining tasks that lie ahead of the Canadian Bahá'ís, in order to complete their Five Year Plan. Shall they then fail? It seems utterly out of the question, and the Guardian is confident they will not.

If each Canadian Bahá'í would decide that the fulfilment of the remaining goals lies solely with him, and no one else, then there would be no room for failure. The Guardian will pray that this consciousness may come to all the friends.

With warm Bahá'í love,
R. Rabbani

May the Almighty bless abundantly your highly meritorious, strenuous, and constant efforts, aid you to win complete victory, and lend a great impetus to the consolidation of the nascent institutions of our glorious Faith,

Your true brother,
Shoghi

৵৽

22 August 1952

To THE NATIONAL SPIRITUAL ASSEMBLY

DELIGHTED RECENT ACHIEVEMENTS PRAYING FERVENTLY MAGNIFICENT SUCCESS HIGH PERSISTENT ENDEAVORS DEEP-EST LOVING APPRECIATION.

SHOGHI

৵৽

24 August 1952

To THE TREASURER OF THE NATIONAL SPIRITUAL ASSEMBLY

Dear Bahá'í Brother:

Your letter of August 12th . . . has been received by the beloved Guardian, and he has asked me to acknowledge it on his behalf.

The contributions made by . . . are very deeply appreciated by him. Receipt is enclosed herewith, which he would ask you to please send to . . . .

The Guardian was very deeply touched that . . . made this very substantial contribution in memory of William Sutherland Maxwell.[22] Mr. Maxwell rendered outstanding and distinguished service to the Cause and to the Guardian during a very difficult period of its development here. Rúḥíyyih Khánum[15] likewise is deeply appreciative of this remembrance of Mr. Maxwell.

The Guardian is praying fervently for the success of the work in . . . . He attaches the utmost importance to the establishment of the Cause in the far-off areas, and particularly in the far north—during the next ten years the Faith is to be established all over the world—and certainly those like . . . , who pioneer so vigorously at this time, are not only helping to achieve great victories now, but are laying the foundation for the success of the great World Crusade which the present efforts will usher in.

The work on the drum of the Shrine is going forward rapidly. The attractiveness of the drum greatly enhances the beauty of the Shrine itself. Not only that, the masons have started to construct the beautiful elaborate masonry surrounding the eighteen windows of the drum, representing the eighteen Letters of the Living.

With warm Bahá'í greetings,
Leroy Ioas

ৡৡ

19 September 1952

To the Bahá'ís who were gathered at the Ontario Summer School Conference

Dear Bahá'í Friends:

The beloved Guardian has received your loving letter of August 9th, and has instructed me to write you on his behalf.

He was most happy to learn that it was possible for so large a number of the friends to attend, and that such a spirit of love and unity was present amongst them; also that a number of the attracted friends have been so touched by the spirit of the Conference, that they have declared their intention of enlisting their services in the Pathway of Bahá'u'lláh.

The Guardian was made happy also to learn that several of the believers have responded to the call for pioneers. A great bounty and a great responsibility will be given the Canadian believers within the coming few months, with the launching of the Ten Year Plan, and a firm foundation in the teaching field must be laid now, so that the friends will be fully equipped to shoulder their tasks, both at home and abroad, during the coming World Crusade.

The Guardian will pray for each one of you.

With loving Bahá'í greetings,
R. Rabbani

May the Almighty guide your steps, remove all obstacles from your path, and enable you to win great and memorable victories in the service of His glorious Faith,

Your true brother,
Shoghi

လ်

19 September 1952

Dear Bahá'í Friends:

Your letter of August 10th has been received by the beloved Guardian, and he has instructed me to answer you on his behalf.

He appreciates your loving greetings; and is confident that those who were privileged to attend this conference have left it, filled with renewed spiritual vitality to do all in their power in the teaching field.

Within a few brief months, the Canadian believers will be called upon to shoulder heavier responsibilities in the Path of Bahá'u'lláh, to be carried during the Ten Year Crusade; and the firmer the foundation laid now, the more confirmed will be the results of their labours both at home and abroad, with the launching of the great World Crusade.

He will remember you all in his loving prayers.

With warm Bahá'í greetings,
R. Rabbani

May the Almighty bless your high and meritorious endeav-ours, guide and sustain you always, and enable you to pro-mote the vital interests of His Faith and of its institutions,

Your true brother,
Shoghi

လ်

29 November 1952

Dear Spiritual Brother:
Your letter dated February 13th, 1952, has been received by
Shoghi Effendi, and he has instructed me to answer you on his
behalf.

We are always happy to have friends of the Bahá'í Faith, and
have counted amongst them many fine souls who for one reason
or another cannot seem to take the step forward of working actively for that which we cherish so highly.

Shoghi Effendi is pleased to see that you are a staunch friend
of the Canadian Bahá'ís; for truly in their struggles, the more friends
they have amongst the general public, the better.

There are, no doubt, always grounds for criticism. The Bahá'ís
are not perfect, and are not able, at present at least, to put into
practice all the things they stand for. However, he feels that if you
compare them to the people of the world in general, you will find
a high average of sincerity and dedication to a great ideal, and a
tangible effort being made on their part to live up to that which
they preach. As time goes by, and there are larger communities of
Bahá'ís believing in the same things, it will obviously become easier
for them to put them into community practice. Perhaps sometime
you will feel moved to help them. Your collaboration would be
most welcome.

He will pray that the dearest wishes of your heart may be realized, and sends you his kind regards.

Yours truly,
R. Rabbani

ᭁᮣ

8 February 1953

Dear Bahá'í Sister:
The beloved Guardian was pleased to receive your letter of
December 20th, also your contribution for the Shrine of the Báb,

which came to him through Mr. and Mrs. Rakovsky,[48] and he has asked me to acknowledge it on his behalf. The receipt for the contribution was taken to you by Mr. Rakovsky.

The Guardian highly values your service and devotion to the Faith. Your letter recalls to his mind the statements of the Master that many people who come to the Holy Land are here in body only, while others, whose body remains away, are here in spirit. The Guardian assures you that your service and devotion to the Faith make your spirit at home in Haifa.

He will continue to pray for your spiritual development, that the gifts of the Holy Spirit may be yours in abundance.

With warm Bahá'í greetings,
Leroy Ioas

✌

5 April 1953

TO THE NATIONAL SPIRITUAL ASSEMBLY

APPEAL ENTIRE COMMUNITY ARISE ELEVENTH HOUR SUPREME EFFORT FILL GAPS ENSURE SUCCESS FIRST COL-LECTIVE ENTERPRISE CANADIAN BAHÁ'Í HISTORY.

SHOGHI

✌

Canada's Part in the
Ten Year World Spiritual Crusade

1953-1957

Canada's Part in the
Ten Year World Spiritual Crusade[49]

19 April 1953

TO THE CANADIAN CONVENTION

OVERJOYED GRATEFUL TRIUMPHANT CONCLUSION FIVE YEAR PLAN MOST MOMENTOUS ENTERPRISE LAUNCHED CANADIAN BAHÁ'Í HISTORY INITIATED MORROW EMERGENCE INDEPENDENT EXISTENCE CANADIAN BAHÁ'Í COMMUNITY CULMINATING CENTENARY BIRTH BAHÁ'U'LLÁH'S MISSION CONSTITUTING PRELUDE MIGHTIER UNDERTAKING DESIGNED CONSOLIDATE MAGNIFICENT VICTORIES ACHIEVED HOMEFRONT INAUGURATE COMMUNITY'S HISTORIC MISSION BEYOND CONFINES DOMINION. TEN YEAR PLAN ITS VALIANT MEMBERS NOW EMBARKING UPON ENABLING THEM PUSH OUTPOSTS FAITH NORTHERNMOST TERRITORIES WESTERN HEMISPHERE ASSOCIATING THEM MEMBERS SEVEN OTHER SISTER COMMUNITIES RAISING ALOFT BANNER FAITH PACIFIC ISLANDS INVOLVES FIRST OPENING FOLLOWING VIRGIN TERRITORIES ELEVEN NORTH AMERICA ANTICOSTI ISLAND BARANOF ISLAND CAPE BRETON ISLAND FRANKLIN GRAND MANAN ISLAND KEEWATIN LABRADOR MAGDALEN ISLANDS MIQUELON ISLAND AND ST. PIERRE ISLAND QUEEN CHARLOTTE ISLANDS YUKON[50] TWO ASIA MARQUESAS ISLANDS SAMOA ISLANDS SECOND CONSOLIDATION FAITH ICELAND GREENLAND MACKENZIE NEWFOUNDLAND THIRD PURCHASE LAND TORONTO ANTICIPATION CONSTRUCTION FIRST MASHRIQU'L-ADHKÁR CANADA FOURTH ESTABLISHMENT NATIONAL BAHÁ'Í ENDOWMENTS FIFTH DOUBLING NUMBER

*LOCAL SPIRITUAL ASSEMBLIES SIXTH RAISING NUMBER IN-
CORPORATED SPIRITUAL ASSEMBLIES NINETEEN SEVENTH
FORMATION ISRAEL BRANCH CANADIAN NATIONAL SPIRI-
TUAL ASSEMBLY EIGHTH ESTABLISHMENT AMERICAN ASIAN
TEACHING COMMITTEES ENTRUSTED TASK STIMULATE CO-
ORDINATE TEACHING ACTIVITIES INITIATED PLAN. APPEAL
MEMBERS ENTIRE COMMUNITY WORTHY ALLIES CHIEF EX-
ECUTORS 'ABDU'L-BAHÁ'S DIVINE PLAN DEDICATE THEM-
SELVES IMMEDIATE REQUIREMENTS STEADILY UNFOLDING
MISSION DISCHARGE NOBLY SACRED STRENUOUS TASKS
AHEAD CONTRIBUTE MEMORABLE SHARE PROSECUTION
DECADE LONG WORLD SPIRITUAL CRUSADE PAY BEFITTING
TRIBUTE THROUGH FUTURE ACCOMPLISHMENTS MEMORY
FOUNDER FAITH OCCASION MOST GREAT JUBILEE COM-
MEMORATING CENTENARY DECLARATION HIS MISSION CITY
BAGHDÁD.*

SHOGHI

 споч

22 April 1953

To the National Spiritual Assembly

PROFOUNDLY IMPRESSED MAGNIFICENT VICTORIES LOVE.

SHOGHI

 споч

1 May 1953

To the National Convention

*DEEPLY TOUCHED MESSAGE FERVENTLY SUPPLICATING
SIGNAL VICTORIES LOVING REMEMBRANCE SHRINES.*

SHOGHI

 споч

9 [May] 1953

To the Montreal Assembly

OCCASION VISIT AMATU'L-BAHÁ[15] MONTREAL ADVISE ALL FRIENDS GATHER GRAVE HAND CAUSE SUTHERLAND MAXWELL[22] PAY TRIBUTE HIS IMMORTAL SERVICES WORLD CENTRE FAITH. INSTRUCTING AMATU'L-BAHÁ MILLY[51] PLACE BLOSSOMS SHRINE AND FRESH FLOWERS MY BEHALF. APPRECIATE PHOTOGRAPH FRIENDS ASSEMBLED GRAVE LOVE.
SHOGHI

৩৵৶

23 May 1953

To Fred Schopflocher[5]

Dear Bahá'í Brother:

The Beloved Guardian sends his loving greetings to you.

Shoghi Effendi asked me to send you with his love the enclosed photograph, which shows the new Gates which have been installed facing the entrance door of the Shrine of Bahá'u'lláh. The Guardian wanted you to know he has used some of the gold you have sent on this Gate, which is clearly visible, and greatly enhances its beauty.

Now that the Ten Year Crusade has been so auspiciously launched, and the confirming spirit of Bahá'u'lláh released in such volume, he hopes the Friends everywhere will arise, and with a superhuman effort, quickly start the initial phase of the Crusade, which is to get their pioneers into the fields assigned to them, and to initiate strong teaching methods at home. Of particular moment now is entering the virgin areas, assigned to each Assembly. He is sure Canada will respond to this urgent need, and lay the firm foundation for its successful prosecution.

The Guardian will pray for the Friends, and for your guidance and confirmation; that the blessings of Bahá'u'lláh may reach you in rich abundance.

Faithfully yours,
Leroy Ioas

৩৵৶

8 June 1953

Dear Bahá'í Friends:

Our Beloved Guardian has been greatly encouraged by reports reaching him from all parts of the Bahá'í World; of the victories already gained, and the plans being laid for the prosecution of the Ten Year Crusade.

They have evoked his awe-inspiring, and soul-stirring cablegram of May 28th, calling for the immediate settlement of all the 131 virgin areas of the Plan, just as quickly as possible. He is convinced, that the Friends will arise and translate their enthusiasm into Action, because the Keynote of the Crusade must be Action, Action, Action!

The Beloved Guardian has directed me to write your Assembly to amplify some of the aspects of his dynamic message.

The settlement of these virgin areas is of such an emergency nature, that he feels pioneering in one of them takes precedence over every other type of Bahá'í service—whether it be in the teaching or administrative fields of the Faith. So important is it that the National Assembly may delay initiation of steps to fulfil other phases of the Plan, until all these areas are conquered for the Faith. Nothing, absolutely nothing, must be allowed to interfere with the placing of pioneers in each of the 131 goal countries.

In the United States some 150 people have volunteered for pioneer service, and some of them already are preparing to leave for their posts. The Beloved Guardian fully expects the dear Friends in Canada, to follow this example, and quickly settle the areas allotted to them.

Because of it being the Chief Executor of the Divine Plan, and having so many pioneers available, the Guardian has given permission to the United States to send pioneers into any area of the Globe regardless of whom it may be assigned to. Thus pioneers from the United States may ask permission to settle in one of the Areas assigned to your Assembly. If this is done, you should assist them in every way possible.

There are some general observations which the Guardian shares with you, and then some specific suggestions which are enumerated below.

1. Every individual who has offered to pioneer must be encouraged in every way by the National Assembly.

2. The National Assembly should assist each pioneer, so they may be placed in their post just as quickly as possible.

3. The handling of each application for pioneering service must be expedited, and not allowed to be bogged down for any reason, or in the hands of Committees.

4. The National Assembly should make it their first order of business to follow up actively this most important task. They must make it the first order of business at each Assembly meeting, to see that each application is being processed rapidly. This does not mean the special committees should not handle the details; but it does mean the Assembly itself must review each application at each meeting; and see that the pioneer gets into the field as soon as possible.

5. A large number of pioneers should not be sent to any one country. One, or even two, will be sufficient for the time being. Later on, if supplementary assistance is needed, that of course can be taken care of. The all important thing now is to get at least one pioneer in each of the 131 virgin areas.

6. The National Assembly may exercise its prerogatives and suggest to applicants where their services are most needed. This, of course, applies particularly to pioneers, where a large number wish to go to the same place.

The specific suggestions of the Guardian are:

a. Areas close at hand and easy of settlement should be filled first. Then the areas more difficult, and finally, those which will be difficult.

b. Whenever a pioneer enters a new territory, a cable should be sent at once to the Guardian, giving the name, place, and any pertinent information.

c. A monthly report of progress is to be sent by your Assembly to the Secretary-General of the International Bahá'í Council. Special matters of [a] report nature, for the Guardian, in connection with the plan of settling these 131 areas, should be sent to the Secretary-General of the Council also.

d. This does not mean that any administrative matters in connection with the settlement of pioneers should be handled with the Council. These should continue to be handled with the Guardian direct. The Council is simply to coordinate reports, consolidate them, keep maps up to date, etc. for the Guardian, and your reports will enable them to do this.

e. The Guardian feels the following areas should be easily settled, and he would appreciate your early cable advice of such new victories: Anticosti Island, Baranof Island, Cape Breton Island, Magdalen Islands, Miquelon Island, and St. Pierre Island, followed by other areas in the American Continent. Precedence should, however, be given to those listed above, as they appear the easiest of accomplishment, at the moment.

f. As his dramatic cable indicates, the Guardian will have prepared an illuminated "Roll of Honour" on which will be inscribed the names of the "Knights of Bahá'u'lláh", who first enter these 131 virgin areas. This "Roll of Honour" will be placed inside the entrance door of the Inner Sanctuary of the Tomb of Bahá'u'lláh.

From time to time, the Guardian will announce to the Bahá'í World the names of those Holy Souls who arise under the conditions outlined in his message, and settle these areas and conquer them for Bahá'u'lláh.

Now is the time for the Bahá'ís of the World to demonstrate the spiritual vitality of the Faith, and to arise as one soul to spread the Glory of the Lord over the face of the Earth. The Guardian is sure that the Bahá'ís of Canada who have served and sacrificed so long for the Faith, will continue their glorious record by winning many new victories for the Faith.

The Guardian will pray fervently for the Bahá'ís of Canada, and for the success of their efforts.

The Guardian will pray for the members of the Assembly, whose sacrificial efforts he greatly values.

Faithfully yours,
Leroy Ioas

ക

20 June 1953

To THE NATIONAL SPIRITUAL ASSEMBLY

Dear Bahá'í Sister:

Your letters of August 18, September 16, October 17, November 17, 1952, and January 19, March 12, 13 and 18 and April 22, 1953 have been received by the beloved Guardian, and he has instructed me to answer you on his behalf.

He regrets very much the delay in answering your letters. Unfortunately he has had to delay in replying to all national bodies during the last year, because of the pressure of work here, which has steadily increased during this Holy Year.

The purchase of your national headquarters,[52] he feels, was an important milestone in the history of the Faith in Canada, and he hopes that it will be put to good use, during the coming years, by your Assembly. To this institution you will soon be adding the Maxwell Home[53] in Montreal, which should be viewed in the nature of a national Shrine, because of its association with the beloved Master, during His visit to Montreal. He sees no objection to having one room in the house being used as a little museum associated with Mr. and Mrs. Maxwell.[4, 22]

He was most happy to hear that all of your goals were achieved. This augurs well for the future of your activities, especially during the Ten Year Plan just launched. He wishes through your body to thank all the pioneers, teachers and Bahá'ís who helped achieve this great victory. They have every reason to feel proud of themselves, and grateful to Bahá'u'lláh. Undoubtedly His divine assistance, combined with their determination and faith, enabled them to fulfil their objectives.

He was very happy to know that Charlottetown not only achieved Assembly status, but that the believers there are mostly self-supporting, as this is a sound basis for the expansion of the work in any place, especially in such a difficult one.

The Bahá'í Exhibit held at the Canadian National Exhibition was an excellent means of obtaining publicity. He hopes that advantage will be taken of similar opportunities in the future.

He urges your Assembly to press for recognition of the Bahá'í marriage in Ontario,[54] and, gradually, where the Cause is strong enough, in other Provinces.

Regarding the question you asked him about one of the believers who seems to be flagrantly a homosexual—although to a certain extent we must be forbearing in the matter of people's moral conduct because of the terrible deterioration in society in general, this does not mean that we can put up indefinitely with conduct which is disgracing the Cause. This person should have it brought to his attention that such acts are condemned by Bahá'u'lláh, and that he must mend his ways, if necessary consult doctors, and make every effort to overcome this affliction, which is corruptive for him and bad for the Cause. If after a period of probation you do not see an improvement, he should have his voting rights taken away. The Guardian does not think, however, that a Bahá'í body should take it upon itself to denounce him to the Authorities unless his conduct borders on insanity.

The Guardian attaches the greatest importance, during this opening year of the Ten Year Campaign, to settling the virgin areas with pioneers. He has informed, or is informing, the other National Assemblies that there is no reason why believers from one country should not fill the goals in other countries. In other words, Canada could receive foreign pioneers for her goals, who would operate under her jurisdiction; likewise, Canadians could go forth and pioneer in other countries' goal territories if the way opened for them to do so. Naturally, they must feel their first responsibility should be toward the Canadian part of the Plan, as they are Canadians, but sometimes health, business openings or family connections might take people into other goal countries.

He realizes that the objectives in the far north are perhaps the hardest. On the other hand, the harder the task, the more glorious the victory.

You may be sure that he is praying for your success, and, what is more, he is confident that this young, virile Canadian Community can and will succeed in carrying out its share of the World Spiritual Crusade, so vast and challenging, upon which we are now launched.

With warmest Bahá'í love,

R. Rabbani

Dear and valued co-workers:

The brilliant success achieved by the Canadian Bahá'í Community, marking the triumphant conclusion of the Plan formulated on the morrow of the emergence of the community as an independent member of the international Bahá'í Family, is to be regarded as a milestone of far-reaching importance in the evolution of the Faith not only in the Dominion of Canada but throughout the entire Western Hemisphere. The vitality displayed so strikingly by this youthful community, the exemplary fidelity demonstrated by its members to the spiritual as well as administrative principles of the Faith in the conduct of their manifold activities; the splendid co-operation with their national and local elected representatives which they have invariably shown, at every stage in the development of the Plan; the sacrifices they have repeatedly made; the vigilance and care which they have exercised while discharging their sacred and weighty responsibilities; the soundness of judgement, the enthusiasm and perseverance that have distinguished them in the pursuance of their tasks—all these have, in recent years, contributed, in no small measure, to the raising of the pres-

tige of this community in the eyes of its sister communities in both the East and the West, and in evoking feelings of profound admiration in the hearts of the followers of the Faith in every continent of the globe.

I myself am deeply touched, and feel a profound gratitude for the superb contribution made by this community, still in the early years of its development, to the world-wide progress of the Faith achieved since the inception of the successive Plans undertaken by various National Assemblies for the systematic propagation of the Faith throughout the world.

The great strides which this virile and highly promising community has made in so short a period, over so vast a continent, despite such formidable obstacles, and in the service of so glorious a Cause, fill my heart with confidence that the tasks it has now assumed, on the morrow of the successful termination of the first collective enterprise undertaken in Canadian Bahá'í history, will be consummated in a manner that will redound to the glory of the Faith to which its members are so wholly dedicated.

The Ten Year Plan which your Assembly has now launched, in its capacity as the elected representatives of the Canadian Bahá'í Community—the recognized allies of the chief executors of Abdu'l-Bahá's Divine Plan—and which constitutes so important a phase of the Global Spiritual Crusade on which the followers of the Faith have embarked, marks the inauguration of the initial stage in the unfoldment of the glorious Mission of this community, a Mission which will enable it to implant, in collaboration with its sister-community in the Great Republic of the West, and with the support of the Latin American Bahá'í Communities associated in the execution of the Divine Plan, the standard of the Faith in all continents of the Globe.

Of all the objectives of this momentous Ten Year Plan, with which the immediate destinies of this firmly-grounded, fully consecrated, high-minded, spiritually quickened community are so closely linked, the purchase of the site of the Mother

Temple[55] *of the Dominion of Canada and the settlement of pioneers in the thirteen virgin territories and islands, eleven of which are situated in North America and two in the South Pacific Ocean, may be regarded as the most important.*

Prompt and effective measures must, no matter how great the sacrifice involved, be taken to ensure that, ere the termination of the first two years of the Plan, these two paramount objectives, which constitute the opening phase of the Plan, will have been fully attained. The entire Community must arise, as it has never risen before, to meet the challenge of the present hour. The time fixed for the achievement of the initial victories of the Plan is admittedly brief. The prizes to be won in distant fields, under the most trying circumstances, by the members of a community so youthful, so circumscribed in number and resources, are so precious that none of them can as yet even dimly imagine their transcendent glory. On the homefront, as well as in the far-off islands of the Pacific Ocean, in both the teaching and administrative fields, the Canadian Bahá'í Community must labour incessantly in anticipation of the fulfilment of the inspiring prophecies made by the Centre of the Covenant Who, repeatedly and in unmistakable language, promised to this Community a glorious future, and predicted both the material and spiritual advancement of the nation of which it forms a part.

On the success of this initial stage in the unfoldment of its Mission in foreign fields—a stage which will witness the departure of the Canadian pioneers from their homeland, in the northern regions of the Western Hemisphere, to the South Sea Islands—must depend the degree to which they will be active in days to come in other continents of the globe and their neighbouring islands. As the chosen allies of the chief executors of the Master's Divine Plan, they shoulder a responsibility which is at once staggering, sacred and inescapable. The greater their exertions, the more abundant will be the outpouring of celestial grace vouchsafed to them by the Author of the Plan Himself, Who in His immortal Tablets has more than once assured of His unfailing aid all who arise to serve His Father's Cause.

Now is the hour to demonstrate to the entire Bahá'í World those qualities which the heroes of God, unfurling in the Western Hemisphere the banners of a world Crusade destined to be carried over the entire surface of the globe, must possess in order to accomplish their exalted Mission. The Canadian Bahá'í Community must stand in the vanguard of this conquering army of Bahá'u'lláh. They must prove themselves increasingly worthy of their high calling as this momentous Crusade steadily unfolds. They must put their entire trust in Him Who guides its destinies from His station on high. They must dedicate themselves heart and soul to the fulfilment of all its objectives without delay, without any exception.

That they may acquit themselves of their task, as befits their high station in this great spiritual adventure, that they may enrich their heritage, and noise abroad the fame of the Cause of Bahá'u'lláh through a whole-hearted and valiant participation in this world-girdling spiritual Crusade, is the object of my constant prayer and one of my most cherished hopes.

Shoghi

❧

3 July 1953

To the National Spiritual Assembly

APPROVE PROVIDED CONSTRUCTION NOT DELAYED CABLE WHENEVER TEMPLE SITE CHOSEN DESIRE PARTICIPATE PURCHASE.

SHOGHI

❧

15 July 1953

To the National Spiritual Assembly

ADVISE HOLD MAXWELL HOME BEFITTING MEMORIAL GATHERING EDDIE ELLIOT[56] FIRST NEGRO CANADIAN BAHÁ'Í.

SHOGHI

❧

26 July 1953

To the Treasurer of the National Spiritual Assembly

Dear Bahá'í Friends:

The beloved Guardian has received your loving letter of June 26th, enclosing contributions from Assemblies and individuals, for the Shrine of the Báb Fund, and has asked me to acknowledge it on his behalf.

He greatly appreciates the devotion which these contributions represent. Enclosed are receipts for them. The Guardian asks that you send them to the contributors, with his loving appreciation.

The reports which are being received in connection with the Ten Year Crusade indicate splendid results. The Guardian has been pleased with the cable which has been received from the Inter-Territorial Committee, telling of the progress of the settlement of the Canadian pioneers. He greatly values the sacrifices and the devotion of the Canadian believers. They have great responsibilities, but he knows they will fulfil all of the tasks assigned to them.

He certainly will pray at the Shrines for the guidance and confirmation of the Canadian Bahá'í Community as a whole, and the Bahá'ís, individually.

The Shrine of the Báb is progressing very rapidly at this time. The golden tiles are more than half laid on the dome, adding to the splendour of the Shrine each day.

The Guardian sends his loving greetings to all of you.

With warm Bahá'í love,
Leroy Ioas

ട്ര⊛ൿ

30 July 1953

To the National Spiritual Assembly

PROFOUNDLY GRIEVED PASSING DEARLY LOVED OUT-STANDINGLY STAUNCH HAND CAUSE FRED SCHOPFLOCHER.[5] NUMEROUS MAGNIFICENT SERVICES EXTENDING OVER THIRTY YEARS ADMINISTRATIVE TEACHING SPHERES UNITED STATES

CANADA INSTITUTIONS BAHÁ'Í WORLD CENTRE GREATLY
ENRICHED ANNALS FORMATIVE AGE FAITH. ABUNDANT RE-
WARD ASSURED ABHÁ KINGDOM. ADVISING AMERICAN NA-
TIONAL ASSEMBLY HOLD BEFITTING MEMORIAL GATHERING
TEMPLE HE GENEROUSLY HELPED RAISE. ADVISE HOLD
MEMORIAL GATHERING MAXWELL HOME COMMEMORATE HIS
EMINENT PART RISE ADMINISTRATIVE ORDER FAITH CANADA.
URGE ENSURE BURIAL CLOSE NEIGHBOURHOOD RESTING
PLACE DISTINGUISHED HAND CAUSE SUTHERLAND MAX-
WELL.[22]

SHOGHI

❦

14 August 1953

To an individual believer

Dear Bahá'í Sister:

Your loving letter of June 19th has been received by the beloved Guardian, and he has instructed me to answer you on his
behalf.

The Guardian was indeed happy to hear of the visit made to
you recently by dear Fred Schopflocher,[5] and of the warm love he
carried to you from the Guardian, and of the happiness and inspiration he brought you in his own loving spirit.

Perhaps you have been informed by this time that this dear
brother and devoted Hand of the Cause has just recently passed to
the Abhá Kingdom. Now he will reap the reward of his years of
ceaseless and outstanding services to our beloved Faith. He was
truly a dedicated soul, and his physical presence will be sadly
missed by all the friends. You should be very happy that you have
such precious memories to cherish, of his visit; which will always
be a source of joy and help to you. No doubt from the invisible
worlds, he will continue to assist you in your work.

If it is not possible for you to be among the pioneers who go
forth to virgin areas, you must not feel disheartened, but must
remember that there must be a strong home-front, as this will aid

those who go forth to foreign fields, in their teaching work. The Guardian urges you to redouble your efforts in the teaching of the Cause, as teaching is of the greatest importance in this day, and it is the power which attracts to the believers the bounties of Bahá'u'lláh.

The Guardian sends you and your dear husband his loving greetings, and assures you of his prayers on your behalf.

With warm Bahá'í love,
R. Rabbani

May the Almighty bless, guide and sustain you, and enable you to promote the best interests of His Faith,

Your true brother,
Shoghi

ৎৎ

20 August 1953

To an individual believer

Dear Bahá'í Brother:

Your letter of October 5th has been received by the beloved Guardian, and he has instructed me to answer you on his behalf.

Regarding your questions: As you know, each Manifestation of God brings secondary laws, suitable for the age in which He appears. The laws of divorce, as given by Christ and Muhammad, have been changed by Bahá'u'lláh.

Divorced people can remarry either other divorced people, or people who have never been divorced; but divorce is strongly condemned in the Teachings, even though it is permitted.

In the Bahá'í Faith, concubinage is not permitted. It is only permitted to have sexual relations with one's own wife or husband.

With Bahá'í greetings,
R. Rabbani

Assuring you of my loving prayers for your success and spiritual advancement,

> *Your true brother,*
> *Shoghi*

꙳

18 September 1953

SETTLEMENT VIRGIN AREAS PREFERABLE CURRENT YEAR.
> *SHOGHI*

꙳

28 December 1953

TO ROSEMARY SALA[10]

Dear Bahá'í Sister:

Your letter of December 10th has been received by the beloved Guardian, and he has instructed me to answer you on his behalf.

He was very happy to learn that you and your dear husband are planning to go to the Comoro Islands. This is a very difficult goal area, to which he attaches the greatest importance.

The Guardian feels you should be very, very wise and discreet in teaching the Faith in that virgin area; otherwise, you may find you have been asked to leave the country, after having, with such difficulty, succeeded in getting into it. . . .

The best thing would be to make friends, and, through your liberality and tolerance of their point of view, . . . win over the hearts of the people, and then gradually, when you find those who have faith and are receptive, to teach them quietly in your home.

You should not give any publicity to your work at all. You should keep in touch with the Guardian, and also with the National Spiritual Assembly of the Bahá'ís of India, Pákistán and Burma.

Your services are very, very deeply appreciated; and the Guardian is very happy indeed that the Canadian National Assembly has had a part through its members in carrying out the work of the great Crusade.

He will pray for your success in your historic venture.

With warm Bahá'í love,

R. Rabbani

May the Almighty bless, guide and sustain you, and enable you to promote, at all times, the vital interests of His Faith,

Your true brother,

Shoghi

꠴꠵

2 January 1954

TO THE TREASURER OF THE NATIONAL SPIRITUAL ASSEMBLY

Dear Bahá'í Friend:

The Beloved Guardian greatly appreciated your loving letter of November 5th, enclosing contribution for various funds on behalf of the Canadian National Spiritual Assembly, as well as various Local Assemblies and individuals. Receipt cards are enclosed herewith.

Will you please send the receipts to the Assemblies and individuals, and express to them the Guardian's appreciation.

The Beloved Guardian is very happy with the development of the teaching work in the virgin areas of the Ten Year Crusade. Over seventy of the countries have now been settled, bringing the number of countries within the pale of the Faith to over two hundred. All the areas have either been settled, or assigned to pioneers, with the exception of the Iron Curtain countries.

The Ten Year Crusade is dual in nature. Teaching in foreign fields, and teaching on the home front. Now that the work is going ahead nicely abroad, the Guardian is hoping the Friends at home will arise with the same spirit of sacrifice and determination as the pioneers abroad have evinced. The reservoir at home must be kept filled to overflowing, if the work abroad is to prosper. More Bahá'ís, more Groups, more Assemblies is the immediate goal before the friends at home. The Guardian feels sure all the Friends will arise as never before, and filled with the gifts of the Holy Spirit, quicken the seeking souls, and lead many to the bourne of Immortality.

Dedication to the heavenly task, complete consecration to the noble mission, and living the Life, are the requirements for success in the teaching field. May we all be confirmed in achieving this glorious goal, so the hosts of heaven may be able to confirm the souls through our humble efforts.

Faithfully yours,
Leroy Ioas

7 February 1954

TO THE SPIRITUAL ASSEMBLY OF THE BAHÁ'ÍS OF ST. LAMBERT

Dear Bahá'í Sister:

Your loving letter of January 24th has been received by the beloved Guardian, and he has instructed me to answer you on his behalf.

The sudden passing of the honoured and greatly confirmed Hand of the Cause of God, dear Dorothy Baker,[57] is a great loss to the work of the Faith, particularly in the teaching field, where she rendered such tireless and invaluable services, and where the need for such dedicated Bahá'ís is at the present time so great. However, we can be sure that her pure spirit can reinforce the work of the believers on this plane, and that she is now receiving her reward.

Such happenings must serve to spur the friends on to ever greater efforts toward the accomplishment of the goals placed before the followers of Bahá'u'lláh in all lands for the historic Ten Year Crusade, which this precious soul was, herself, pursuing.

With warm Bahá'í love,
R. Rabbani

Assuring you of my loving prayers for your success in the

*service of our beloved Faith and of its divinely-appointed in-
stitutions,*

> *Your true brother,*
> *Shoghi*

ༀ

8 February 1954

To Rosemary Sala[10]

Dear Bahá'í Sister:

Your letter of January 15th has been received, and, as the beloved Guardian has been very busy, that is why you have not heard from him before, about your plans.

He is very happy to hear that there seems a prospect of useful occupation for your dear husband, once you reach the Comoro Islands. To get settled permanently on a sound basis is certainly one of the most important aspects of pioneering.

He has been deeply moved by this self-sacrificing response you have both made to the demands of the Ten Year Plan; and he feels sure that this will be in the end a great bounty and blessing to both of you, as well as to the work of the Cause.

He feels that if it is at all possible for you to arrive in the Comoro Islands before the end of this Bahá'í year, which is the first year of the Ten Year Plan, that this would be highly meritorious. He hopes that all of the goals, outside those of the Soviet and satellite countries, will be filled, and thus establish a glorious record at the beginning of this great World Campaign; but, if all are not feasible, then he is hoping that most of the posts will be filled by their pioneers.

No doubt the Canadian Bahá'ís will feel your absence keenly. On the other hand, it will force others to arise and take your place; and this is always stimulating in the Community life.

You may be sure that his loving prayers will surround you both, and that he will supplicate in the Holy Shrines that your way may be smooth, and your services meet with speedy success.

> With warm Bahá'í love,
> R. Rabbani

May the Almighty bless, guide and sustain you and your dear husband in your high endeavours, guide every step you take, and enable you to win great and memorable victories in the days to come,

Your true and grateful brother,
Shoghi

თოთ

19 March 1954

PROPOSED AREA[58] TOO FAR TOO EXPENSIVE LOVE.

SHOGHI

თოთ

22 March 1954

To THE NATIONAL SPIRITUAL ASSEMBLY

GUARDIAN ANXIOUS ALL AFRICAN AREAS SETTLED RIḌVÁN. URGES SALAS[10] SETTLE COMORO BY THEN LOVING GREET-INGS.

IOAS

თოთ

27 March 1954

To THE NATIONAL SPIRITUAL ASSEMBLY

ENTRY PIONEER ANTICOSTI LABRADOR BEFORE RIḌVÁN. ESSENTIAL GREAT VICTORY.

SHOGHI

თოთ

29 March 1954

To THE NEW TERRITORIES COMMITTEE

Dear Bahá'í Friends:

Your letter of March 15th has been received by the beloved Guardian, and he has instructed me to answer you on his behalf.

He is very sorry to hear that Anticosti is proving so extremely difficult to get into. Perhaps if Mr. Rakovsky[48] succeeds in going on a hunting trip there (providing his recent flight there has not shown him some other way of ingress to the land, or one of the other friends), he will find some means of contact and a possible opening.

There is no doubt that a few of the islands and territories embodied in the Plan are extremely difficult "nuts to crack". As he attaches great importance to filling all the goals as soon as possible, he feels sure your Committee will continue to do its utmost.

He was very happy to hear of the pioneers who are going to Labrador and Magdalen Islands. The Canadian Bahá'ís are certainly pushing their Plan forward successfully and effectively.

He assures you of his loving prayers for your success, and his appreciation of your unflagging efforts.

With warm Bahá'í love,
R. Rabbani

May the Beloved bless, guide and sustain you in your meritorious activities, and aid you to promote, at all times, the vital interests of His Faith,

Your true brother,
Shoghi

ৡৢ

12 April 1954

To the National Spiritual Assembly

MY MESSAGE SETTLEMENT VIRGIN AREAS UTMOST IMPORTANCE ANTICOSTI BE SETTLED PROMPTLY. CAN YOU NOT DELEGATE ONE MEMBER NATIONAL ASSEMBLY WORK EXCLUSIVELY THIS MATTER AND SECURE PERMIT ENTRY. UNDERSTAND RAKOVSKY[48] HAS CONTACTS ADVISE.

IOAS

ৡৢ

12 April 1954

To the National Spiritual Assembly

BELOVED GUARDIAN FEELS UTMOST IMPORTANCE ALL VIRGIN AREAS SUSCEPTIBLE BE SETTLED BEFORE END RIḌVÁN. NINETY-EIGHT AREAS SETTLED. TEN OF REMAINING EIGHTEEN OUTSIDE IRON CURTAIN CAN SHOULD BE SETTLED DURING FIRST YEAR CRUSADE GUARDIAN URGES YOU CONSIDER SETTLEMENT FOLLOWING AREAS MOST IMPORTANT TASK NEXT THREE WEEKS ADMIRALTY ANTICOSTI CHAGOS ARCHIPELAGO COCOS COMORO HAINAN LOYALTY MARIANA MARSHALL PORTUGUESE TIMOR. IN ORDER ASSURE SPIRITUAL VICTORY GUARDIAN EXTENDING SETTLEMENT PRIOR TO END RIḌVÁN. THIS EMERGENCY SHOULD BE FOLLOWED VIGOROUSLY DAILY BY ASSEMBLY IN CONJUNCTION APPROPRIATE TEACHING COMMITTEE. CABLE PROGRESS FULFILLMENT STRATEGIC GOALS THIS CABLE SENT NATIONAL ASSEMBLIES AMERICA CANADA AUSTRALIA INDIA.

IOAS

ço&ç

18 April 1954

To the Treasurer of the National Spiritual Assembly

Dear Bahá'í Brother:

Your loving letter of March 9th to the beloved Guardian has been received by him. He has directed me to answer you on his behalf.

The contributions which have been made by the National Assembly of Canada, various Assemblies and individuals are deeply appreciated by the Guardian. Receipts are enclosed herewith. Will you please pass them on to each Assembly or individual concerned.

As previously advised, the Shrine of the Báb Fund does not exist any longer, inasmuch as the Shrine has been finished. However, these contributions have been placed in the International Fund, which is being used for the development of the Faith at the World Centre.

The beloved Guardian has been greatly pleased with the results of the first year of the Ten Year Crusade. He feels that even greater victories will be achieved as the Crusade is underway.

Now that the initial task of introducing the Faith in the virgin areas has been virtually concluded, he feels the friends one and all must turn their attention to teaching on the home front, and consolidating the victories won in the virgin areas. He feels sure the friends will arise to the opportunity afforded them, and achieve even greater victories in this second phase of our work.

With warm Bahá'í greetings,

Faithfully yours,
Leroy Ioas

2 May 1954

To THE NATIONAL CONVENTION

DEEPLY APPRECIATE SENTIMENTS DELEGATES FERVENTLY SUPPLICATING MIGHTY VICTORIES URGE REDOUBLE EFFORTS ATTAINMENT GOALS DEEPEST LOVE.

SHOGHI

4 May 1954

To THE NATIONAL SPIRITUAL ASSEMBLY

PRAYING FERVENTLY SUCCESS NEW ASSEMBLY URGE REDOUBLE EFFORTS PROSECUTE VIGOROUSLY PLAN DEEPEST LOVE.

SHOGHI

5 May 1954

To EMERIC AND ROSEMARY SALA[10]

Dear Bahá'í Friends:

Your letters, one from Mrs. Sala, dated February 20th, and two from Mr. Sala, dated March 25th and April 15th, have been received by the beloved Guardian, and he has instructed me to answer you on his behalf.

He fully realizes how deep your disappointment has been that you are not able to secure your visa for the Comoro Islands. He himself was deeply disappointed also. However, some of these places are extremely difficult to enter; and he hopes that where you have failed, at least for the time being, someone else will prove successful at a later date.

He urges you, upon your arrival in Zululand, to find out the status of the Cause in neighbouring places, and, if it is possible for you to settle in one of the neighbouring countries where the Centre is much weaker, and where it is more difficult for people to get established, and there is a better possibility for people like yourselves to build up a business and remain, that you by all means go to the weaker Centre, in preference to Zululand, which now has a certain number of pioneers.

He assures you that the example that you and the Robarts[18] have shown has moved him very deeply, and he hopes it will stir the Canadian Community, and impress upon them the advisability of answering the pioneer call now, while the field is open, and the opportunities and the rewards so glorious.

You are often remembered in his prayers in the Holy Shrines, and he is supplicating that you may be richly blessed, and meet with success in both your teaching efforts and in your personal affairs.

With warmest Bahá'í love,
R. Rabbani

May the Beloved bless your constant endeavours, remove all obstacles from your path, and enable you to enrich the record of your meritorious services to His Faith,

Your true brother,
Shoghi

৩৶৶

6 May 1954

TO THE NEW TERRITORIES COMMITTEE

Dear Bahá'í Friend:

Thank you for your loving letter of April 26th, giving a detailed report concerning the settlement work carried forward so efficiently by your important committee.

The Guardian wishes to have a street address in all of the countries where Bahá'ís are located; and for that reason, he would appreciate it if it is possible for you to give him the street address or Post Office address in Labrador of Mr. Gilliland.[59] Of course, being in the military service, this may be impossible. On the other hand, perhaps you can give the exact location of Bruce Matthew,[60] who is in Goose Bay.

The Guardian has been hoping that Mr. Rakovsky[48] might be able to achieve success in connection with the location of someone in Anticosti. He realizes that this is a very difficult assignment, but feels that the hand of Bahá'u'lláh will assist those who arise to carry on this work, and that the doors will open, somehow or other. He hopes your committee and the National Assembly will realize the great importance of someone being settled in Anticosti, and will continue to press the matter.

With regard to the plan of Miss Edythe MacArthur[61] to leave the Queen Charlotte Islands in order to settle in some more distant area, it appears that Miss MacArthur is the only Bahá'í in the Queen Charlotte Islands and, inasmuch as this is one of the virgin areas of the Crusade, it would seem inadvisable for her to leave unless of course there are other pioneers who could enter it, or unless she has confirmed two or three of the people living permanently in that island.

As I have written all National Assemblies, the Guardian attaches the greatest importance to the teaching work in these newly-settled virgin areas, and has written every National Assembly to see that the pioneers do not leave unless there is some emergency involved.

So far as Africa is concerned, the countries are now fairly well settled on an initial basis. The only area not settled is Spanish

Guinea, and if Miss MacArthur could settle there, and your committee can send another pioneer to the Queen Charlotte Islands, he feels that would be permissible and highly meritorious.

As you know, the Guardian attaches the utmost importance to Greenland, and he therefore hopes that if Mr. Palle Bischoff[43] does leave Greenland this summer, that your committee will undertake to have a new pioneer there before he leaves. The teaching work in that important country must go forward, and the Guardian is hopeful that nothing whatsoever will prevent this being done.

With loving Bahá'í greetings, I am,

Faithfully yours,
Leroy Ioas

ço~ç

14 May 1954

To Mr. and Mrs. Rowland Estall[23]

Dear Bahá'í Friends:
Your letter of March 17th has been received by the beloved Guardian, and he has instructed me to answer you on his behalf.

He deeply appreciates your desire to pioneer, and your unrestricted offer to do whatever you can in whatever field he advises.

He will be very happy to see you in the pioneer field. However, he considers that at the present time the national work in Canada has been weakened through Freddie's[5] death, Rosemary and Emeric Sala's[10] departure and that of John Robarts[18] and his family.

In view of this, he advises you to continue living where you are and helping with the national work, which, if weakened to too great an extent through the departure of all the most active members of the National Assembly, will suffer spiritually, and even endanger, he fears, the success of their part of the Ten Year Plan. Perhaps, at a later date, when the national work is in a stronger position, it will be possible for you to enter the pioneering field.

As to your investments, he does not feel this is a subject on which he is qualified to give you advice. You should consult financial experts there, and act wisely.

James and Melba Loft,
Tyendinaga Reserve, Ontario, 1960

Allan Raynor, c.1954

First incorporated Spiritual Assembly of the Bahá'ís of North York, Ontario, 1956

Seated: Emily Roberts, Doreen Willis, Gisele Muhlschlegel Liedtke, Evelyn Raynor, Margaret Roberts
Standing: Klaus (Harry) Liedtke, George Spendlove, Allan Raynor, Charles Roberts, Jr.

Western Canada Conference, Banff, Alberta, 1954

Bahá'ís of Forest, Ontario on the occasion of the visit of Hand of
the Cause Zikrullah Khadem (seated, centre), 1957
(Charles Willey, Photographer)

First incorporated Spiritual Assembly of the Bahá'ís of Vernon,
British Columbia, 1957
Seated: Alice Mann, Knute Westman, Elizabeth Varley, Helen Worth
Standing: Atha MacLean, William MacLean, Catherine Saunders, Austin
Collin, Edna Montfort

National Spiritual Assembly of the Bahá'ís of Canada, 1957
Seated: Rowland Estall, Hartwell Bowsfield, Lloyd Gardner, Allan Raynor
Standing: Harold Moscrop, Audrey Westheuser, Peggy Ross, Winnifred
Harvey, Fred Graham

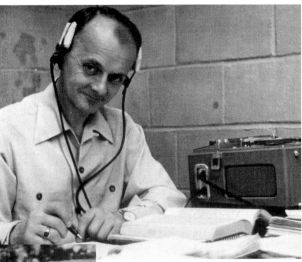

Bruce Matthew in his pioneer post, Labrador City, during the Ten Year Crusade

Clifford and Catherine Huxtable, Saltspring Island, British Columbia, 1967

Joan and Ted Anderson with sons Chris and Mark, Whitehorse, Yukon, 1958

188 St. George Street, Toronto, Ontario, first for national Ḥaẓíratu'l-Quds, 1952

274 Huron Street. Toronto, Ontario second property used as national Ḥaẓíratu'l-Quds, 1956

15 Lola Road,
Toronto, Ontario,
third national
Ḥaẓíratu'l-Quds,
ʁuired September 1957

First land acquired for the Mashriqu'l-Adhkár, Cummer Ave. at
Bayview Ave., Toronto, Ontario, 1958

THE SENATE OF CANADA

BILL I⁷.

Assented to April 30th, 1949.

An Act to incorporate the National Spiritual Assembly
of the Bahá'ís of Canada.

Preamble.

WHEREAS a petition has been presented praying that
it be enacted as hereinafter set forth, and it is expedient
to grant the prayer of the petition: Therefore His Majesty,
by and with the advice and consent of the Senate and
House of Commons of Canada, enacts as follows:— 5

Incorpora-
tion.

1. John Aldham Robarts, of the city of Toronto, province
of Ontario, manager; Emeric Sala, of the city of St. Lambert,
province of Quebec, manufacturer; Dame Laura Romney
Davis, wife of Victor Davis, of the city of Toronto, province
of Ontario; Siegfried Schopflocher, of the city of Montreal, 10
province of Quebec, manufacturer; Rowland Ardouin
Estall, of the city of Montreal, province of Quebec, insur-
ance broker; Ross Greig Woodman, of the city of Toronto,
province of Ontario, lecturer; Lloyd George Gardner, of
the city of Toronto, province of Ontario, wholesaler; Dame 15
Doris Cecilia Richardson, wife of J. P. Richardson, of the
city of Toronto, province of Ontario; and Dame Rosemary
Scott Sala, wife of the said Emeric Sala, of the city of St.
Lambert, province of Quebec, and their successors are con-

Corporate
name.

stituted a body politic and corporate under the name of 20
"National Spiritual Assembly of the Bahá'ís of Canada",
hereinafter called the "National Assembly".

Officers.

2. The persons named in s
the first directors of the N
Aldham Robarts, Emeric
Davis and Siegfried Schopfloc
vice-president, secretary and
hold office until their success

Passed by the Senate, Wednesday, 27th April, 1949.

Clerk of the Senate.

Wednesday, 27th April, 1949.

ORDERED: That the Clerk do carry this Bill to the Commons
and acquaint them that the Senate desires their
concurrence thereto.

Clerk of the Senate.

H OUSE OF COMMONS,
Friday, 29th April, 1949.

ORDERED: That the Clerk do carry back this Bill to the
Senate and acquaint Their Honours that this House
hath passed the same without any amendment.

Clerk of the House.

I assent to this Bill in His Majesty's name.

Act of Parliament incorporating the National Spiritual Assembly
of the Bahá'ís of Canada, 1949

Your tireless and devoted services to our beloved Faith are very deeply appreciated, and he will remember you and your family in his prayers in the Holy Shrines.

With warm Bahá'í love,
R. Rabbani

Assuring you of my loving prayers for your success and for the realization of every hope you cherish for the promotion of our beloved Faith,

Your true brother,
Shoghi

ঙ৵৻ঌ

21 May 1954

To an individual believer

Dear Bahá'í Sister:

Your letter of April 19th has been received by the beloved Guardian, and he has instructed me to answer you on his behalf.

He is very happy to have this opportunity of welcoming you personally into the service of our Faith; and hopes that, both in your professional career as a social worker, and in your life as a Bahá'í, you will be able to help many needy and troubled souls.

Amongst the many other evils afflicting society in this spiritual low water mark in history, is the question of immorality, and over-emphasis of sex. Homosexuality, according to the Writings of Bahá'u'lláh, is spiritually condemned. This does not mean that people so afflicted must not be helped and advised and sympathized with. It does mean that we do not believe it is a permissible way of life; which, alas, is all too often the accepted attitude nowadays.

We must struggle against the evils in society by spiritual means, and medical and social ones as well. We must be tolerant but uncompromising, understanding but immovable in our point of view.

The thing people need to meet this type of trouble, as well as every other type, is greater spiritual understanding and stability; and of course we Bahá'ís believe that ultimately this can only be given to mankind through the Teachings of the Manifestation of God for this Day.

He will pray that you may be successful in your services to mankind as a Bahá'í.

With kind regards,
R. Rabbani

Assuring you of my loving prayers for your success and spiritual advancement,

Your true brother,
Shoghi

༄༅

23 May 1954

To an individual believer

Dear Bahá'í Brother:

Your letter of May 13th with enclosures has been received by the beloved Guardian, and he has instructed me to answer you on his behalf.

The Bahá'í rosary has no significance, whatsoever, except to enable the person who is repeating something a set number of times to concentrate on the meaning of the words, and not have to count at the same time.

It does not matter in the least how the rosaries are made up, or whether one uses one or not. Some people seem to be able to concentrate, and at the same time remember the number, without any difficulty.

If you like to make rosaries and share them with your friends, that is your privilege. He certainly, however, does not see why it should in any way be a bone of contention.

With warm Bahá'í greetings,
R. Rabbani

Assuring you of my loving prayers for your success and spiritual advancement,

> *Your true brother,*
> *Shoghi*

ᛐᛞ

4 June 1954

To Mr. and Mrs. Ted Anderson[62]

Dear Bahá'í Friends:

Your loving letter of May 18th, giving your permanent postal address, has just come to hand.

The Beloved Guardian was very happy to learn of the recovery of Ted, and of your happiness, and feeling of being at "home" in the far north country.

The Guardian assures you of his prayers in your behalf; that every obstacle may be overcome, and you win new and fresh victories for the Faith. The Guardian welcomed advice of the teaching work you are doing. He urges you to concentrate on the native population, as it is for that reason that we have opened new countries to the Faith. After all, Europeans, Americans, etc., can become Bahá'ís in their home lands. We have entered new fields all over the world, to bring the light of Divine Guidance, to the native populations; who have thus far been deprived of the spiritual teachings of Bahá'u'lláh.

May you be confirmed in this teaching effort among the natives. The great goal would be an Assembly in Whitehorse, made up of native Bahá'ís, or at least the majority natives.

The Guardian sends you his loving greetings.

> Faithfully yours,
> Leroy Ioas

ᛐᛞ

5 June 1954

To the Treasurer of the National Spiritual Assembly

Dear Bahá'í Friends:

Your loving letter of April 26th, enclosing contribution to the

International Fund of $355.00, which included contributions from the Assemblies of Ottawa and Hamilton, and gifts from Miss . . . , and Mr. . . . , has been received by the Beloved Guardian, and he has directed me to acknowledge it on his behalf. The contributions to the International Fund are deeply appreciated. Receipts are enclosed herewith. Will you please send them on to the donors, with the Guardian's appreciation.

The Friends in Canada have acquitted themselves marvellously during the First Year of the Ten Year Crusade, which has given the Guardian much happiness. He is looking expectantly to Canada, and the Canadian friends to carry the Banner of the Faith, to new heights, during the second phase of the Crusade, now opening. The keynote of this second phase, is more Assemblies, more Groups, more Isolated Centres. A rapid multiplication of Bahá'í Centres is most important. The peoples of the world are now prepared for the Message. It remains for the Bahá'ís to arise with determination, consecration, and devotion, to zealously teach the Faith and quicken the souls.

The Guardian will pray for the success of the sacrificing efforts of the Friends. He sends the members of the National Assembly, his loving greetings.

Leroy Ioas

ৡৡ

15 June 1954

To the National Spiritual Assembly

Dear Bahá'í Sister:

The letters of your Assembly dated June 1, July 1 and 29, August 7 and 31, October 4 and 19 and November 27, 1953, and January 27, March 25 and 29, April 2 and 22 and May 8, and May 18, May 25 (two), 1954, with enclosures, have all been safely received, and the beloved Guardian has instructed me to answer you on his behalf.

Although a number of the matters raised in your various letters have been attended to by cable, he is sorry that he has not been able to answer the letters of your Assembly sooner. It is becoming increasingly difficult for him to get around to National Assembly letters at all.

During the past year, the Canadian Bahá'í Community has gone through a great many experiences of both a sad nature and a pleasant one.

The loss of the dear Hand of the Cause, Freddie Schopflocher,[5] is going to be much felt. He was so intensely loyal, so vigilant in watching over the interests of the Faith, so steadfast and tenacious in serving it, that he will be much missed in the national work. For over thirty years, he promoted, not only the interests of the Faith, but those of the Canadian Bahá'í Community, and rendered on a national and an international scale, through contributions and many teaching trips, valuable services to the Cause of God.

The Guardian was very happy that dear Fred could be buried so close to Sutherland Maxwell.[22] Montreal has indeed been blessed in more ways than one; and, as the Mother Community of Canada, should become increasingly active and united, and live up to the high expectations the Master cherished for her future, and prove herself worthy of the many blessings she has already received. . . .

Another thing which your community has had to pass through this year—both a blessing and a calamity—is the departure of so many active members[10, 18] of your National Body for pioneer fields abroad. It should be a source of great pride that one-third of the membership of your Body set sail for such distant goals, and will render services during the Ten Year Crusade, of such a nature, he feels sure, as to bestow honour upon the entire Canadian Community.

He likewise feels that you have every reason to be satisfied over the progress which has been made during the first year of the Plan in settling the goals entrusted to your care. It is very unfortunate that Anticosti should prove such a hard nut to crack. He appreciates very much the determined efforts which your Body, and particularly Mr. Rakovsky,[48] made to get a pioneer into it before last Riḍván. No doubt eventually your efforts will be crowned with success; but you will have to be very tactful and careful in order not to arouse a permanently resistant attitude on the part of the Company that owns the Island.

In regard to the question you asked about jurisdiction, the area of jurisdiction is related to the National Spiritual Assembly responsible for the teaching work in the goal country in question, and has nothing to do with what nation the territory belongs to. All Canadian goals are therefore under the jurisdiction of your National Body, and their pioneers must report to you, and people, whose declarations are accepted, should be registered by your National Body, or the Committee in charge of the work, as the case may be.

Regarding the question as to whether your Assembly need do anything about its Israel Branch here: this is a matter which concerns entirely local legal procedures. Your Canadian Branch has now been legally established, and is entitled to hold property in this country; and he is planning at an early date to register a piece of land in its name. He will send you the title deed as soon as all formalities have been carried out.

As he has already informed you by cable, he feels that the land which you proposed as a Temple and National Ḥaẓíratu'l-Quds site was altogether too large, too expensive, and above all, too far from the city limits. He has given similar instructions to a number of other national bodies who were pursuing their investigations in a direction much the same as your own. He realizes that it is difficult, and much more expensive, to find a plot close to the heart of the city. On the other hand, he feels that even a small plot, near to town, is much more reasonable from every standpoint than a large plot way out in the country. The friends must remember that they have to be able to get out to their National Centre and their National Temple and use them; and, as Bahá'ís are all busy, hardworking people for the most part, the time involved must inevitably influence their attendance at Bahá'í meetings in the Ḥaẓíratu'l-Quds, and later, Bahá'í services in the Temple.

If the filling of the goals and the purchase of the Temple site can be accomplished before the lapse of two years from the inception of the Plan, he feels you will have carried out his instructions to the letter, and he will indeed be very happy.

He thinks that it is very befitting that your Body, as representatives of the Canadian Bahá'ís, should be responsible for the erection of a tombstone over dear Fred Schopflocher's grave.[5]

As you no doubt are aware, he cherishes the very brightest hopes for the future of the Canadian Bahá'ís. They are a fortunate people, possessing many of the virtues and few of the faults of both the new and old worlds. He remembers them in his prayers in the Holy Shrines, and prays that they may speedily advance in the service of the Cause, and accomplish the tasks outlined in the Ten Year Plan as their particular portion of the work.

He would like to call your attention, and indeed the attention of all the friends, to the fact that it is time for the Bahá'ís everywhere, including Canada, to devote themselves to the consolidation work. The goals on the homefront are going to be, in some ways, even harder to achieve than those abroad. They will require an increase of membership in the community, which means patient and devoted teaching, the multiplication of both Assemblies and groups, the incorporation of many Spiritual Assemblies, etc. They now have nine years in which to do it, but the sooner they get some of the work finished and behind them, the better! We can never tell what the situation may be at a later date, and whether we will not have to carry on our labours under much more difficult circumstances than those prevailing at present.

With warmest Bahá'í love,
R. Rabbani

P.S.—Regarding the contribution which Mrs. . . . wishes to make to the Faith, the Guardian is deeply touched by the spirit which has motivated her; and he feels that she could spend it in no better way than to give it to the British National Spiritual Assembly for their National Ḥaẓíratu'l-Quds. They are much in need of money, and it would be of real help in purchasing this important and historic institution.

Please assure her of his admiration for her services, and his loving prayers.

I notice that I have neglected to answer your question concerning Mrs. . . . consent to her daughter's marriage: this must be given in order to be a Bahá'í Marriage. Bahá'u'lláh requires this and makes no provision about a parent changing his or her mind. So they are free to do so. Once the written consent is given and the marriage takes place, the parents have no right to interfere any more.

P.S.—The Guardian was very pleased about the publications in Ukrainian and will place copies in the Mansion Library. Please thank the dear believer[63] responsible for this work on behalf of the Guardian.

Dear and valued co-workers:
The Canadian Bahá'í Community, having recently entered the second phase of the world Spiritual Crusade so auspiciously launched by the followers of the Faith of Bahá'u'lláh, on the morrow of the hundredth anniversary of the birth of His prophetic Mission, may well pride itself on the quality as well as the number of achievements which, in both the teaching and administrative spheres of Bahá'í activity, have distinguished its stewardship to His Cause ever since its emergence as an independent national entity in the world-encompassing Bahá'í Brotherhood. Its mission in foreign lands has been befittingly inaugurated in the course of the opening phase of this world-girdling Crusade. The expansion and consolidation of its activities on the homefront have kept pace with the progress of the work initiated by its pioneers beyond the borders of its homeland in both the Western Hemisphere and the Pacific Islands. It has, moreover, launched upon its twofold historic enterprise aiming at the acquisition of its new national administrative Headquarters and the purchase of the site of its future Temple. It has, in addition, been enriched through the donation and legal transfer of a House[53] uniquely associated with 'Abdu'l-Bahá's historic visit to the Dominion of Canada, and destined to be regarded as the foremost Bahá'í Shrine throughout that Dominion.
The years immediately ahead must witness an intensification of effort, on the part of all of its members, as well as its

elected national representatives, which will at once safeguard the prizes won in distant fields, and lend a notable impetus to the consolidation of its administrative institutions within its borders.

The selection of the site for the national Ḥaẓíratu'l-Quds and for the first Mashriqu'l-Adhkár in Canada must be made with the utmost care and promptitude. Measures must, without delay, be taken for the construction of the administrative Headquarters of its National Assembly. The process of multiplication of isolated centres, groups and Assemblies must gather momentum in the course of the current year. The incorporation of firmly established Local Spiritual Assemblies must simultaneously be accelerated, in order to strengthen the structure of these newly established institutions, and pave the way for the establishment of local Bahá'í endowments. The one remaining virgin territory assigned to it must be speedily opened, and every precaution taken to ensure its preservation in the future. Particular attention should be directed to Iceland and Greenland, as the two foremost objectives of this community in connection with the work of consolidation assigned to its members. The meritorious effort exerted so devotedly and patiently by its national elected representatives for the purpose of obtaining official recognition by the Civil Authorities for the Bahá'í Marriage Certificate[54] should be pursued with the utmost diligence, vigilance and caution.

While the members of this valiant, this highly gifted, forward marching and deeply consecrated community, and particularly its alert and zealous national representatives, labour to attain these immediate goals, that constitute the distinguishing features and the prime objectives of this newly opened phase of the Crusade, the measures initiated recently in the Holy Land to transfer eventually part of the international Bahá'í endowments on Mount Carmel to the name of the newly-established Branch of the Canadian National Spiritual Assembly will be steadily and energetically pursued, as a mark of abiding appreciation of the magnificent and exemplary achievements of this Community in recent years in the service of the Cause of Bahá'u'lláh.

A Community, whose founder[4] has conferred upon it such splendid benefits and whose dust now lies on the far-off shores of the South American continent; which has been exalted by reason of the eminent services which two other members[22,15] of her family have rendered, in the Holy Land, to the world Bahá'í community; which can, moreover boast of the endur-ing and historic achievements of yet another Hand of the Cause[5]—the third nominated from the ranks of its members; and which, in the course of the past year, has set a further example of steadfastness and devotion through the action of outstanding members[10, 18] of its National Assembly who have forsaken their homes to settle in the African continent—such a community can well assert its capacity and determination to consummate, within the allotted time, the laborious and mighty task it has risen to shoulder.

The rapidity of its expansion, its sound development, the steadiness, the single-mindedness, the tenacity, the enthusi-asm, the unity and staunchness of its members, augur well for the remarkable material and spiritual progress which the na-tion to which it belongs must achieve in the years to come, in accordance with the explicit promise enshrined in the Tablets of the Divine Plan by the Centre of Bahá'u'lláh's Covenant.

May this community march forward on its destined path with renewed vigour, with undimmed vision, with complete unity, with utter consecration, and be enabled to play an im-mortal part in the execution of the great tasks ahead, and worthily contribute to the prodigious efforts now being collec-tively exerted by the followers of the Most Great Name, in every continent of the globe, for the world-wide establishment and ultimate triumph of a long-persecuted, divinely impelled, world-redeeming Faith.

Your true brother,
Shoghi

30 June 1954

To an individual believer

Dear Bahá'í Sister:

Your loving letter of June 14th has been received by the beloved Guardian, and he has directed me to answer it on his behalf.

Your contribution to the International Interests of the Faith, made in memory of your mother, is deeply appreciated. Receipt is enclosed. This gift will certainly help your dear one to progress in the realms beyond.

The Guardian is very happy with the results of the first year of the Ten Year Crusade. 101 virgin areas have been settled, bringing the number of countries within the Faith up to 229.

The second year of the Crusade calls for the rapid growth and expansion of the Faith in the consolidation areas, and on the home fronts. Each person must arise with renewed vigour to teach the Cause of God. Everyone who possibly can should disperse to one of the goal cities, either on the home front or in the consolidation areas abroad. If the friends everywhere arise with the same spirit of devotion, sacrifice and dedication as the pioneers in the virgin areas, then victory will surely be achieved in many fields during the coming year.

The beloved Guardian assures you of prayers in your behalf. He will pray that every obstacle may be removed from your path, so that you may be able to serve the Cause diligently and effectively.

The true goal for an individual to seek is to become so filled with the spirit that it radiates through him at all times. Dedication and consecration are necessary. As one applies himself, gradually what is hard at first becomes a habit, and then it becomes a simple matter to carry on with good deeds and good service.

You should not become discouraged in any way, but you should each day endeavour to become more centred in the Faith; and as you become more centred, you will find it becomes a part of your life, and thus there will be no difficulty because of outside distractions.

The Guardian will pray for the progress of the soul of your dear mother in the realms beyond.

Faithfully yours,
Leroy Ioas

ᘯᕉᕉᒧ

5 September 1954

Dear Bahá'í Friends:

Your loving letter of August 3rd came duly to hand, and the questions which you have raised were presented to our beloved Guardian.

About a year ago, there was some correspondence with your Assembly with regard to the Bahá'ís who are in the virgin territories of the Ten Year Crusade, etc.

The Guardian renews the advice given at that time, that all pioneers in virgin areas, or new Bahá'ís who are confirmed in those virgin areas, are not part of the National Canadian Bahá'í Community, and cannot vote in elections.

The virgin areas are separate, administratively, and under the jurisdiction of the National Spiritual Assembly responsible for their development. The same ruling applies to any Assemblies which might develop in these virgin areas. They do not become part of the National Canadian Bahá'í Community.

The Guardian was distressed to learn of the problems which arose concerning the election of the Spiritual Assembly of . . . However, the ruling is quite definite, that an Assembly must be elected on the first day of Riḍván, April 21st. Regretful as it is, . . . must now be considered a Group, until the elections which take place April 21, 1955.

The beloved Guardian assures you all of his prayers in your behalf. He sends you his loving greetings.

Faithfully yours,
Leroy Ioas

ᘯᕉᕉᒧ

19 September 1954

TO THE NATIONAL SPIRITUAL ASSEMBLY

DISAPPROVE OWING EXPENSE INVOLVED CONTINUE SEARCH[58] PRAYING SUCCESS LOVE.

SHOGHI

꧁꧂

22 October 1954

TO AN INDIVIDUAL BELIEVER

Dear Bahá'í Sister:

Your letter of September 17th has been received by the beloved Guardian, and he has instructed me to answer you on his behalf.

He considers it will be excellent if you go to Windhoek, as much help is needed there.

On your arrival, you should exert every effort to secure some sort of employment and establish yourself, so that you may be in a position to lend your assistance to the work there, and help to confirm in the Faith a number of native believers.

His loving prayers will surround you as you go forth on your noble mission.

The Guardian urges you to use great caution and tact in making contacts in this new field, to proceed with your teaching work with great wisdom; but, at the same time, with persistence and perseverance. You should have complete confidence in the power of Bahá'u'lláh, regardless of whatever difficulties may be encountered.

With warm Bahá'í greetings,
R. Rabbani

May the Almighty bless, guide and sustain you, and enable you to fulfil your heart's desire, and to promote the vital interests of His Faith,

Your true brother,
Shoghi

꧁꧂

27 October 1954

ADVISE SUGGESTED TEMPLE SITE ABOUT NINE MILES FROM HEART TORONTO AREA ABOUT THREE ACRES.
                      SHOGHI

૭∘ᐨ

1 November 1954

Dear Bahá'í Sister:

Your letter of August 31st has been received by the beloved Guardian, enclosing contributions from the National Assembly, various Local Assemblies and individuals, to the International Bahá'í Fund.

These contributions are deeply appreciated by the beloved Guardian. Receipts are enclosed herewith. Will you please send them on to the donors, expressing to them the Guardian's appreciation?

The beloved Guardian greatly values the devoted services of the Canadian Bahá'ís, and the remarkable manner in which they are arising to fulfil their many obligations under the Ten Year Plan.

As you know, the time is ripe for the wide-spread diffusion of the Faith throughout the homeland. The Guardian is looking forward to reports from you of many great victories being won. He sends each of you his loving greetings.

                            Faithfully yours,
                            Leroy Ioas

૭∘ᐨ

24 November 1954

Dear Bahá'í Brother:

Your letter of October 28th has been received by the beloved Guardian, and he has instructed me to answer you on his behalf.

The Guardian would advise that you endeavour to secure a position in Canada, in a town or city where you will be strengthening a weak centre, or opening up a new centre to the Faith.

He hopes that, by the time your school term is ended, you will have found a location where you can earn your livelihood and at the same time serve the Cause of God.

He assures you of his prayers.

With warm Bahá'í greetings,
R. Rabbani

Assuring you of my loving prayers for your success and spiritual advancement,

Your true brother,
Shoghi

ৡৢৢ

4 December 1954

To THE NATIONAL SPIRITUAL ASSEMBLY

Dear Bahá'í Friends:

The beloved Guardian has directed me to write you in connection with a recent communication you submitted to him, in which you stated that you were pleased to note that the Israel Branch of the National Spiritual Assembly of the Bahá'ís of Canada was to be established, and land on Mount Carmel registered in your name.

In the Guardian's Riḍván Message of April, 1954, you will note he has advised that the Israel Branch of the Bahá'ís of Canada was formed. The actual date of the formation was November 20, 1953.

The land on Mount Carmel, which the Guardian had instructed be registered in the name of the Israel Branch of the Canadian Assembly, was transferred to the title of the National Spiritual Assembly of the Bahá'ís of Canada, Israel Branch, on October 1, 1954.

I am attaching hereto, for preservation in your files, the title deed covering this particular piece of land, which is Parcel No.

304, Block 10811, Mount Carmel, Haifa.
With loving Bahá'í greetings, I am,

Faithfully yours,
Leroy Ioas

༄༅

4 December 1954

To the New Territories Committee

Dear Bahá'í Sister:
In your letter of November 16, 1954, giving the record of the settlement of various virgin areas, it is noted that Miss Mary Zabolotny,[64] of Verdun, Quebec, is making arrangements to go to Anticosti Island as the guest of a family living there.

The beloved Guardian is anxious to know if this represents permanent settlement of the Anticosti Islands by Miss Zabolotny, or if this arrangement simply contemplates a short stay in the Islands.

If it consists of permanent settlement, the Guardian would appreciate definite advice to that effect.

With loving Bahá'í greetings, I am,

Faithfully yours,
Leroy Ioas

༄༅

22 February 1955

To the Treasurer of the National Spiritual Assembly

Dear Bahá'í Friends:
Your letter of January 8th with enclosures has been received by the beloved Guardian, and he has instructed me to acknowledge it on his behalf.

He deeply appreciates the various contributions to the International Interests of the Faith. Receipts are enclosed herewith. Will you please send to each one of the donors his receipt, with the Guardian's appreciation.

The beloved Guardian has been greatly encouraged by the reports reaching him from all parts of the world in connection with the various goals of the Ten Year Crusade. The one remaining area of service which is lagging is teaching on the home front. He sincerely hopes that all the friends will arise as never before and, while there is yet time, actively carry the banner of the Faith to new heights.

The Bahá'ís of Canada have shown great strength in their teaching work. He feels that the spiritual future of Canada is very bright. The degree to which the friends disperse and teach is the degree to which the spirit of Bahá'u'lláh will quicken all of Canada. This is the hour of dispersal, and the Guardian hopes your Assembly will be able to encourage the friends everywhere to open up new cities, towns and villages.

He will pray for the success of your work, and sends you his loving greetings.

Faithfully yours,
Leroy Ioas

ﻌ

23 February 1955

TO AN INDIVIDUAL BELIEVER

Dear Bahá'í Sister:

Your letter of January 16th with enclosure has been received by the beloved Guardian, and he has instructed me to answer you on his behalf.

He assures you that he will pray for your health and for the success of your devoted and constant services to the Faith.

With warmest Bahá'í greetings,
R. Rabbani

Assuring you of my loving prayers for your success and spiritual advancement,

Your true brother,
Shoghi

ﻌ

3 March 1955

Dear Bahá'í Friends:

Our beloved Guardian has instructed me to write you on his behalf and bring to your attention a certain matter.

He has heard from a number of sources that some of the Canadian believers have been deprived of their voting rights; and he feels that all National Spiritual Assemblies should bear in mind that this is the heaviest sanction we possess at present in the Faith, short of excommunication, which lies within the powers of the Guardian alone; and is consequently a very weighty weapon to wield.

He considers that under no circumstances should any Bahá'í ever be suspended from the voting list and deprived of his administrative privileges for a matter which is not of the utmost gravity. By that he means breaking of laws, such as the consent of parents to marriage etc., or acts of such an immoral character as to damage the good name of the Faith.

He has informed, some years ago, the American National Spiritual Assembly that, before anyone is deprived of their voting rights, they should be consulted with and lovingly admonished at first, given repeated warnings if they do not mend their immoral ways, or whatever other extremely serious misdemeanour they are committing, and finally, after these repeated warnings, be deprived of their voting rights.

He feels that a great many problems within the Communities would be solved if the believers would more constructively devote their attention to the teaching work and carrying out the provisions of the Ten Year Plan as they affect Canada. The leadership of your Assembly in these matters will no doubt be of great help and inspiration to the friends; and he on his part will reinforce you with his prayers.

With warm Bahá'í love,
R. Rabbani

11 March 1955

Dearly beloved co-workers:
The beloved Guardian is anxious to learn the exact status of the translation and publication of Bahá'í literature into various languages; the work of which was begun before the Ten Year Crusade.

The Guardian has been informed by the American National Spiritual Assembly that your Assembly has undertaken the translation of some literature into Mohawk. Will you please give me by return airmail a detailed report for the beloved Guardian?

Faithfully yours,
Leroy Ioas

෨෧

20 March 1955

Dear Bahá'í Friends:
The beloved Guardian has been very anxious indeed, as you know, to see the purchase of the Ḥaẓíratu'l-Quds and Temple Land in Toronto concluded at the earliest possible date. He certainly felt that both of these transactions would be concluded before the close of the present Bahá'í year. The Guardian feels the Faith will be harmed if they are not consummated promptly. He feels the prestige of the Cause is at stake.

The Guardian requests that the National Spiritual Assembly itself consider these projects the most important of any of their responsibilities at the present time, and devote such time as is necessary to their conclusions.

The Guardian has written to the American National Spiritual Assembly as per attached copy of letter, asking that they arrange to assist in every way possible in the attainment of these goals, either through advice, or the assistance of one of their expert real estate operators.

The Guardian assures you of his prayers in your behalf. He sends you his loving greetings.

Faithfully yours,
Leroy Ioas

20 March 1955

NATIONAL SPIRITUAL ASSEMBLY OF THE BAHÁ'ÍS OF THE UNITED STATES

c/o MR. HORACE HOLLEY, SECRETARY

Dear Horace:

The beloved Guardian has been greatly concerned over the delay in the purchase of an Ḥaẓíratu'l-Quds and the Temple land in Toronto.

The Canadian National Spiritual Assembly has the funds for these projects, but for some reason, the goals are not attained.

The Guardian has requested your Assembly to render the Canadian Assembly every assistance, either through advice or through the visit of one of your members, particularly one who has real estate experience, so that these projects can be concluded at an early date. He has been hoping they would have been concluded quite some time ago, and certainly during the present Bahá'í year. At this late date that seems very difficult; but action should be taken to conclude them as quickly as possible.

The Guardian sends his loving greetings to the members of the American National Spiritual Assembly, and assures them of his prayers in their behalf.

Faithfully yours,
Leroy Ioas

৩৶৶

5 April 1955

To the National Spiritual Assembly

URGE TRANSLATE WITHOUT DELAY ARTICLE MESSAGE
TO INDIANS INTO BLACKFOOT AND IROQUOIS.
SHOGHI

ໆ

23 April 1955

To individual believers

Dear Bahá'í Friends:
Your letter of April 10th has been received, and the beloved Guardian was very touched by the sentiments you expressed in it, and he has instructed me to answer you on his behalf.

He suggests that you get in touch with Mr. John Robarts,[18] and discuss with him the possibility of . . . getting a job in Bechuanaland, a difficult territory, and where there are only the Robarts pioneering at present.

If the way opened, and this seemed the right move for you to take, it might lead to greater service to the Faith throughout the African area, at least the southern part of it.

If it is not possible to secure a job in Bechuanaland or neighbouring territories needing pioneers, he certainly approves of your moving to Calgary, and helping to reestablish the Assembly there.

You may be sure he will pray that your services to the Faith may be richly blessed wherever you are, and that the way may open for you to render ever greater service as time goes by. Wherever you are, you can all be of help to the Cause, in Canada with the Indians, or if possible in Africa with the Negroes.

With warmest Bahá'í greetings,
R. Rabbani

Assuring you of my loving prayers for your success and

spiritual advancement,

> *Your true brother,*
> *Shoghi*

❧

26 April 1955

CABLE IMMEDIATELY NAMES NEW CANADIAN ASSEMBLIES.
SHOGHI

❧

1 May 1955

DEEPLY APPRECIATE MESSAGE DELEGATES. URGE EN-
TIRE COMMUNITY EXERT SUPREME EFFORT LAST YEAR SEC-
OND PHASE PLAN MULTIPLICATION LOCALITIES ASSEMBLIES
INTENSIFICATION TEACHING ACTIVITIES PURCHASE LAND
TEMPLE ḤAẒÍRA INCORPORATION ASSEMBLIES TRANSLATION
LITERATURE INDIAN LANGUAGES CONSOLIDATION ALLOTTED
NEWLY OPENED TERRITORIES. CALL URGENT TIME SHORT
RESPONSIBILITIES GREAT.

> *SHOGHI*

❧

3 May 1955

Dear Bahá'í Sister:

Your letter of April 21st with photographs enclosed has been received, and, in spite of the fact that he is extremely busy, the beloved Guardian has instructed me to answer you on his behalf.

He was very happy to see that you and your husband are united in serving the Faith in Prince Edward Island, a centre which is very important, as it has been very hard to establish the Assembly there and maintain it. He hopes that you both will be instrumental in bringing in new souls, and in promoting unity amongst the be-lievers, as this is the basis of all healthy Bahá'í community life.

He will pray for you both, for your daughter, and for your success in the teaching work.

With Bahá'í greetings,
R. Rabbani

Assuring you of my loving prayers for your success and spiritual advancement,

Your true brother,
Shoghi

ೞ~ಬ

24 May 1955

Dear Bahá'í Friends:

Your loving letter of April 27th has been received by the beloved Guardian, together with enclosures; and he has asked me to thank you for the contributions which have been made by the National Spiritual Assembly to the National Fund, likewise from various individuals, Groups and Assemblies, all of which are deeply appreciated by him. Receipts are enclosed herewith. He would appreciate your sending the receipts to the various contributors.

The entire world is saddened by the reports that have been received of the persecutions of the firm believers in Persia, the Cradle of the Faith. Certainly these persecutions will release a very strong spiritual influence throughout the world; and the Bahá'ís everywhere, outside of Persia, should arise with renewed effort, in order to take advantage of this spiritual power, and teach the Cause very vigorously. If the Faith spreads rapidly in all other parts of the world, then it will mean that the Persian believers will not have suffered in vain.

The Guardian hopes that the believers who have relative freedom will realize under what difficulties the main body of believers are serving in Persia, and will therefore arise, in accordance with the spirit of the time, to disperse to new centres, to establish Spiritual Assemblies and to increase the Bahá'í fold.

Faithfully yours,
Leroy Ioas

ço⌘

16 July 1955

Dear Bahá'í Sister:

Your letters of July 12, August 15 with enclosures, October 5, 11 (two) and 26, and December 15, 1954, and February 18 (two), March 23, 31, April 6, May 3, 25, 26 1955, have been received by the beloved Guardian, and he has instructed me to answer you on his behalf.

He considers the revised criteria you sent him for the Temple and Ḥaẓíratu'l-Quds land, as outlined in your letter of December 15, satisfactory.

He is extremely anxious to have these properties purchased, either together in one place, or if this is not feasible, then in two separate places, as he has already informed you. Eight of the eleven Temple sites have been purchased, and many of them in very difficult places; and he feels very strongly that it is a great pity that Canada should be behind-hand in this matter, in view of the fact that she is one of the oldest Bahá'í Communities in the western world. No doubt the problem is more difficult for you to solve, owing to special conditions in Toronto and vicinity; but we know that all problems are solvable for the Bahá'ís, with the power of God to help them; and he is eagerly awaiting news of your success.

As regards your question about the nature of the endowment, which is one of the objectives of your part of the Ten Year Crusade: although the Maxwell house[53] in Montreal is really a national endowment he feels in conformity to the policy being pursued in other countries Canada should acquire one also at this time. This may be a small piece of land purchased for Two Thousand Dollars or even less, or for that matter, given to the National

Assembly as a gift. The important point is that Canada should have its own National Endowment, as distinguished from the school property.

The Guardian does not feel that it is possible or right to change Anticosti and to substitute another goal in its place. He fully realizes the difficulties involved; but feels convinced that sooner or later, through perseverance and prayer, a way will open and a believer will be able to get into the Island on a more-or-less permanent basis.

As regards the money you have received on account of the estate of dear Fred Schopflocher:[5] this your Body is free to use for the purposes of the Faith, at its discretion.

He hopes that the National Assembly, through its love, wisdom, patience and leadership, will carry the members of the Canadian Community forward during the coming year on the difficult road leading to the achievement of their goals. The spirit of enthusiasm and consecration which animates the Canadian Bahá'ís will, he feels sure, bring forth a warm and generous response to all the plans made by your Assembly for obtaining your objectives.

He assures you, and through you all the members of the Canadian Community, that the work in Canada is very dear to his heart, and that he will remember you all in his loving prayers in the Holy Shrines.

With warm Bahá'í love,
R. Rabbani

P.S.—He is very happy to see you are expediting building Mr. Schopflocher's grave. The details he leaves to the discretion of your Assembly, as he is too busy to go into such matters. The most suitable passages should be chosen from his cable regarding Freddie at the time of his death, and engraved on the tombstone of this distinguished Hand of the Cause.

As regards building the grave of Mr. Maxwell,[22] this has already been taken care of by his family. However, he thanks you for the loving offer.

He approves of your taking steps right away to erect a worthy monument on the grave of dear and heroic Marion Jack.[42]

Dear and valued co-workers:
The steady progress of the manifold activities in which the
Canadian Bahá'í Community is now so devotedly and
unflaggingly engaged is a source of great joy and satisfaction
to all who have, in recent years, observed its growth and noted
its consolidation throughout that vast and promising Domin-
ion.
Though some of its most capable and active members have,
urged by a compelling force to forsake their homes and settle
in distant fields, ceased to lend to the members of this brave
and greatly consecrated community their valued support, and
though a few others to be reckoned among its oldest and most
distinguished supporters have passed to the Abhá Kingdom,
leaving a gap difficult indeed to fill, yet the body of the Cana-
dian believers, far from flinching or relaxing in its noble en-
deavours, has amply demonstrated its capacity to assume and
discharge its heavy and multiple responsibilities, has steadily
enlarged the scope of its achievements, has preserved its unity,
and coherence, and set an inspiring example to Bahá'í com-
munities, both young and old, throughout all the continents
of the globe.
The superb feats achieved by this community's indomi-
table pioneers far beyond the Arctic Circle, in neighbouring
islands of both the Atlantic and Pacific Oceans, as well as in
far off isolated territories; the incorporation of the elected body
of its national representatives; the notable increase in the
number of its members; its response to the urgent needs of the
National Fund; and the rapid enlargement in the scope of its
teaching and administrative activities, are all evidences of the
intense vitality of the faith which animates it, and of the firm
attachment of its members to the Cause which it has espoused.
Though much has been achieved in various fields, the work
that still remains unaccomplished is so vital and urgent that
none of its members can afford to relax for a moment, or to

lose sight of the significance and sacredness of the immediate tasks now confronting it.

The virgin areas, so laboriously opened, must, under no circumstances, be neglected; nay rather constant attention must be focused upon them in order to consolidate the glorious historic work initiated in those areas. The island of Anticosti, the one remaining goal as yet unattained, and the only island in the Atlantic Ocean as yet unopened in pursuance of the Ten Year Plan, should continue to be the object of the special solicitude of the national elected representatives of this community. The purchase of the site of the Mother Temple of the Dominion of Canada and the establishment of the national Ḥaẓíratu'l-Quds constitute a double task that can brook no further delay, as the entire Bahá'í World, having hailed the erection of such an indispensable institution in no less than eighteen countries scattered throughout the continents and oceans of the Globe, is now intently fixing its eyes on this community, so richly blessed by 'Abdu'l-Bahá, eager to witness this twofold consummation destined to considerably enrich the record of the services rendered by its members. The acceleration in the process of incorporating firmly established Local Assemblies is yet another objective to which the closest attention must be paid—a task which will, to a very great extent, contribute, from a legal standpoint, to the consolidation of these Assemblies. No less important and vital is the multiplication of isolated centres and groups, the rapid increase in the number of Local Assemblies, and the steady numerical growth of the community—the one enduring foundation on which the security and future prosperity of the community must ultimately rest.

The sudden and indeed tragic turn of events in the land of the birth of our Faith[65] must act as an unprecedented and powerful stimulus to the spirit which animates the members of the Canadian Bahá'í Community. It must not, indeed it cannot for a moment, dampen their ardour, deflect them from their purpose, or weaken their resolve to accomplish the tasks as-

signed to them under the Ten Year Plan.

Conscious of their inescapable, their sacred and multiple responsibilities; spurred on by the realization of the great and varied sacrifices being made, and the vicissitudes experienced, by the great mass of their long-suffering brethren in Bahá'u'lláh's native land; mindful of the prophecies made by the Centre of the Covenant regarding the spiritual and material destiny of their country; following the noble and immortal example set by the founder[4] of their community and by the two Hands of the Cause[66] ranking among its foremost members; encouraged by their own splendid achievements in recent years; thankful for the unrestricted freedom enabling them to proclaim, unreservedly and far and wide, the fundamental verities of their Faith; and fully aware of the shortness of the time allotted to them for the performance of their arduous and mighty task, the members of the Canadian Bahá'í Community must arise, at this very hour, and evince such a wholehearted dedication to the mission they have pledged themselves to carry out as to astonish the entire Bahá'í World, and bring everlasting consolation to the hearts of the persecuted followers of the Faith in the land of its birth.

That this community may rise to this occasion, and may befittingly fulfil this glorious mission, and enrich immeasurably the record of its splendid and unforgettable achievements is the object of my constant prayer and the dearest wish of my heart.

Your true brother,
Shoghi

 formula

3 September 1955

Dear Bahá'í Friends:

The beloved Guardian has received your letter of August 8th, and has instructed me to answer you on his behalf.

He urges you to strive in every possible way to arrange to settle in Bechuanaland. This country should be given preference, as it is most important to place pioneers there now.

If you find, after making every effort, that you cannot accomplish this, then you should bend all your energies toward settling in one of the Rhodesias.

He deeply appreciates your devotion to the Faith, and will remember you in his ardent prayers, that you may be guided and assisted in the accomplishment of this noble undertaking.

With warm Bahá'í greetings,
R. Rabbani

May the Almighty guide your steps, remove all obstacles from your path, and enable you to fulfil your heart's desire in the service of His Faith,

Your true brother,
Shoghi

ഊഛ

14 September 1955

To THE NEW TERRITORIES COMMITTEE

Dear Bahá'í Sister:

Your loving letter of August 21st came duly to hand.

In the meantime the Guardian had cabled to the Bonds[39] that their return to Franklin was essential, and that his fervent prayers would accompany them.

I take it there is no further comment to be made concerning the matter, as it has been decided and determined by the Guardian.

We hope that the Bonds will have no difficulty in carrying out the Guardian's wishes in the matter. Surely with his prayers, every obstacle will be removed from their path.

With loving Bahá'í greetings, I am,

Faithfully yours,
Leroy Ioas

ഊഛ

7 October 1955

Dear Bahá'í Sister:

Your loving letter of September 16th came duly to hand with regard to the books published by the Rotary Club of the city of 'Akká.

I find that the dispatch of these books from Haifa was delayed, through a series of mishaps.

They have now gone forward; and I hope will reach you in good shape in due course, and be helpful to you.

With every good wish to you and all the members of the National Assembly, I am,

Faithfully yours,
Leroy Ioas

ৼৡ

19 October 1955

Dear Bahá'í Friends:

Your loving letter of September 21st has come duly to hand, with contributions totalling $419. The receipts for the money are enclosed herewith. Will you please send them on to each individual, Assembly or Group, expressing the Guardian's appreciation of their gift to the International Fund.

The beloved Guardian is hopeful that all of the friends in Canada will redouble or even treble their efforts to spread the Faith promptly throughout Canada, and to build up the key cities, so that all of the goals of the Ten Year Crusade may easily be won.

He assures the National Spiritual Assembly and the Canadian Bahá'ís of his prayers in their behalf. He sends them his loving greetings.

Faithfully yours,
Leroy Ioas

P.S.—It is entirely satisfactory for contributions to be made to the International Fund by bank cheque.

ഗൈ

20 October 1955

To THE NATIONAL SPIRITUAL ASSEMBLY

ADVISE USE SCHOPFLOCHER FUND SEND PIONEERS GOAL AREAS PARTICULARLY ICELAND MARQUESAS.

SHOGHI

ഗൈ

21 October 1955

To ARTHUR IRWIN[67]

Dear Bahá'í Brother:

The beloved Guardian has received your letter of September 25th, and has instructed me to answer you on his behalf.

As he has already cabled you, he approves of your moving to Calgary, from which point you will be working with the Indians in Alberta and Saskatchewan, and at the same time reinforcing the efforts of the friends in Calgary.

The teaching of the Indians is of the utmost importance. Although much contact work has been done, yet the Red Indian believers are very few in number. The Guardian would be very happy indeed to see a large number of the Indian race become Bahá'ís, so that the Indians may be properly represented within the Faith.

He is most happy that you will be engaged in this work, for which you are evidently so well qualified.

He deeply appreciates your spirit of devotion, and assures you of his prayers for the abundant success of your labours for the Faith.

With warm Bahá'í greetings,
R. Rabbani

May the Beloved bless, guide and sustain you, and enable

you to promote the vital interests of His Faith,
                                              Your true brother,
                                                    Shoghi

                              ৩৹৵

                                        10 November 1955

To the New Territories Committee

Dear Bahá'í Sister:

Your loving letter of October 19th came duly to hand, and its contents were presented to the beloved Guardian. The Guardian has instructed me to give you the following answers to the questions which you raised:

1. Special situations exist in Alaska, in consideration of which the Guardian permitted individuals living in military establishments situated close to cities with Bahá'ís to be included in the area of the Assembly of that city.

He feels the same situation does not exist in the Yukon, and therefore does not approve of this principle for the Yukon Territory. He feels that the Bahá'ís must be resident in any city in order to be members of that Assembly.

2. The Guardian instructs that in Samoa all of the Holy Days should be celebrated in accordance with the Solar calendar, in accordance with the practice of the Western Bahá'ís. The Guardian of course has in mind that the Bahá'ís in the East follow the Lunar calendar, for certain of the Holy Days. He has in mind especially the instructions in the *Aqdas* with regard to the Twin Festivals. However as the Faith develops around the world there are many problems involved in the observance of certain of the Holy Days, particularly the Twin Festivals according to the Lunar Calendar.

In the future, no doubt all of the Holy Days will follow the Solar calendar, and provisions be made as to how the Twin Festivals will be celebrated universally.

As indicated above, there are many problems involved in the application of the statements concerning the Twin Festivals, which will have to be worked out by the House of Justice.

Thus for the present, in all of the western world, and in all of the virgin areas as they become settled, even if by pioneers from the East and the West, the Solar or Western calendar should be observed.

The Guardian sends you and the members of your distinguished Committee his loving greetings.

Faithfully yours,
Leroy Ioas

ஒல

14 December 1955

To the National Spiritual Assembly

Dearly beloved Friends:

The beloved Guardian is very anxious that the purchase of the Temple land and the Ḥaẓíratu'l-Quds be concluded at an early date.

Canada is the only country which has had funds available for both of these important projects. Eleven Temple lands were to be purchased during the Ten Year Crusade; and while funds were not available for the other Temple lands, yet nine of them have been purchased, and the tenth one is under negotiation at the present time.

The entire Bahá'í world is waiting for word that the Temple Lands goal of the Ten Year Crusade has been won—and therefore he hopes your Assembly itself will look upon this project as its most important task at the present time.

Will you please write me for the Guardian just what the present status is, and what the National Spiritual Assembly itself can do to bring these matters to a successful conclusion—both the purchase of the Temple Land—and the Ḥaẓíra.

The Guardian will pray for the success of your efforts.

Faithfully yours,
Leroy Ioas

ஒல

15 December 1955

Dear Bahá'í Friends:

The beloved Guardian has directed me to communicate with you with regard to the incorporation of Local Assemblies.

Notwithstanding three years of the Ten Year Crusade have passed, there has only been one additional Assembly incorporated.

The Guardian sees little reason why many Assemblies should not be incorporated in Canada; and hopes your Assembly will be able to deal with this matter specifically, so that the Local Assemblies may be encouraged to incorporate as rapidly as possible.

Faithfully yours,
Leroy Ioas

ை

13 January 1956

Dear Bahá'í Friends:

The beloved Guardian has instructed me to write you the following:

He was sorry to hear that the piece of plaster from the walls of the Prison of Máh-kú had not been placed in the grave of Mr. Maxwell;[22] and he would like the National Assembly, with the greatest of care, to see that somehow or other in the foundation of the monument this piece of plaster is carefully inserted and preserved; if necessary, the head-stone can be removed, and it can be put under it, and the head-stone rebuilt in such a way as not to damage the head-stone.

He has decided that, in view of the fact that Anticosti is so extremely difficult to get into, the Canadian Assembly can choose some other goal as substitute for Anticosti. In other words, a territory or an island in the vicinity of Canada, which has never been opened to the Faith, may be opened in the place of Anticosti, and thus the goals of the Ten Year Plan will not be decreased.[68] On the other hand, Anticosti should be maintained as an objective; and every effort be made to get a Bahá'í in there.

At present, Mr. Allan Raynor[69] of your Assembly is visiting here, and, although unfortunately he has been laid up with a cold, it has been a great pleasure to have a Canadian Assembly member here.

With warmest Bahá'í greetings,
R. Rabbani

ৡৄৡ

30 January 1956

TO THE TREASURER OF THE NATIONAL SPIRITUAL ASSEMBLY

Dear Bahá'í Friends:

Your loving letters of January 14th have been received by the Beloved Guardian, and he has directed me to respond in his behalf. The contributions made to the International Fund are greatly appreciated. Receipts are enclosed herewith. Will you please send these receipts to the donors, with a note of his appreciation.

The Cause of God is moving rapidly everywhere, especially in the foreign fields. The goals in the new countries are rapidly being won. On the home fronts, however, the Teaching work seems not to go forward, and the Guardian therefore hopes everyone at home will arise with renewed effort to teach the Faith and convey the message. Dedication, consecration, and perseverance are essential. Until the Friends become reeds through which the confirming power of the Holy Spirit may flow, the victories will not be won.

The Guardian assures you of his prayers in your behalf, and in behalf of all the Friends. He hopes they will be guided and confirmed in their work. He sends each and all his loving greetings.

Faithfully yours,
Leroy Ioas

ৡৄৡ

2 February 1956

TO AN INDIVIDUAL BELIEVER

Dear Bahá'í Sister:

Our beloved Guardian wishes me to thank you on his behalf for your note of January 19th and the material on teaching which you sent. It was delivered through the kindness of dear Mr. Spendlove[11] who is here at present.

He hopes that this book, which you have worked so hard to produce, will be of great help in the teaching work.

With warmest Bahá'í love,
R. Rabbani

Assuring you of my loving prayers for your success and spiritual advancement,

Your true brother,
Shoghi

ഇൟ

24 February 1956

APPROVE DESIGN JACK'S[42] GRAVE ALSO STAR.
SHOGHI

ഇൟ

10 March 1956

Dear Bahá'í Friends:

The beloved Guardian has been reviewing the progress of the teaching work, particularly in the goal areas during the Ten Year Crusade.

Tremendous progress has been achieved. If the few remaining virgin goals of the Ten Year Crusade could be promptly settled, and those which were settled and again became virgin areas, could again be settled, it would be a great victory at this time.

The virgin areas coming under the jurisdiction of the Canadian National Spiritual Assembly are Anticosti and Marquesas Islands. Likewise he feels it important that Greenland, Newfoundland, Mackenzie and the Yukon be reinforced.

It will be appreciated if you will let me know as promptly as possible what can be done to establish the Faith solidly in these areas.

Faithfully yours,
Leroy Ioas

࿆

20 March 1956

To Mr. and Mrs. Arthur Irwin[67]

Dear Bahá'í Friends:
Your letter of March 6th has been received by the beloved Guardian; and he has instructed me to answer you on his behalf.

He is very happy to hear that you are going to be able to assist in the re-establishment of the Calgary Assembly, which is certainly one of the important ones of Canada.

He hopes that your presence in that city will be a means of attracting many new souls to the Faith and of founding the Community on a firmer and wider basis.

He assures you of his prayers for your success and his deep appreciation of the spirit which animates you.

With loving Naw-Rúz greetings,
R. Rabbani

Assuring you of my loving prayers for the success of your meritorious efforts for the promotion of our beloved Faith,
Your true brother,
Shoghi

࿆

23 March 1956

To the Bahá'ís of Forest, Ontario

Dear Bahá'í Friends:
The beloved Guardian thanks you for your loving Naw-Rúz greetings, which he reciprocates.

He trusts that God will bless your efforts to teach His Cause, so that the number of the believers in your vicinity may be greatly augmented during this year.

With Bahá'í love,
R. Rabbani

Assuring you of my loving prayers for your success and spiritual advancement,

Your true brother,
Shoghi

ৠৄ৶

28 April 1956

To THE NATIONAL SPIRITUAL ASSEMBLY

DEEPLY APPRECIATE MESSAGE WELCOME REDEDICATION TASKS FERVENTLY SUPPLICATING ABUNDANT BLESSINGS.
SHOGHI

ৠৄ৶

3 May 1956

To ALLAN F. RAYNOR[69]

Dear Bahá'í Brother:

Your letter of January 25th has been received by the beloved Guardian, and he has instructed me to answer you on his behalf. . . .

He was very happy to have you here as his guest and as a member of the Canadian National Assembly. As you know, he cherishes bright hopes for the future of the work in Canada, and is proud of the achievements of the Canadian National Spiritual Assembly to date, a young but virile body.

He hopes that you have entirely recovered from the effects of the cold you had when you were here; and he sends you and your dear family his loving greetings and his appreciation of your tireless services.

With warm Bahá'í love,
R. Rabbani

May the Almighty bless your high endeavours, guide your steps, and aid you to promote the vital interests of His Faith and of its institutions,

Your true brother,
Shoghi

ৡ৵

6 May 1956

TO THE TREASURER OF THE NATIONAL SPIRITUAL ASSEMBLY

Dear Bahá'í Sister:

Your loving letter of April 20th enclosing contributions from individuals, Groups and Local Assemblies in Canada was duly received. The beloved Guardian has instructed me to acknowledge it on his behalf.

Receipts are enclosed herewith. He asks that you send each individual, Group or Assembly the receipt for them.

The beloved Guardian greatly values the devoted services of the Canadian believers. With little resources they have undertaken great responsibilities and are carrying them through to a glorious victory in an exemplary manner. This is only due to their devotion and sacrifice for the Cause of God.

The Guardian assures you of his prayers in your behalf. He sends you his loving greetings.

Faithfully yours,
Leroy Ioas

ৡ৵

10 June 1956

TO THE TREASURER OF THE NATIONAL SPIRITUAL ASSEMBLY

Dear Bahá'í Friend:

Your loving letter of May 30th was received by the Beloved Guardian, and he has directed me to acknowledge it on his behalf. Your contributions sent by Mr. . . . , Mr. . . . , Mr. . . . , the Magdalen Islands Group and the Ottawa Local Spiritual Assembly, are greatly appreciated. Receipts are enclosed.

The spirit of the hour is teaching on the Home Fronts. Its goal can only be won by a new spirit of dedication and consecration on the part of the Friends at home. Miraculous victories are being won, in the difficult virgin areas, because the pioneers have consecrated their lives to the Noble Mission they have embarked upon. The Friends at home must display this same consecration and dedication. Never must they let a day pass, without teaching some soul, hoping that Bahá'u'lláh will cause each seed to grow. The Friends should seek pure souls, gain their confidence and then teach that person carefully until he becomes a Bahá'í—and then nurture him until he becomes a firm and active supporter of the Faith.

The Guardian assures each of you of his prayers in your behalf; that you may become a channel for the Holy Spirit, so it may quicken many souls through you.

The Guardian asks that you express his appreciation of the devotion of the Friends making these contributions. Above all he values the spirit that animates them. This spirit is the basis of true Bahá'í service. He will pray for them and the success of their work.

Faithfully yours,
Leroy Ioas

ৎ৹৵

26 June 1956

Dear Bahá'í Friends:

Your communications with their enclosures and material sent under separate cover have all been safely received by the beloved Guardian; and he has instructed me to answer you on his behalf, and to acknowledge receipt of your letters dated: June 1 and 29, July 5, August 5, September 1, October 6 (two), November 29 and December 2 (three), 1955, and January 30, February 11 and 29, May 1 (two).

The recent news that Anticosti had at last received a pioneer[64] was immensely welcome, and enabled the Guardian to take off his list one of the few remaining virgin territories (aside from those under Soviet domination) on the list of countries to be opened to the Faith under the Ten Year Plan.

The remarkable achievements of the friends during the last three years in opening the virgin areas no doubt will be looked back upon by posterity with astonishment and admiration; and the Canadian friends have certainly played an active part in this process and forged ahead in carrying out their own Plan.

He is particularly eager that Iceland should have a Bahá'í nucleus formed, a country which has for many years had the blessing of knowing about the Faith,[70] but never the blessing of resident local Bahá'ís. It deserves particular attention at this time.

The achievement of the friends in the far northern territories is a source of great pride to him; and his warm admiration surrounds the valiant pioneers who, forgetful of self, have arisen to follow 'Abdu'l-Bahá's expressed wishes.

Another achievement during the past year of the Canadian friends has been the publication of literature in Ukrainian and in some of the Indian languages. He feels sure that this will speed up their teaching work immensely amongst both of these minorities; and he hopes that more of the Bahá'ís will make a special effort to get jobs in the reservations or amongst Indian people, so that they can carry to them the Message of Bahá'u'lláh.

He was glad to know that a number of Spiritual Assemblies have been incorporated, and hopes that this process will also be accelerated during the coming months, and that all of the Assemblies that seem to have a firm foundation, however small the community may be, will take out their incorporation papers.

He hopes that it has been possible to make the arrangements to have Miss Jack's[42] grave built. This is a task which is indeed a precious trust for your Assembly. When the friends realize that her grave will become in the future a place of visitation, they will appreciate the bounty bestowed upon the Canadian Community through being able to claim one of the most distinguished of all pioneers as a member of their Community.

It was a great pleasure to him to have Mr. Raynor,[69] a member of your Assembly, as his guest here in the Holy Land, and he feels sure that this contact has forged yet another link between the Canadian Bahá'ís and the World Centre.

Regarding various matters raised in your letters: there is nothing in the Teachings to prevent a Bahá'í from willing his body for medical research after death. However, it should be made clear that the remains must be buried eventually and not cremated, as this is according to Bahá'í law.

He was very sorry to hear of the prolonged inharmony in the . . . Bahá'í Community. . . . Some of the younger believers, from letters and reports received here, seem to lack a firm grounding on such matters as the Will and Testament and the deeper spiritual teachings of the Faith. Whenever the grasp of these fundamentals is weak, the friends are almost sure to pay undue attention to secondary procedures, to quibble over details, to lose themselves in personalities, and to founder in a sea of unnecessary inharmony. This has nothing to do with their devotion, their loyalty, their zeal, their eagerness to serve. It is merely a question of not having received, perhaps through lack of sufficient teachers to carry on the all-important work of deepening the friends in their own faith, a strong enough education in the Covenant before the duties and responsibilities of the Administrative Order were thrust upon them.

He has the greatest confidence in the abilities, and the loyalty and devotion of the Canadian friends. They have proved themselves over and over again, and distinguished their community through acts of great sacrifice, vision, courage and devotion. He hopes that, during the coming year, your Assembly will be able to send out more teachers, to assist the friends in grasping the fundamentals of the Faith, in uniting them, and stimulating their desire to do more in the teaching field. If the supply of teachers is limited in Canada—and the area to be covered is certainly vast!—perhaps your Sister Assembly in the United States can help through lending visiting teachers.

He assures all the members of the National Assembly of his loving prayers for the success of your indefatigable labours.

With warm Bahá'í love,
R. Rabbani

P.S.—As regards the question about a person who is mentally ill attending the Feasts, anybody who is well enough mentally to attend a Bahá'í Feast and understand what it is all about is certainly well enough to be a voting member. Only people who are very seriously deranged mentally and confined to institutions or under constant supervision should be deprived of their voting rights.

Regarding your question of applying the sanction of suspension of voting rights to people who marry without the consent of parents, this should be done from now on. The law of the *Aqdas* is explicit and not open to any ambiguity at all. As long as the parents are alive, the consent must be obtained; it is not conditioned on their relationship to their children. If the whereabouts of the parents is not known legally, in other words, if they are legally dead, then it is not necessary for the children to obtain their consent, obviously. It is not a question of the child not knowing the present whereabouts of its parents, it is a question of a legal thing— if the parents are alive, they must be asked.

As regards the question of alcohol, the Guardian explained this to Mr. Raynor,[69] and he feels that his understanding of it is quite correct. The Assemblies must be wise and gentle in dealing with such cases, but at the same time must not tolerate a prolonged and flagrant disregard of the Bahá'í Teachings as regards alcohol.

Dear and valued co-workers:
The Canadian Bahá'í Community, whose members are so valiantly participating in the furtherance of the World Spiritual Crusade, now claiming the attention of the entire body of followers of the Faith of Bahá'u'lláh in all continents of the globe, has ever since the inception of this world-embracing enterprise, proved itself capable of carrying its share of responsibility in the accomplishment of this collective, colossal task, and has rendered services that have enriched the annals

of the Faith, not only in a land so dear to the heart of 'Abdu'l-Bahá, but in far-off islands and territories which it is the mission of this Community to illuminate and conquer.

Ever since the emergence of this progressive, youthful and dynamic community, as an independent entity, and particularly since the inception of the Ten Year Plan, it has demonstrated, on several occasions, those qualities which alone can provide the guarantee of success in carrying out, as a worthy ally of her sister community in the Great Republic of the West, the sacred and historic Mission assigned to it by the Author of the Tablets of the Divine Plan. The staunchness of the faith of its members, their unyielding resolve, their ceaseless efforts, their willingness to sacrifice, their exemplary loyalty, their steadfast courage, have, time and again, been strikingly displayed, and served to fortify the hopes which I have always cherished for their future destiny.

The vastness of the field in which this firmly knit, irresistibly advancing, steadily consolidating community now operates, stretching as it does from the Atlantic to the Pacific seaboards, and touching, on the one hand, the fringes of the Arctic Region, and extending, on the other, as far as the islands of the South Pacific, contrasts with the extremely restricted area, in which, for so many years, and until recently, the administrative activities of this community were confined. The diversity and multiplicity of the enterprises in which it finds itself now engaged, the manner in which it is consolidating its strength, enlarging its membership, safeguarding the unity of its members, and noising abroad its fame, may be regarded as additional evidences of its spiritual vigour, and of its rapid rise to maturity at so significant a period in the evolution of the Faith throughout the Western Hemisphere.

At this crucial hour, when the Plan to which this highly promising community stands committed is entering on the third phase in its unfoldment, the responsibilities confronting its members are at once manifold, pressing and inescapable. The situation on the homefront, so extensive and so varied in character, calls for careful consideration and energetic action on the part of your Assembly. The steady increase in the num-

ber of those enlisted under the banner of the Faith must be paralleled by a multiplication of Assemblies, groups and isolated centres. The incorporation of all firmly established Assemblies must simultaneously be accelerated. The virgin areas now opened, and particularly Anticosti, Greenland, Iceland and Franklin, as well as those territories deprived recently of the benefits of a resident pioneer, must be made the object of the special attention and solicitude of your Assembly, for upon the preservation of these hard-won prizes must depend the ultimate triumph of this community's collective and historic task, and the enhancement of the prestige it has deservedly won in recent years throughout the Bahá'í World.

Of equal importance is the strenuous yet highly meritorious obligation to add, steadily and rapidly, to the number of the American Indian and Eskimo adherents of the Faith, and to ensure their active participation in both the teaching and administrative spheres of Bahá'í activity—a task so clearly emphasized by the Pen of the Centre of the Covenant, and in the consummation of which the Canadian Bahá'í Community is destined to play so conspicuous a part.

Above all, the utmost endeavour should be exerted by your Assembly to familiarize the newly enrolled believers with the fundamental and spiritual verities of the Faith, and with the origins, the aims and purposes, as well as the processes of a divinely appointed Administrative Order, to acquaint them more fully with the history of the Faith, to instil in them a deeper understanding of the Covenants of both Bahá'u'lláh and of 'Abdu'l-Bahá, to enrich their spiritual life, to rouse them to a greater effort and a closer participation in both the teaching of the Faith and the administration of its activities, and to inspire them to make the necessary sacrifices for the furtherance of its vital interests. For as the body of the avowed supporters of the Faith is enlarged, and the basis of the structure of its Administrative Order is broadened, and the fame of the rising community spreads far and wide, a parallel progress must be achieved, if the fruits already garnered are to endure, in the spiritual quickening of its members and the deepening *of their inner life.*

The duties incumbent upon this community, and particularly its elected national representatives, multiply with every passing day. Heavy is the burden they carry. Rich and immense are the possibilities stretching before them. Priceless are the rewards which a befitting discharge of their multiple responsibilities must bring in its wake. Boundless are the favours and bestowals which a loving and watchful Providence is ready to confer upon those who will arise to meet the challenge of the present hour.

May the members of this community, as well as its elected representatives, consecrate themselves anew to the mission which 'Abdu'l-Bahá has conferred upon them, and immortalize their stewardship to the Faith of His Father through acts which future generations will unanimously acclaim and for which they will feel eternally grateful.

Shoghi

৩৯৯

1 July 1956

TO THE TREASURER OF THE NATIONAL SPIRITUAL ASSEMBLY

Dear Bahá'í Sister:

Your loving letter of June 20th has come to hand, and the Guardian has directed me to acknowledge it on his behalf. The contributions to the International Fund are greatly appreciated. Receipts are enclosed herewith, which please send to the donors with the appreciation of the Guardian; especially the pioneers in the Magdalen Islands, and in Newfoundland. He has written a letter directly to Mr. Harrison,[24] in which he has acknowledged the gift made in behalf of his wife, for the work in Africa.

The work of the Canadian Bahá'ís is exemplary, and through their sacrificial devotion, many victories are being won for the Faith. He is hopeful, that the new Bahá'í Year we are entering will see rapid spread of the Faith in Canada, with Groups being developed into Assemblies, Isolated Centres into Groups, and many new

Centres opened.

The Guardian assures you of his prayers in your behalf. He sends loving greetings.

Faithfully yours,
Leroy Ioas

ৡৣ

1 July 1956

TO ERNEST HARRISON[24]

Dear Bahá'í Brother:

The Beloved Guardian has received your kind gift to be used for the progress of the Faith in Africa. He has directed me to acknowledge it on his behalf, and to inform you that it will be used as you wish, in memory of your dear wife. Receipt is enclosed herewith.

The Beloved Guardian wishes you to know how deeply he cherishes and values your long and devoted services to the Cause of God. You are one of the pioneers of the Faith in Canada, in the days of the Beloved Master. Now you are pioneering in a virgin area, in the days of the Guardian, who is striving so diligently to fulfil all the Master's instructions; especially in the teaching field. Well is it with you, that you have arisen to win the goals the Master has set before us. The Guardian is sure the Master will both guide and confirm you in this noble mission.

The Guardian assures you of his prayers in your behalf; that every obstacle will be overcome, and you win many souls to the Water of Life, and Eternal Salvation, through the Outpourings of the Holy Spirit, through Bahá'u'lláh. He sends you his loving Greetings.

The Guardian feels this gift for the African work, made in the name of your wife, will give her great happiness in the realms beyond. It will be a means for the progress of her soul in the Abhá

Kingdom. He assures you of his prayers in her behalf, and for the progress of her soul.

With loving Bahá'í greetings, I am,

Faithfully yours,
Leroy Ioas

ᔥᕊᕖ

30 July 1956

To AN INDIVIDUAL BELIEVER

Dear Bahá'í Sister:

Your letter of June 25 has been received, and the beloved Guardian has instructed me to answer it on his behalf.

As regards the questions you have asked:

We should try not to introduce any set patterns into our teaching methods; however, if this form of group meditation produces unity and a deeper understanding of the teachings, he sees no reason why it should be not used at least in the beginning of a teaching class—providing the people want to, like it, and fully understand it has nothing to do with the teachings of the Faith, but is a method which sometimes proves helpful.

Fruitless sciences is what Bahá'u'lláh refers to, like metaphysical hair splittings, and other abstract things carried to the extreme.

The friends should be encouraged not to waste time on such things as astrology, etc., which you mention. They cannot be forbidden to do so. The exercise of our free will to choose to do the right thing is much more important.

There is no "grace" in the Bahá'í teachings; the Guardian doubts if the words are those of the Báb, they may be, but, unless he saw the source in the original, he could not be sure.

You should try to reactivate those you taught, but if there continues to be no response you had better concentrate on more receptive souls. He thinks your teaching efforts have been very fruitful, and you should be very happy.

He feels you should consult with the Canadian National Spiritual Assembly as to whether you could do more good by pioneering or remaining where you are, presenting to them your situation in detail, as they best know the needs of the Faith in Canada at the present time.

He will certainly pray that your labours may continue to be blessed, and you may confirm many more people in our beloved Faith.

With warmest Bahá'í greetings,
R. Rabbani

May the Beloved aid you to deepen your understanding of the essential verities of His Faith, remove every obstacle from your path, and enable you to win great victories in the service of His glorious Faith,

Your true brother,
Shoghi

ৎৡৢ

25 August 1956

To AN INDIVIDUAL BELIEVER

Dear Bahá'í Sister:

Your loving letter of August 16th has been received by the beloved Guardian. He has asked me to acknowledge it on his behalf. The contribution you have made to the International Fund is greatly appreciated. Receipt is enclosed.

The Guardian has been following your teaching activities in Canada with interest, through reports being received. It is most encouraging to get your word of the confirmation of six souls, and great interest on the part of others, who may also become Bahá'ís. This indicates the wisdom of visiting teachers, who will settle for a time in a goal city or area, so the fruits of their labours are developed. Too often our teachers enter a city, assist the local friends, stir up interest, and then leave, before the results are known. The Guardian hopes more teachers may be able to remain in a city, until the fruit is garnered.

The Guardian is happy also that you are to devote time now in the southern States, which are so pregnant with the clamour of interracial unity. If properly taught to the seeking Negro, many souls will enter the Faith. The Guardian hopes you will be most successful, so a new movement may take place in the teaching work in the South, which has lagged so badly of late.

The Guardian will pray for the success of your work, that many seeking souls may find eternal life through your sacrificial and devoted services.

The Guardian sends you his loving greetings.

Faithfully yours,
Leroy Ioas

ᭀᨄᨛ

16 September 1956

To Ernest V. Harrison[24]

Dear Bahá'í Brother:

The beloved Guardian has received your letter of August 11th, and has instructed me to answer you on his behalf.

·He wants you to know he deeply appreciates your services and your example as an old Bahá'í in going forth to pioneer and settle and labour for the Faith in such an important and difficult Province.

The work of the pioneers is very close to his heart, and he remembers you in his loving prayers, that Bahá'u'lláh may strengthen and guide you, and enable you to meet and teach those of His servants in that land whose hearts will be receptive to the news of His appearance.

With warmest Bahá'í greetings,
R. Rabbani

ᭀᨄᨛ

10 October 1956

To the Treasurer of the National Spiritual Assembly

Dear Bahá'í Sister:

Your loving letter of September 1st has been received by the Beloved Guardian, and he has directed me to acknowledge it on his behalf. The contribution of the National Assembly, and various Assemblies, Groups, and Individuals, to the International Fund is greatly appreciated. Receipts are enclosed. Will you please send them on to the dear friends, etc.

The Guardian is urgently anticipating word of the renewed teaching efforts of the Friends on the "Home Front", where a stirring impetus is needed. The world is today seeking; the Faith is the goal of their search; the Friends are the light bearers, showing the way to the Kingdom. If the Friends do not arise with enthusiasm and vigour and their light is not burning brightly; then the world suffers, and the Faith as well.

The Guardian assures the Assembly of his prayers in their behalf. He sends to each, his loving Greeting.

Faithfully yours,
Leroy Ioas

ာ

20 October 1956

To the National Spiritual Assembly

Dear Bahá'í Sister:

In reading the minutes of the June National Spiritual Assembly meeting which the Guardian recently received he noticed something which he wishes to call to the attention of the Canadian National Spiritual Assembly.

He feels that to distribute Bahá'í pamphlets from door to door, as prepared by [a Local Spiritual Assembly], is undignified and might create a bad impression of the Faith. No doubt, it is the eagerness and devotion of the friends there that led them to make this proposal, but he does not think the best interests of the Cause are served by such a method. Please inform them of this in a loving way.

With the assurance of his prayers for the success of the Assembly's work,

Yours in His service,
R. Rabbani

3 December 1956

Dear Bahá'í Sister:

The Beloved Guardian has directed me to write you concerning the Temple Land for the Temple in Canada.

He would like you to send me a report just as quickly as possible, of the present status of this important matter.

Has the land been purchased, and if so when, and what is the cost.

If it has not been purchased, when will it be accomplished.

Your early full advice will be appreciated by him.

With loving Bahá'í greetings, I am,

Faithfully yours,
Leroy Ioas

༄

14 December 1956

Dear Bahá'í Sister:

The Beloved Guardian has directed me to write you, that he feels it is time for the Canadian Bahá'ís, in their teaching work, to concentrate, to the extent possible, on bringing Catholics into the Faith.

There are the vast number of French Canadians who are of Catholic persuasion. They would make fine Bahá'ís, and if representative members could be brought into the Faith, it will add prestige to the Faith, and help solidify its institutions.

Thus, to the extent possible, the friends should do what they can to attract Catholics and then confirm them in the Faith.

He sends the members of the National Assembly his loving greetings.

Faithfully yours,
Leroy Ioas

20 December 1956

Dear Bahá'í Friends:

The beloved Guardian was pleased to see the work is going well in the new territories, and particularly to see the post mark "Saint Pierre & Miquelon" on your post card of October 22nd.

He is happy to know that Mrs. Pawlowska[71] is continuing her valuable pioneer service there, to which he attaches great importance.

He assures you both of his loving prayers for the success of your devoted labours.

With warm Bahá'í greetings,
R. Rabbani

May the Beloved, Whose Cause you promote with such splendid devotion, constancy and vigilance, reward you for your past achievements, and enable you to enrich the record of your meritorious services to His Faith,

Your true brother,
Shoghi

ᑭᕐ

22 December 1956

Dear Bahá'í Friends:

I have been instructed on behalf of our beloved Guardian to answer the questions raised in your recent letter.

There are two things which he wishes to impress upon you. The first is that depriving people of their voting rights is the heaviest sanction which can be imposed at the present time (with the exception of excommunication, which is a right the Guardian has never permitted anyone else to exercise). Therefore, the greatest care should be exerted to try and remedy a situation before depriving anybody of their voting rights, and the action itself should only be taken if absolutely necessary.

The other point is that the Guardian is very anxious that no more rules and regulations should be introduced by any National Spiritual Assemblies. He has continually impressed this upon the American, the British and other National Bodies. The spirit of the Cause will be stifled, the initiative of the friends killed, and the teaching work come to a stand-still if the friends are continually hemmed in by instructions. In view of this, he has instructed the National Bodies to deal with each case as it arises.

The understanding conveyed in the quotation from *Principles of Bahá'í Administration* is correct; also people who are deprived of their voting rights should not receive *Bahá'í News* or Bulletins, as they are no longer active in the administrative affairs of the Faith.

He is very happy at present to have a member[32] of your Assembly visiting Haifa, and hopes that Miss Harvey will carry back to you a fresh impetus from the Holy Land, which will assist the Canadian Assembly members in carrying on their many heavy burdens in the service of the Faith.

With warm Bahá'í greetings,
R. Rabbani

ﻌﻮﻋ

27 December 1956

To the National Spiritual Assembly

Dear Bahá'í Friends:

The Beloved Guardian has directed me to write you concerning the important matter of teaching the minorities of Canada.

He has spoken in some detail to Miss Harvey[32] concerning the subject, and she can and will amplify this communication.

He feels it most important that active work be done in connection with the French Canadians, Eskimos, and Indians. You are also now actively in touch with the Poles and Ukrainians in your country.

In order to intensify this work, the Guardian feels you should establish a Minorities Teaching Committee, with sub-committees to specialize in the teaching of the French Canadians, Eskimos, and Indians. As the work spreads, you can add other sub-committees, such as one for Eastern Europe, or the countries under active consideration. In other words, sub-committees might be formed for regional areas of the globe, where their people form a goodly number of inhabitants of Canada.

Thus you would now have a Minorities Committee, with sub-committees to specialize in the teaching work of the Eskimos, another sub-committee for the Indians, another for the French Canadians, and another one for the Poles and Ukrainians.

With loving Bahá'í greetings, I am,

Faithfully yours,
Leroy Ioas

〜

27 December 1956

To the National Spiritual Assembly

Dear Bahá'í Friends:
The Beloved Guardian has directed me to write you concerning the manner of reporting information to him of the Bahá'í population of Canada.

In such reports sent him of the Assemblies, Groups, and Isolated Centres, as well as the number of Bahá'ís, in Canada, you should not include data concerning the virgin areas without Canada such as Baranof Island, Greenland, etc. These should be kept separately, and reported separately to him.

Later, it will be decided just what National Bodies these virgin areas will report to, but for the present, they are to be considered independent administrative units, under the direction of the appropriate national body set up in the Ten Year Crusade, but not a part of the Bahá'í population of Canada.

With loving Bahá'í greetings, I am,

Faithfully yours,
Leroy Ioas

〜

15 January 1957

To INDIVIDUAL BELIEVERS

Dear Bahá'í Friends:

Your letter of December 31st with enclosure has been received by the beloved Guardian, and he has instructed me to answer you on his behalf.

He was very happy to see what you have been able to achieve on your recent teaching trip.

He feels that the work in Canada is certainly very urgent, and hopes that you will be able to assist on the Home Front. However, if you have to make a choice between teaching at a summer school or going to Austria and helping with the work there, he would certainly recommend Austria. The prospects are good in many towns there at present; and the help of a German-speaking Bahá'í, who can give a lecture and who has the added attraction of coming from far away, would undoubtedly lend an impetus to the work at this time.

He does not advise your trying to get into any of the Iron Curtain countries at this point, owing to the international situation.

Assuring you of his loving prayers and his deep appreciation of your united and tireless services to the Faith,

With warm Bahá'í love,
R. Rabbani

May the Beloved of our hearts, Whose Cause you promote with such assiduous care, exemplary devotion and perseverance, reward you for your meritorious labours, and enable you to enrich the record of your various accomplishments in the service of His glorious Faith,

Your true brother,
Shoghi

26 January 1957

Dear Bahá'í Sister:

Your loving letter of January 7th was duly received by the Guardian, and he has directed me to acknowledge it in his behalf. The contributions of the Friends in Canada are greatly appreciated. Receipts are enclosed, which please send on to the individuals, groups, and Assemblies, with the Guardian's appreciation.

The Guardian is ever hopeful the Friends "at home" will arise with the same ardour, dedication, and selflessness as those in the pioneering fields. When this is done, the Faith will grow on the home front, to the same extent as in the virgin areas.

He hopes your Assembly will be able to stimulate the Friends to loftier goals, and more dedicated service; so the reservoir of the home front may be richly replenished with new souls anxious to carry the Faith to new horizons.

The Guardian will pray for you, and for the success of your work. He sends loving greetings.

Faithfully yours,
Leroy Ioas

ໞ

2 February 1957

TO AN INDIVIDUAL BELIEVER

Dear Bahá'í Sister:

Your letter of January 17th has been received by the beloved Guardian, and he has instructed me to answer you on his behalf.

He is very sorry that it will not be possible to have you make the pilgrimage in August or September; and hopes that, at some future date, if you see your way to coming during the winter months you will let him know, and he will put your name on the list. Let him know however well in advance, as there are many friends waiting to come.

He was very happy to know that you are in Labrador, and hopes you are able to teach the Faith there.

Assuring you of his loving prayers for your success,

With warm Bahá'í greetings,
R. Rabbani

May the Beloved bless, guide and sustain you, and enable you to promote the vital interests of His Faith, and win memorable victories in its service,

Your true brother,
Shoghi

৩০৫

7 February 1957

TO THE SPIRITUAL ASSEMBLY OF THE BAHÁ'ÍS OF OTTAWA

Dear Bahá'í Sister:

Your letter of January 26th has been received by the beloved Guardian, and he has instructed me to answer you on his behalf.

He was very happy to hear of the response of the Ottawa Community to the messages which Miss Winnifred Harvey[32] conveyed to them. It makes a great difference to make the personal contact of a returning pilgrim, and the Guardian feels sure that many of the friends would arise and do pioneer work if they grasped the privilege and the importance of it. The contact with a visitor from Haifa is naturally a vivid experience, and he feels sure will be a great stimulation to not only the Ottawa friends but others.

He appreciates very deeply your sending him the maps, and will be happy to receive them.

Please convey to those who have responded to the teaching call his sincere appreciation.

He assures you one and all of his loving prayers for the success of your devoted labours.

With warm Bahá'í greetings,
R. Rabbani

May the Almighty bless your efforts, guide your steps, and aid you and your co-workers to win great victories in the service of His Faith,

> *Your true brother,*
> *Shoghi*

〜〜

30 March 1957

To the National Spiritual Assembly

Dear Bahá'í Friends:

The beloved Guardian has instructed me to answer certain matters raised in your recent correspondence with him.

He is delighted to see that substantial progress is being made in Samoa. It is too early for him to say under whose administrative jurisdiction the Samoan Bahá'ís will come in the future. It will probably be Australia, but at the present time, these things have not been definitely settled.

People who have withdrawn from the Cause because they no longer feel that they can support its Teachings and Institutions sincerely are not Covenant-breakers—they are non-Bahá'ís and should just be treated as such. Only those who ally themselves actively with known enemies of the Faith who are Covenant-breakers, and who attack the Faith in the same spirit as these people, can be considered, themselves, to be Covenant-breakers. As you know, up to the present time, no one has been permitted to pronounce anybody a Covenant-breaker but the Guardian himself.

With warm Bahá'í greetings, and assuring you all of his prayers for the success of your important work,

> R. Rabbani

〜〜

30 April 1957

Dear Bahá'í Friends:

The Beloved Guardian thanks you for your loving Riḍván greetings, which he heartily reciprocates.

He hopes that the work in Hamilton and its vicinity will advance rapidly during the coming year, and that, through the efforts of the Hamilton Bahá'ís, a new Spiritual Assembly in that region will come into existence by next Riḍván. This might well be your private one year plan!

He will pray for your success in the Holy Shrines.

With loving greetings,
R. Rabbani

May the Beloved bless, guide and sustain you, aid you to extend the range of your valued services, and win great victories in the days to come,

Your true brother,
Shoghi

ை‑‑ை

17 May 1957

Dear Bahá'í Sister:

Your loving letter of May 2nd, was duly received by the Beloved Guardian and he has directed me to acknowledge it in his behalf.

Enclosed are receipts for the contributions made to the International Fund. Will you please send these on to the donors with the Guardian's appreciation.

The Guardian is well pleased with the active teaching work of the Canadian Believers. He hopes that they will redouble their efforts however because the world is being shaken to its foundations and the people are seeking. If the Bahá'ís will arise as never before to teach the Cause they will find many listeners and many will find eternal life through their sacrificial efforts.

The Guardian will pray for you, for the members of the National Assembly and for the success of the teaching work throughout Canada.

He sends his loving greetings to you.

Faithfully yours,
Leroy Ioas

ço-ço

21 May 1957

Dear Bahá'í Sister:

Your letter dated May 9, 1957, with enclosures, has been received, and the beloved Guardian has instructed me to answer you on his behalf.

He has read your letter and the sheets of correspondence with the European Teaching Committee which you enclosed, and he feels that you are not seeing the situation in a clear light; according to the Administrative Order laid down by the Master it is the bodies responsible for the work who bear the full responsibility. Now that you have in full detail acquainted the European Teaching Committee—and through them the American National Spiritual Assembly—with the situation as you see it, your duty is done, and you should stop worrying over the Cause there and leave the entire matter to the new National Spiritual Assembly for Scandinavia and Finland. In fact, as this entire situation has upset you so deeply, he advises you to pioneer elsewhere, if not in Europe then on the Home Front in Canada, where the need is also great. As the European Teaching Committee is willing to pay your fare home he thinks this may be the best plan for you. As I said, Canada needs workers very much at this time.

Of course, if you get a favourable reply regarding Spitsbergen that would have first priority as far as your future plans go. However, as it is exceedingly difficult to get in there, particularly, he understands for a woman, to return to Canada will probably be your wisest course of action.

He deeply appreciates the spirit of service which animates you, and will pray for the success of your future work for our beloved Faith.

With warm Bahá'í greetings,
R. Rabbani

May the Beloved bless your efforts, guide your steps, and aid you to promote the vital interests of His Faith,
Your true brother,
Shoghi

ﻖ﮺

4 June 1957

To the National Spiritual Assembly

Dear Bahá'í Friends:

The Beloved Guardian has noted your letter of February 15th, addressed to the National Teaching Committee, other committees and Local Assemblies giving advice concerning Teaching methods in Canada.

The Beloved Guardian noted that in paragraph 3 you mention that no teachers have the authority to interpret more accurately than others: that every teacher is bound to interpret to some degree but the more he appreciates the Faith, the less will he be inclined to be dogmatic, etc.

The Guardian feels that this paragraph will cause great confusion amongst the friends.

The Will and Testament of Bahá'u'lláh and the Will and Testament of the Master clearly and explicitly indicate that the Interpreter of the Word was the Centre of the Covenant and now is the

Guardian. There are no other Interpreters whatsoever and no individual may interpret. This is strictly forbidden.

No doubt the intent of this paragraph was to indicate that the Bahá'í teachers in making explanation of Divine Truths must give their understanding of the Divine Truths: explanations that have been clarified for them in study classes, summer schools, etc.

Divine Truth is relative and that is why we are enjoined to constantly refer the seeker to the Word itself—and why any explanations we make to ease the journey of the soul of any individual must be based on the Word and the Word alone.

If there is a wide divergence in the understandings of the Friends of the Teachings then the National Assembly should arrange for study classes on such points—and particularly the Summer Schools.

The Guardian feels the letter of February 15th should be withdrawn.

Faithfully yours,
Leroy Ioas

ﻉﻉ

7 July 1957

To AN INDIVIDUAL BELIEVER

Dear Bahá'í Brother:

Your letter of June 10th has been received, and the beloved Guardian has instructed me to answer you on his behalf.

He advises you not to make a teaching trip around the world, as the results of such a trip would not justify the expense it would entail.

He feels you should concentrate on northern European countries and Austria, staying longer, and visiting the small places as well as the larger ones where Bahá'ís reside.

Those Bahá'ís who have not yet made the pilgrimage have priority. However, he hopes at a future date it will be possible for you to come.

With warm Bahá'í greetings,
R. Rabbani

May the Almighty bless your noble endeavours, guide and sustain you in your meritorious and constant activities, and enable you to extend the range of your splendid services and accomplishments,

Your true brother,
Shoghi

ഗ~ഗ

18 July 1957

Dear Bahá'í Sister:

Your Assembly's communications with their enclosures have all arrived safely, and the beloved Guardian has instructed me to answer you on his behalf, and to acknowledge receipt of your letters dated: June 28, August 26, September 25 and December 7, 14 and 17, 1956, and February 15, March 19 and 21, May 15 and 31.

As many of the questions mentioned in your letters have been answered, I will not repeat them here.

It is a pity that the Canadian believers are having so much difficulty settling the question of both their Temple land and their National Headquarters. He was very surprised and distressed to learn that the Temple site you had chosen has entirely fallen through, and that you have to begin all over again looking for a Temple site. He feels that your Assembly should appreciate the fact that the important thing at this time is to acquire a Temple site. It does not have to be a very large piece of land, and, if the worst comes to the worst, at a future date, when the time comes to build a Temple in Canada, it can be exchanged or sold and a better site procured; but the question for this present National Body to settle once and for all is the purchase of a Temple plot as a beginning in order to remove from the Ten Year Plan one of its most important goals, and one the accomplishment of which has been dragging too long. He feels that your Assembly should also look around for a suitable and permanent Ḥaẓíratu'l-Quds in Toronto, and try and dispose of the one you have without loss, if possible, in order to enable you to acquire the new and he hopes permanent one at once.

As regards the matter of those who have withdrawn from the Faith on the west coast: as you know, no one has the right to excommunicate anybody except the Guardian of the Faith, himself. Those people who have withdrawn from the Faith, though critical of it and disgruntled, are not necessarily Covenant-breakers. If they were associating with Ahmad Sohrab[72] and upholding his claims actively, then they would come into an entirely different category. If this is the case, you should inform the Guardian, but otherwise the friends should be advised to just leave these people alone, for their influence can be nothing but negative and destructive, and the less they breathe the breath, so to speak, of those who have turned their back on the light of this Faith, the better.

It is not enough to bring people into the Faith, one must educate them and deepen their love for it and their knowledge of its teachings, after they declare themselves. As the Bahá'ís are few in number, especially the active teachers, and there is a great deal of work to be done, the education of these new believers is often sadly neglected, and then results are seen such as the resignations you have had recently. In this respect, the Summer Schools can be of the greatest help to the friends, new and old Bahá'ís alike, for in them they can study, and enjoy the feeling of Bahá'í companionship which is, alas, usually lacking in their home communities, owing to the smallness of their numbers.

He is very happy to see that the friends are making every effort to execute the provisions of the Ten Year Plan, as they apply to the Canadian Community. The most urgent of all tasks facing them in connection with the execution of their part of the Ten Year Plan is to increase the number of Spiritual Assemblies.

The Bahá'ís should realize that today's intensely materialistic civilization, alas, most perfectly exemplified by the United States, has far exceeded the bounds of moderation, and, as Bahá'u'lláh has pointed out in His Writings, civilization itself, when carried to extremes, leads to destruction. The Canadian friends should be on their guard against this deadly influence to which they are so constantly exposed, and which we can see is undermining the moral strength of not only America, but indeed of Europe and other parts of the world to which it is rapidly spreading.

The fortuitous combination of British solidity and good judgement and American get-up-and-go and enthusiasm, which has characterized Canada, must not be lost in the Canadian Bahá'í Community. Its members must demonstrate their outstanding abilities, and, through a greater vision, more consecration and renewed self-sacrifice, arise and attain their goals.

He is very happy over the work in the Pacific region in general, and was glad to receive word recently of the formation of the Samoan Assembly, a feat of which your Assembly can be duly proud. However, the situation in the Marquesas needs immediate attention, and every effort should be exerted to reinforce the work initiated there, at the cost of much self-sacrifice, by the first pioneer.[47]

The work in the north should likewise be consolidated, and every effort made to get more pioneers to join those heroic souls already labouring in such an infertile field. This applies equally to Labrador and Greenland, where Bill Carr,[73] the lone Canadian pioneer, is demonstrating the Bahá'í spirit in such an exemplary manner. It is hard for the friends to appreciate, when they are isolated in one of these goal territories, and see that they are making no progress in teaching others, are living in inhospitable climes for the most part, and are lonesome for Bahá'í companionship and activity, that they represent a force for good, that they are like a light-house of Bahá'u'lláh shining at a strategic point and casting its beam out into the darkness. This is why he so consistently urges these pioneers not to abandon their posts. Apropos of this, he hopes that it will again be possible in the near future to get someone into Anticosti. It is a great pity that the friend[64] who went there could not remain.

The beloved Guardian sends all the members of your Assembly his loving greetings and assures you all of his ardent prayers for your success.

With warm Bahá'í love,

R. Rabbani

Dear and valued co-workers:

The opening of the second year of the third phase of the Ten Year Bahá'í spiritual Crusade presents the entire Canadian Bahá'í Community, and, particularly, its elected representatives, with an opportunity, and brings them face to face with a challenge, unique since its inception over half a century ago.

The achievements that have distinguished the record of its stewardship, ever since its founding, and particularly since the launching of the world Bahá'í Crusade, both on the homefront and beyond its confines, have been such as to ennoble the annals of the Faith to which it is so whole-heartedly dedicated, and to arouse in the hearts of all those who have watched, throughout succeeding decades, its rise, its emergence into independent existence, and its rapid consolidation, feelings of profound admiration, of pride and of thankfulness.

The distance that has been traversed, in the course of the four brief years since the inauguration of the Ten Year Plan, by a community, still highly restricted in numbers and circumscribed in resources, and faced with tremendous responsibilities, as a result of the colossal task it has willingly shouldered, is admittedly great, and augurs well for its further advancement along the path traced for it by the pen of the Centre of Bahá'u'lláh's Covenant in His immortal Tablets.[28]

The utmost care and vigilance, however, should be exercised by this youthful and dynamic community, so richly laden with the prizes it has so deservedly won, lest the momentum, so painstakingly gained in recent years, in both the teaching and administrative spheres of Bahá'í activity, be lost or reduced. The standard of dedication and of efficiency, attained, while pursuing the goals it has pledged itself to achieve, must never be allowed, through apathy, neglect or faint-heartedness, to be lowered. The vision that has fired its members, on the occasion of the centenary celebrations which witnessed the launching of the Ten Year Plan must, no matter how prolonged or arduous the task, never grow dim. Their unswerving fidel-

ity to the Covenant established by the Author of their Faith, and their attachment to the ideals and precepts enshrined in His Revelation, should, under no circumstances, no matter how active and subtle the machinations of its enemies, both within and without, be weakened. The momentous and highly exacting task, initiated far beyond the confines of their home-land—a task which posterity will recognize as the opening chapter of their glorious Mission overseas—must be pursued with undiminished diligence, nay with redoubled zeal, and renewed determination and dedication. The no less vital obligation to expand, and consolidate the manifold activities conducted on the homefront, from the Atlantic to the Pacific seaboard, and from the northern confines of the Great Republic of the West to the fringes of the Arctic Ocean, must be faithfully discharged. The setbacks and difficulties that have, unexpectedly and most unfortunately, been recently experienced in connection with the acquisition of both the national Ḥaẓíratu'l-Quds and the site of the future Mother Temple of Canada, must be faced with resolution and vigour, and a definite and permanent solution be found which will ensure the full attainment of these twofold primary objectives. The long overdue conversion of the American Indians, the Eskimos and French Canadians, as well as the representatives of other minorities permanently residing within the borders of that vast Dominion, must receive, in the months immediately ahead, such an impetus as to astonish and stimulate the members of all Bahá'í communities throughout the length and breadth of the Western Hemisphere. The independent character of the Faith they profess and champion must, moreover, be fully vindicated through a closer adherence, on the part of the rank and file of the believers, to its distinguishing tenets and precepts, as well as through a fuller recognition by the civil authorities[74] concerned of the Bahá'í Marriage Certificate and of the Bahá'í Holy Days. The integrity of the fundamental teachings of the Faith, its security, the healthy and steady development, and ultimate fruition, of its nascent institutions, must, above all, be ensured and safeguarded, for upon these will depend the consummation of the Mission with which the Author of the Tablets of the Divine Plan has chosen to entrust them.

The few remaining years, separating the steadfast and high-minded members of the Canadian Bahá'í Community, striving so assiduously to achieve their goals, from the time fixed for the termination of a swiftly unfolding Crusade, are rapidly slipping by. A community which, ever since its inception, has, through the instrumentality of its most distinguished members, and particularly its founder[4] and those nearest to her, as well as a number of her spiritual children and associates, won such prizes at the world Centre of the Faith, in Latin America, in Europe, in Africa and in the Pacific area—such a community, at this crucial hour, cannot afford to either stand still, falter or hesitate. As this world Crusade sweeps majestically forward and draws nearer to its close, exploits, as superb as those its sons and daughters have successively achieved in widely scattered areas of the globe, must continue to distinguish and ennoble the imperishable record of its services.

'Abdu'l-Bahá's prophetic words regarding the future of its homeland, spiritually as well as materially—the initial evidences of which are becoming more apparent every day, must not be lost sight of for a moment, however exacting and all-absorbing the strenuous task ahead, however complex the problems its prosecution involves, however burdensome the preoccupations which it must needs engender.

Afire with that same love that burned so brightly in the hearts of its earliest pioneers, holding fast to the strong cord of the spiritual precepts and administrative principles of the Faith it has so whole-heartedly espoused, confident of its ability to achieve, in its entirety, the Mission entrusted to it by the Author of the Tablets of the Divine Plan, this community must forge ahead, with undeviating loyalty, with indomitable courage, with unbreakable unity, and exemplary consecration, striving to scale loftier heights, and widening constantly the range of its operations, on the American mainland as well as in neighbouring and distant islands, until each and every ob-

jective of its allotted task has been triumphantly attained.
                                                    Shoghi

❧

2 September 1957

To the WESTERN CANADIAN CONFERENCE

ASSURE LOVING FERVENT PRAYERS SUCCESS DELIBERA-
TIONS.
                                                    SHOGHI

❧

9 September 1957

To the NATIONAL SPIRITUAL ASSEMBLY

Dear Bahá'í Friends:

The beloved Guardian is very anxious to secure information as to the Indian tribes (native) and Eskimos, which have been contacted by any of the Believers in your area; or of course if there are any Believers from these Tribes, that would be even more interesting.

Can you prepare a list showing the number of Tribes that have been contacted and, of these Tribes, the number who have become Believers. This would be very interesting information.

Can you secure it at an early date and send it on to me for the Beloved Guardian.

With loving Bahá'í greetings, I am,

                                                    Faithfully yours,
                                                    Leroy Ioas

❧

18 September 1957

To AMY E.V. PUTNAM[75]

Dear Bahá'í Sister:

Your letter of July 31st with enclosures has been received by the beloved Guardian, and he has instructed me to answer you on his behalf.

The services you have rendered the Faith since leaving Haifa are deeply appreciated by him, you may be sure.

He feels the Laurentian School is an important institution and serves a wide area. He was most happy to know that this year's Conference was so successful.

With loving Bahá'í greetings,
R. Rabbani

Assuring you of my loving prayers for your success and spiritual advancement,

Your true brother,
Shoghi

ৡ৹ঌ

18 September 1957

To David D. Bowie[76]

Dear Bahá'í Brother:

The beloved Guardian has received your letter of July 9th, and has instructed me to answer you on his behalf.

He was happy to learn that you experienced such spiritual joy and exhilaration from the visit of the honored Hand of the Cause, Mr. Khadem.[77]

The Guardian hopes you will exert your utmost endeavour toward the establishment of a strong Community in Niagara Falls. He will pray that you may receive Divine assistance in your efforts towards this goal.

With warm Bahá'í greetings,
R. Rabbani

May the Almighty bless your efforts, guide your steps, and enable you to win great victories in the days to come,

Your true brother,
Shoghi

ᗯᝒ

22 September 1957

To the National Spiritual Assembly

GUARDIAN ADVISES PAWLOWSKA[71] REMAIN MIQUELON UNTIL REPLACEMENT ARRIVES HE SENDS HER LOVING APPRECIATION.

IOAS

ᗯᝒ

26 September 1957

To an individual believer

Dear Bahá'í Brother:
The beloved Guardian has received your letter of August 25th, and has instructed me to answer you on his behalf.
Because Bahá'u'lláh lived in the Middle East, and addressed himself mostly to Moslems, Christians and Jews, His proofs had reference mostly to these Faiths.

With warm Bahá'í greetings,
R. Rabbani

Assuring you of my loving prayers for your success and spiritual advancement,

Your true brother,
Shoghi

ᗯᝒ

3 October 1957

To an individual believer

Dear Bahá'í Brother:
The beloved Guardian has received your recent letter with greeting card enclosed from the children, which he appreciated.
He was happy to learn that you and your wife are teaching the children. This is most important. He hopes you will encourage them, in addition to acquiring a knowledge of the Teachings, to endeavour to fit themselves for future Bahá'í work, either in their homeland or on foreign soil. The Faith will need many workers in

all countries as time goes on, and it will be the children of today who will carry forward the Torch of Bahá'u'lláh in the days to come.

Your Committee was fortunate indeed to have had a visit from the revered Hand of the Cause, Mr. Khadem.[77] He is truly one who kindles a new flame of love and longing to serve the Cause in the hearts of the believers wherever he goes.

With warm Bahá'í greetings,

R. Rabbani

*May the Almighty bless, guide and sustain you, and enable
you to promote effectively the vital interests of His Faith,*

Your true brother,

Shoghi

෧෧෧

19 October 1957

TO THE NATIONAL SPIRITUAL ASSEMBLY

Dear Bahá'í Sister:
Your loving letter of October 5th was duly received and its contents have been presented to the Beloved Guardian.

He was very happy indeed to learn of the very active manner in which the Canadian Bahá'ís have taken hold of this most important subject of teaching the Indians.

He attaches the greatest importance to this matter as the Master has spoken of the latent strength of character of these people and feels that when the Spirit of the Faith has a chance to work in their midst, it will produce remarkable results.

You[78] yourself are to be congratulated on the very wonderful work you have been doing with the Indians on the Tyendinaga Reserve. The Guardian greatly appreciates this service, and wishes you to know that he values it very highly. He hopes nothing will interfere with your carrying it forward to the fine conclusion which you hope will be the establishment of an Assembly on this reserve. It would be a distinct victory for the Faith if that is accomplished.

The Guardian will pray for you and for the success of your work.

Faithfully yours,
Leroy Ioas

ᖁᎦᎦᏋ

7 November 1957

To the Treasurer of the National Spiritual Assembly

Dear Bahá'í Brother:

Your loving letter of October 12th was duly received by the Beloved Guardian and he has directed me to acknowledge it in his behalf. The contributions which were made by various Assemblies, Groups and individuals to the International Fund are greatly appreciated. Receipts are enclosed herewith.

Will you please send these receipts to each Assembly, Group or individual concerned expressing the Guardian's appreciation to them.

The Beloved Guardian is directing exclusive attention at this time to the great importance of teaching the Cause of God. The Divine confirmations are descending in torrents, particularly on those who arise to teach the Faith. He is hoping there will be a new movement amongst the Friends in Canada so that many thirsty souls may find eternal life through the selfless deeds of the Canadian Bahá'ís.

He will pray for you, for the Believers and for the success of their work. He sends you his loving greetings.

Faithfully yours,
Leroy Ioas

P.S. This is one of the few letters I received instruction from the Guardian to write shortly before his Ascension.

ᖁᎦᎦᏋ

5 November 1957

To all National Assemblies (via Haifa)

SHOGHI EFFENDI BELOVED OF ALL HEARTS SACRED TRUST GIVEN BELIEVERS BY MASTER PASSED AWAY SUDDEN HEART ATTACK IN SLEEP FOLLOWING ASIATIC FLU. URGE BELIEVERS REMAIN STEADFAST CLING INSTITUTION HANDS LOVINGLY REARED RECENTLY REINFORCED EMPHASIZED BY BELOVED GUARDIAN. ONLY ONENESS HEART ONENESS PURPOSE CAN BEFITTINGLY TESTIFY LOYALTY ALL NATIONAL ASSEMBLIES BELIEVERS DEPARTED GUARDIAN WHO SACRIFICED SELF UTTERLY FOR SERVICE FAITH.

RÚḤÍYYIH

Appendix: Knights of Bahá'u'lláh

Shoghi Effendi announced in May 1953[†] that those believers who arose to pioneer to goals outlined in the Ten Year Crusade, would be designated "Knights of Bahá'u'lláh", and would have their names inscribed on a "Roll of Honour". This Roll was placed at the entrance door of the Shrine of Bahá'u'lláh in 1992, as instructed by the Guardian and noted in the 8 June 1953 letter in this book. Several of these Knights were Canadian, and others fulfilled Canadian goals.

Knights of Canadian origin

Ile d'Anticosti: Mary Zabolotny McCulloch

Bechuanaland (now Botswana): Audrey, John and Patrick Robarts

Cape Breton Island: Fred and Jean Allen, Grace and Irving Geary

District of Franklin: Gale and Jameson Bond

District of Keewatin: Richard Stanton

Grand Manan Island: Doris Richardson

Gulf Islands: Cliff and Catherine Huxtable

Iles de la Madeleine (Magdalen Islands): Kathy Weston McLeod

Iles Marquises (Marquesas Islands): Greta Jankko

Labrador: Bruce Matthew

Saint-Pierre et Miquelon: Ola Pawlowska

Queen Charlotte Islands: Edythe MacArthur

Yukon: Joan Anderson

---

†*Messages to the Bahá'í World, p.49*

Knights who pioneered to Canadian goals
from other national communities

Baranof Island: Gail Avery, Helen Robinson

Iles de la Madeleine (Magdalen Islands): Kay Zinky

Labrador: Howard Gilliland

Samoa: Lillian Wyss Ala'i

Yukon: Ted Anderson

Notes

1   Douglas Martin—member of the National Spiritual Assembly of the Bahá'ís of Canada from 1960-85, elected to the Universal House of Justice in 1993.

2   A "message" is a letter or cablegram which has been addressed to an individual, group or Assembly, and which was written by the Guardian, by a secretary on behalf of the Guardian, or which includes portions written both by the Guardian and his secretary.

3   Florence Evaline (Lorol/Kitty) Schopflocher—an early Montreal believer who travelled to 86 countries on behalf of the Cause. Her life and travels are described in *The Bahá'í World* Vol. XV, 488-489, "In Memoriam".

4   May Ellis Maxwell—spiritual mother of the Canadian Bahá'í community, became a believer in 1898, visited 'Abdu'l-Bahá in Haifa in 1899 and returned to Paris to found the first Bahá'í centre on the European continent, married Sutherland Maxwell and settled in Montreal in 1902, achieved "the priceless honour" of a "martyr's death" in Argentina in 1940. For a review of the vast range of her contributions to the Faith in Europe and America, see *The Bahá'í World* Vol. VIII, 631-642, "In Memoriam".

5   Siegfried Schopflocher—known as the "Temple Builder" because of his great contributions to the completion of the first Mashriqu'l-Adhkár of the West, appointed a Hand of the Cause of God in 1952, died in Montreal in 1953. For a review of his "numerous, magnificent services" see *The Bahá'í World* Vol. XII, 664-666, "In Memoriam".

6   Roy Wilhelm—an American believer whom Shoghi Effendi appointed as a Hand of the Cause of God after his passing in 1951. See *The Bahá'í World* Vol. XII, 662-664, "In Memoriam".

7   Horace Holley— Secretary of the National Spiritual Assembly of the Bahá'ís of the United States and Canada, appointed a Hand of the Cause of God in 1951. See *The Bahá'í World* Vol. XIII, 849-858, "In Memoriam".

8   The Universal House of Justice has provided clarification on this issue: "It is clear from further elucidations given by Shoghi Effendi that Bahá'ís may vote for political posts only when they can do so

upon a non-party line, without affiliating themselves with any political party or organization." (Letter dated 13 September 1998 to the National Spiritual Assembly of the Bahá'ís of Canada)

9   Charles Murray—native of Montreal who became a Bahá'í in Washington, D.C., and lived in Prince Edward Island 1932-42.

10   Emeric and Rosemary Sala—members of the National Spiritual Assembly 1948-53. During the first and second Seven Year Plans, they pioneered to Venezuela (1940-41) and travelled throughout Latin America. In 1953 they pioneered to South Africa, and returned to Canada in 1968. In 1971 they pioneered to Mexico, where Rosemary died in 1980. Emeric passed away in 1990. See *The Bahá'í World* Vol. XVIII, 713-715, and Vol. XX, "In Memoriam".

11   F. St. George Spendlove—a Montreal believer who served on the National Spiritual Assembly of the British Isles (1935-36), and settled in Toronto. His many services and accomplishments are described in *The Bahá'í World* Vol. XIII, 895-899, "In Memoriam".

12   William Suter—Swiss-born member of the Montreal Bahá'í youth group who moved to Toronto in 1936, later was caretaker at the Laurentian Bahá'í School until his death in 1966.

13   Gerrard Sluter-Schlutius—German-born member of the Montreal Bahá'í youth group who moved to Toronto in 1935, and to Guatemala in 1939. Shoghi Effendi later declared him a Covenant-breaker for his persistent political involvement.

14   This period covers the first (1937-44) and second (1946-53) Seven Year Plans assigned to the United States and Canada. Canada was assigned its own Five Year Plan in 1948.

15   Amatu'l-Bahá Rúḥíyyih Khánum Rabbani (Mary Maxwell)—daughter of May and Sutherland Maxwell, became the wife of Shoghi Effendi in 1937, appointed a Hand of the Cause of God in 1952.

16   Mabel Rice-Wray Ives—an American believer who taught the Faith in central and eastern Canada. For more details, see *The Bahá'í World* Vol. IX, 616-623, "In Memoriam".

17   Howard Colby Ives—a former Unitarian minister, this American believer published *Portals to Freedom* and *The Song Celestial*, died in 1941. See *The Bahá'í World* Vol. IX, 608-613, "In Memoriam" for an account of his life.

18   John and Audrey Robarts—John was a member of the National Spiritual Assembly from 1948-53. In 1953 they became Knights of Bahá'u'lláh when they pioneered to Bechuanaland. In 1957 John Robarts was appointed a Hand of the Cause of God. He passed

away in Rawdon, Québec in 1991. See *The Bahá'í World* Vol. XX, "In Memoriam".

19 Beulah S. Proctor—American believer who was the first pioneer, with her daughter, to Halifax (1939), died 1958.

20 Doris Skinner—Bahá'í from Vancouver who was the first pioneer to Calgary in 1939, until 1949, when she pioneered to Newfoundland.

21 Dorothy Sheets—first Bahá'í to declare her belief in Bahá'u'lláh in Calgary, later pioneered to Regina, Saskatchewan and to Newfoundland, passed away in 1997.

22 William Sutherland Maxwell—architect of the Shrine of the Báb, appointed a Hand of the Cause of God in 1951, died in Montreal in 1952. His "saintly life" is described in *The Bahá'í World* Vol. XII, 657-662, "In Memoriam".

23 Rowland Estall—a founding member of the Montreal youth group, homefront pioneer to Vancouver and Winnipeg, served on the National Spiritual Assembly of the Bahá'ís of Canada (1948-1972), the Auxiliary Board (1954-63), and as a Counsellor for the Americas for several years in the Caribbean beginning 1973, passed away in 1993.

24 Ernest Vernon Harrison—this early Montreal Bahá'í (confirmed 1921) pioneered to Prince Edward Island in the early 1950s, where he passed away in 1959.

25 Emeric Sala's book was *This Earth One Country* (1945).

26 Elsa Vento—a native of Finland who became a Bahá'í in Toronto in 1938, pioneered to Prince Edward Island in 1944, and returned to Finland in 1953. For more details see *The Bahá'í World* Vol. XIII, 900-901, "In Memoriam".

27 Elizabeth Cowles—an early Montreal believer.

28 The Tablets of the Divine Plan, revealed by 'Abdu'l-Bahá in 1916-17, and addressed severally to the Bahá'ís of the United States and Canada, constitute the authority for the successive Plans inaugurated by the Guardian for the spread of the Faith and the establishment of its Institutions throughout the world.

29 Laura Davis—Secretary of the National Spiritual Assembly of the Bahá'ís of Canada, 1948-54, passed away 1990.

30 The city of Montreal, Quebec, visited by 'Abdu'l-Bahá August 30—September 12, 1912.

31 The Bill to incorporate the National Spiritual Assembly of the Bahá'ís of Canada was passed by both Houses of the Canadian Parliament, and given Royal assent on April 30, 1949.

32 Winnifred Harvey—member of the National Spiritual Assembly 1950-61, passed away in Haifa in 1990.

33 Although Newfoundland was first visited by Marion Jack and Kate Cowan Ives in 1917, the first pioneers to Newfoundland, arriving in 1949, were Margaret Reid, Dorothy Sheets, and Doris Skinner (who remained there until 1955).

34 Nancy Gates—American pioneer to Denmark who attempted to pioneer to Greenland, but was unable to do so.

35 The question concerned tie votes when motions are introduced in Assembly meetings.

36 The question concerned who should chair Feasts.

37 James and Melba Loft—Mohawk and Ojibwa believers who returned to Canada from the United States to pioneer to the Tyendinaga (Mohawk) Indian Reserve, near Shannonville, Ontario, in 1949, where James passed away in 1973, and Melba in 1985. Melba was the first Canadian native believer. See *The Bahá'í World* Vol. XVI, 514-516, and Vol. XIX, 697-699, "In Memoriam".

38 E. Blair Fuller—a believer serving in the United States armed forces.

39 Jameson Bond—first pioneer to the Canadian Arctic (District of Keewatin 1950-53, District of Franklin with Mrs. Gale Bond, 1953-63). They were named Knights of Bahá'u'lláh for Franklin. Jameson served on the National Spiritual Assembly of the Bahá'ís of Canada 1967-82.

40 Nan Brandle—beginning in 1950 served several years as a pioneer to the native people in Department of Indian Affairs hospitals at Fisher River and Hodgson, Manitoba and at Moose Factory and Ohsweken, Ontario.

41 Louis Bourgeois—architect of the Mother Temple of the West, in Wilmette, Illinois, the construction of which was the first collective enterprise undertaken by the Bahá'ís of America. He died in 1930.

42 Marion Jack—"immortal heroine" and "shining example to pioneers", who remained at her post in Sofia, Bulgaria from 1930 until her death in 1954. Her imperishable services are recorded in *The Bahá'í World* Vol. XII, 674-677, "In Memoriam".

43 Palle Bischoff—Danish believer, the first pioneer to Greenland (1951-54).

44 Laurentian Bahá'í School, near Beaulac, Quebec—founded 1946, transferred in 1949 to the National Spiritual Assembly, the first national endowment.

45 Ross Woodman—member of the National Spiritual Assembly of

the Bahá'ís of Canada, 1948-51, 1952-53.

46 Dr. Ali Kuli Khan—a Persian believer who lived in the United States and, amongst many other services, translated the Bahá'í Writings into English. More details may be found in *The Bahá'í World* Vol. XIV, 351-353, "In Memoriam".

47 Greta Jankko—Knight of Bahá'u'lláh for the Marquesas Islands (1954). See *The Bahá'í World* Vol. XV, 543-545, "In Memoriam".

48 Albert Rakovsky—first Bahá'í to visit Anticosti Island, member of the National Spiritual Assembly 1953-56.

49 The Ten Year Crusade lasted from 1953-63.

50 Although Yukon had been visited by Susan Rice (1916), Marion Jack and Emogene Hoagg (1919), and Orcella Rexford (1922), no one resident there had outwardly responded to the Faith.

51 Amelia Collins—an American believer appointed by the Guardian as Hand of the Cause in 1951, whose outstanding contributions and services are described in *The Bahá'í World* Vol. XIII, 834-841, "In Memoriam".

52 The first building purchased for the National Ḥaẓíratu'l-Quds (188 St. George Street, Toronto, 1952-53) was unsuitable. So was the second (539 Mount Pleasant Road, 1955-56). The third building (274 Huron Street, 1956-57) was expropriated. The building at 15 Lola Road, Toronto was acquired in 1957 and served as the National Ḥaẓíratu'l-Quds until 1969.

53 Maxwell Home, 1548 Pine Avenue West, Montreal, Québec—'Abdu'l-Bahá stayed in this house during His visit to Montreal in 1912. It was given to the Canadian Bahá'í community by Hand of the Cause Rúḥíyyih Khánum in 1953.

54 The Bahá'í marriage ceremony was first legally recognized in Ontario and British Columbia in 1958.

55 The first Temple site was purchased in 1957 in North York, and replaced by the site in Markham Township in 1969.

56 Eddie Elliot—a childhood friend of Mary Maxwell, the first African Canadian to become a Bahá'í (1929), member of the Montreal Spiritual Assembly, died 1953.

57 Dorothy Baker—A "remarkably gifted" American teacher who was appointed as a Hand of the Cause by the Guardian, passed away in a plane crash in 1954. See *The Bahá'í World* Vol. XII, 670-674, "In Memoriam".

58 See 15 June 1954 message, page 204.

59 Howard Gilliland—Knight of Bahá'u'lláh for Labrador (1954).

60 Bruce Matthew—Knight of Bahá'u'lláh for Labrador (1954).

61 Edythe MacArthur—Knight of Bahá'u'lláh for the Queen Charlotte Islands (1953). She pioneered to southern Africa later in the Ten Year Crusade. Passed away 1994. See her obituary in *The Bahá'í*

World 1993-94, 321.

62 R. Ted and Joan Anderson—Knights of Bahá'u'lláh for the Yukon Territory (1953), where they remained until 1972.

63 Peter Pihichyn—a believer of Ukrainian descent.

64 Mary Zabolotny (McCulloch)—Knight of Bahá'u'lláh for Anticosti Island (1956), passed away 1996.

65 The resurgence of persecution of the Bahá'í community in Írán during 1955 is described in *The Bahá'í World* Vol. XIII, 291-296.

66 Sutherland Maxwell and Siegfried Schopflocher.

67 Arthur and Lily Ann Irwin—among the first believers who contributed to the establishment of the Bahá'í Faith in native communities. Arthur passed away in 1994; see his obituary in *The Bahá'í World* 1994-95, 314.

68 The Gulf Islands were later selected as a substitute for Anticosti Island, and opened by Cliff and Catherine Huxtable (1960-66).

69 Allan Raynor—member of the National Spiritual Assembly 1954-60 and 1963-64, passed away in 1979. See *The Bahá'í World* Vol. XVIII, 696-698, "In Memoriam".

70 Iceland appears to have been visited first by Amelia Collins in 1924. Martha Root spent a month in Iceland in 1935.

71 Ola Pawlowska—Knight of Bahá'u'lláh for St. Pierre and Miquelon Islands (1953-58), later pioneered to Luxembourg, Poland and Congo (Zaire).

72 Ahmad Sohrab—former secretary of 'Abdu'l-Bahá, declared a Covenant-breaker by the Guardian, died 1958.

73 William Carr—Canadian pioneer to Thule Air Base, Greenland 1955-72. From 1958 to 1963 Mrs. Kaya Holck, a Danish believer, pioneered among the Greenlanders.

74 The decision by the Superior Court in Montreal in 1958 which recognized the independent character of the Bahá'í Faith and exempted the Bahá'í Shrine from taxation is recorded in *The Bahá'í World* Vol. XIII, 662-664.

75 Amy Putnam—one of the earliest believers to enrol in the Bahá'í Faith in Hamilton, later pioneered to St. Pierre and Miquelon Islands.

76 David Bowie—a believer who has served, in Canada and overseas, as a local and travelling teacher.

77 Zikrullah Khadem (Ḏhikru'lláh Ḵhádim)—Persian believer appointed Hand of the Cause by the Guardian in 1952, visited over fifty countries during the Ten Year Crusade, including Canada, passed away 1986. See *The Bahá'í World* Vol. XX, "In Memoriam".

78 Peggy Ross—member of the National Spiritual Assembly, 1953-63, and of the Auxiliary Board, 1957-86.

Index